DATA FILE PROGRAMMING IN BASIC

DATA FILE PROGRAMMING IN BASIC

LEROY FINKEL

San Carlos High School

and

JERALD R. BROWN

Educational Consultant

John Wiley & Sons, Inc.

New York • Chichester • Brisbane • Toronto

Publisher: Judy V. Wilson
Editors: Dianne Littwin and Karen Hess
Composition and Make-up: Trotta Composition

Library of Congress Cataloging in Publication Data

Finkel, LeRoy.
Data files programming BASIC.

(Wiley Self-Teaching Guides)
Includes index.
1. Basic (Computer program language) – Programmed instruction. 2. File organization (Computer science) – Programmed instruction. I. Brown, Jerald, joint author. II. Title.
QA76.73.B3F53 001.64'24 80-39790
ISBN 0-471-08333-X

Printed in the United States of America

81 82 10 9 8 7 6 5 4 3 2 1

How To Use This Book

When you use the self-instruction format in this book, you will be actively involved in learning data file programming in BASIC. Most of the material is presented in sections called frames, each of which teaches you something new or provides practice. Each frame also gives you questions to answer or asks you to write a program or program segment.

You will learn best if you actually write out the answers and try the programs on your computer. The questions are carefully designed to call your attention to important points in the examples and explanations, and to help you apply what is being explained or demonstrated. We cannot urge you too strongly to really "fill in the blanks" for rapid and accurate learning.

Each chapter begins with a list of objectives – what you will be able to do after completing that chapter. At the end of each chapter is a self-test to provide valuable practice.

The self-tests do triple duty. They can be used as a review of the material covered in the chapter. Or you can read and work through a chapter, take a break, and save the self-test as a review before you begin the next chapter. The self-tests also provide valuable practice, for maximum retention of the material learned. Starting with the Chapter Four Self-test, you are asked to write programs that can be used to either create data files or display the contents of data files. These data files are then used by other programs in later chapters, so please don't skip the self-tests! At the end of the book is a final self-test to assess your overall understanding of data file programming. You will find it easy, if you have worked through this self-instruction format without skipping over the practice programs.

Instructors will find this book to be an excellent text for intermediate or advanced courses in BASIC programming at the high school and college levels, as well as for computer center classes, university extension workshops, and in-house instructional settings.

This book is designed to be used with a computer close at hand. What you learn will be theoretical only until you actually sit down at a computer and apply your knowledge "hands-on." We strongly recommend that you and this book get together with a computer! Learning data file programming in BASIC will be easier and clearer if you have regular access to a computer so you can try the examples and exercises, make your own modifications, and invent programs for your own purposes. You are now ready to use data files in BASIC.

Preface

This text will teach you to program data files in BASIC. As a prerequisite to its use, you should have already completed an introductory course or book in BASIC programming and be able to read program listings and write simple programs: This is not a book for the absolute novice in BASIC. You should already be comfortable writing your own programs that use statements including string variables, string functions, and arrays. We do start the book with a review of statements that you already know, though we cover them in more depth and show you new ways to use them.

The book is designed for use by readers who have little or no experience using data files in BASIC (or elsewhere, for that matter). We take you slowly and carefully through experiences that "teach by doing." You will be asked to complete many programs and program segments. By doing so, you will learn the essentials and a lot more. If you already have data file experience, you can use this book to learn about data files in more depth.

The particular data files explained in this text are for the Radio Shack TRS-80 computer Model I and Model III, with one or more disk drives or else a cassette recorder. Data file programming in other versions of BASIC will be similar, but not identical, to those taught in this book. You will find this book most useful when used in conjunction with the appropriate reference materials for your computer system.

Data files are used to store quantities of information that you may want to use now and later; for example, mailing addresses, numeric or statistical information, or tax and bookkeeping data. The examples presented in this book will help you use files for home applications, for home business applications, and for your small business or profession. When you have completed this book, you will be able to write your own programs, modify programs purchased from commercial sources, and adapt programs using data files that you find in magazines and other sources.

Contents

CHAPTER ONE

Writing BASIC Programs for Clarity, Readability, and Logic

Objectives: When you have completed this chapter you will be able to:

1. describe how a program can be written using a top-to-bottom format.
2. write an introductory module using REMARK statements.
3. describe six prettyprinting rules.
4. describe seven rules to write programs that save memory space.

INTRODUCTION

This text will teach you to use data files in BASIC. You should have already completed an introductory course or book in BASIC programming, and be able to read program listings and write simple programs.. This is not a book for the absolute novice in BASIC, but is for those who have never used data files in BASIC (or elsewhere, for that matter). The particular data files explained in this text are for TRS-80 BASIC and MICROSOFT BASIC.

Data files in other versions of BASIC will be similar, but not identical, to those taught in this book. You will find this book most useful when used in conjunction with the reference manual for your computer system.

Since it is assumed you have some knowledge of programming in BASIC and have practiced by writing small programs, the next step is for you to begin thinking about program organization and clarity. Because data file programs can become fairly large and complex, the inevitable debugging process – making the program actually work – can be proportionately complex. Therefore, this chapter is important to you because it provides some program organization methods to help make your future programming easier.

THE BASIC LANGUAGE

The computer language called BASIC was developed at Dartmouth College in the early 1960s. It was intended for use by people with little or no previous computer experience who were not necessarily adept at mathematics. The original language syntax included only those functions that a beginner would need. As other colleges, computer manufacturers, and institutions began to adopt BASIC, they added embellishments to meet their own needs. Soon BASIC grew in syntax to what various sources called Extended BASIC, Expanded BASIC, SUPERBASIC, XBASIC, BASIC PLUS, and so on. Finally, in 1978 an industry standard was developed for BASIC, but that standard was for only a "minimal BASIC," as defined by the American National Standards Institute (ANSI). Despite the ANSI standard, today we have a plethora of different BASIC languages, most of which "look alike," but each with its own special characteristics and quirks.

In the microcomputer field, the most widely used versions of BASIC were developed by the Microsoft Company and are generally referred to as MICROSOFT BASIC. These BASICs are available on a variety of microcomputers but, unfortunately, the language is implemented differently on each computer system. Microsoft also sells its own version of BASIC, called BASIC-80, useable on many microcomputers.

The programs and runs shown in the main text were actually performed by a Radio Shack TRS-80 with DOS and disk BASIC. Where possible, we used only those language features that appear to be common in ALL versions of MICROSOFT BASIC. We have also tried to use BASIC language features common to all versions of BASIC, regardless of manufacturer. We did not attempt to show off all the bells and whistles found in MICROSOFT BASIC, but rather, to present easy-to-understand programs that will run on or be easily adapted to a variety of computers.

THE BASIC LANGUAGE YOU SHOULD USE

Conservative Programming

Since you will now be writing longer and more complex programs, *you should adopt conservative programming techniques so that errors will be easier to isolate and locate.* (Yes, you will still make errors. We all do!) This means that you should NOT use all the fanciest features available in your version of BASIC until you have tested the features to be sure they work the way you think they work. Even then, you still might decide against using your fancy features, many of which relate to printing or graphic output and do not work the same on other computers. Some might be special functions that simply do not exist on other computers. Leave them out of your programs unless you feel you must include them.

We have found that not all software (BASIC) features work EXACTLY as described in the manufacturer's reference materials, or that the description may be subject to misinterpretation. Thus, *the more conservative your programming techniques, the less chance there is of running into a software "glitch."* This chapter discusses a program format that, in itself, is a conservative programming technique.

One reason for conservative programming is that your programs will be more portable or transportable to other computers. "Why should I care about portability?" you ask. Perhaps the most important reason is that you will want to trade programs with friends. But do all of your friends have a computer IDENTICAL to yours? Unless they do, they will probably be unable to use your programs without modifying them. Conservative programming techniques will minimize the number of changes required.

Portability is also important for your own convenience. The computer you use or own today may not be the one you will use one year from now, or you may enhance your system. In order to use today's programs on tomorrow's computer be conservative in your programming.

> Use conservative programming to:
>
> - Isolate and locate errors more easily.
> - Avoid software "glitch."
> - Enhance portability.

WRITING READABLE PROGRAMS

Look at the sample programs throughout this book and you will see that they are easy to read and understand because the programs and the individual statements are written in simple, straight-line BASIC code without fancy methodology or language syntax. It is as if the statements are written with the READER rather than the computer in mind.

Writing readable BASIC programs requires thinking ahead, planning your program in a logical flow, and using a few special formats that make the program listing easier to the eye. If you plan to program for a living, you may find yourself bound by your employer's programming style. However, if you program for pleasure, adding readable style to your programs will make them that much easier to debug or change later, not to mention the pride inherent in trading a clean, readable program to someone else.

A readable programming style provides its own documentation. Such self-documentation is not only pleasing to the eye, it provides the reader/user with sufficient information to understand exactly how the program works. This style is not as precise as "structured programming," though we have borrowed features usually promoted by structured programming enthusiasts. *Our format organizes programs in MODULES, each module containing one major function or program activity.* We also include techniques long accepted as good programming, but for some reason forgotten in recent years. Most of our suggestions do NOT save memory space or speed up the program run. Rather, readability is our primary concern, at the expense of memory space. Later in this chapter, we will show some procedures to shorten and speed up your programs. Modular style programs will usually be better running programs and will effectively communicate your thought processes to a reader.

THE TOP-TO-BOTTOM ORGANIZATION

When planning your program, think in terms of major program functions. These might include some or all of the functions from this list:

DATA ENTRY
DATA ANALYSIS
COMPUTATION
FILE UPDATE
EDITING
REPORT GENERATION

Using our modular process, divide your program into modules, each containing one of these functions. Your program should flow from module one to module two and continue to the next higher numbered module. *This "top-to-bottom organization" makes your program easy to follow.* Program modules might be broken up into smaller "blocks", each containing one procedure or computation. The size or scope of a program block within a module is determined by the programmer and the task to be accomplished. Block style will vary from person to person, and perhaps from program to program.

USE A MODULAR FORMAT AND TOP-TO-BOTTOM APPROACH

REMARK Statements

Separate program modules and blocks from each other by REMARK statements or blank program lines. Since blank numbered lines are eliminated by many BASICs when the program is listed, test your version of BASIC to see how blank lines are printed in a listing. In general, programs designed for readability make liberal use of REMARK statements, but do not be overzealous. A blank line (or nearly blank) can be induced using an apostrophe (') as a substitute for the word REMARK, or by merely typing a line number followed by a colon (:). A line number followed by REM (e.g., 150 REM) can also be used. Experiment with your computer to see what works.

```
100 REMARK        DATA ENTRY MODULE
110 REMARK **** READ DATA FROM DATA STATEMENTS 9000-9090
120 '
130 :
140 REM
.
.
190 '
200 REMARK   COMPUTATION MODULE
```

Begin each program module, block, or subroutine with an explanatory REMARK and end it with a blank line or blank REMARK statement indicating the end (see line 190 above).

Consistency in your use of REMARKs enhances readability. Use REM or REMARK, but be consistent. Use an apostrophe or colon consistently. Some writers use the **** shown in line 110 above to set off REMARK statements containing comments from other REMARK statements; others use spaces four to six places after the REMARK before they add a comment (line 100). Both formats effectively separate REMARK comments from BASIC code.

You can place remarks on the same line as BASIC code using multiple statement lines, but be sure your REMARK is the LAST statement on the line. Such "on-line" remarks can be used to explain what a particular statement is doing. A common practice is to leave considerable space between an on-line remark and the BASIC code, as shown in line 240 below.

```
220 LET C(X) = C(X) + U: REM***COUNT UNITS IN C ARRAY
240 LET T(X) = T(X) + C(X): REM***INCREASE TOTAL ARRAY
```

Liberal use of REMARK statements to separate program modules and blocks is desirable. Using REMARKs to explain what the program is doing is also desirable, but don't be overzealous or simplistic (LET C = A + B does not require a REMARK or explanation!). REM should add information, not merely state an obvious step.

Like everything else said in these first chapters, there will be exceptions to what we say here. Keep in mind that we are trying to get you to think through your programming techniques and formats a little more than you are probably accustomed to doing. Thus, our suggested "rules" are just that – suggestions to which there will be exceptions.

GOTO STATEMENTS

Perhaps the most controversial statement in the BASIC language is the unconditional GOTO statement. Its use and abuse causes more controversy than any other statement. Purists say you would NEVER use an unconditional GOTO statement such as GOTO 100. A more realistic approach suggests that all GOTOs and GOSUBs go DOWN the page to a line number larger than the line number where the GOTO or GOSUB appears. This is consistent with the "top-to-bottom" program organization. This same approach, down the page, also applies to using IF. . .THEN statements (there will be obvious exceptions to this rule).

```
140 GOTO 210
150 IF X < Y THEN 800
160 GOSUB 8000
```

A final suggestion: A GOTO, GOSUB, or IF. . .THEN should not go to a statement containing *only* a REMARK. If you or the next user of your program run short of memory space you will delete extra REMARK statements. This, in turn, requires you to change all your GOTOs line numbers, so plan ahead first. Not all BASICs even allow a program to branch to a statement starting with REM.

Bad	Good
150 GOTO 300	150 GOTO 300
•	•
	•
•	•
	•
•	•
300 REM DATA ENTRY	299 REM DATA ENTRY
310 LINE INPUT "NAME";N$	300 LINE INPUT "NAME";N$

A FORMAT FOR THE INTRODUCTORY MODULE

The first module of BASIC code (lines 100 through 199 or 1000 through 1999) should contain a brief description of the program, user instructions when needed, a list of all variables used, and the initialization of constants, variables, and arrays.

The very first program statement should be a REMARK statement containing the program name. Carefully choose a name that tells the reader what the program does, not just a randomly selected name. After the program's name comes the author or programmer's name and the date. For the benefit of someone else who may like to use your program, include a REMARK describing the computer system and/or software system used when writing the program. Whenever the program is altered or updated, the opening remarks should reflect the change.

```
100 REMARK    PAYROLL SUBSYSTEM
110 REMARK    COPYRIGHT CONSUMER PROGRAMMING CORP 12/79
120 REMARK
130 REMARK    HP 2000 BASIC
140 REMARK    MODIFIED FOR MICROSOFT BASIC BY J. BROWN
150 REMARK    ON TRS-80, 16K, LEVEL II BASIC
160 REMARK
```

Follow these remarks with a brief explanation of what the program does, contained either in REMARK statements or in PRINT statements. Next add user instructions. For some programs you might offer the user the choice of having instructions printed or not. If instructions are long, place the request for instructions in the introductory module and the actual printed instructions in a subroutine toward the end of your program. That way, the long instructions will not be listed each time you LIST your program.

```
170 REMARK   THIS PROGRAM WILL COMPUTE PAY AND PRODUCE PRINTED PAYROLL
180 REMARK   REGISTER USING DATA ENTERED BY OPERATOR
190 REMARK
200 LINE INPUT "DO YOU NEED INSTRUCTIONS?"; R$
210 IF R$ = "YES" THEN GOSUB 800
220 REMARK
```

Follow the description/instructions with a series of statements to identify the variables, string variables, arrays, constants, and files used in the program. Again, these statements communicate information to a READER, making it that much easier for you or someone else to modify the program later. We usually complete this section AFTER we have completed the program so we don't forget to include anything.

Assign a variable name to all "constants" used. Even though a constant will not change during the run of the program, a constant may change values between runs. By assigning it a variable name, you make it that much easier to change the value; that is, by merely changing one statement in the program. It is a good idea to jot down notes while writing the program so important details do not slip your mind or escape notice. When the program has been written and tested (debugged), go back through it, bring your notes up-to-date, and polish the descriptions in the REMARKs.

```
220 REM    VARIABLES/STRING VARIABLES
230 REM      G = GROSS PAY
240 REM      N = NET PAY
250 REM      IT1 = FEDL. INCOME TAX
260 REM      IT2 = STATE INCOME TAX
270 REM      F = SOC. SEC. TAX
280 REM      D = DISABILITY TAX
290 REM      X,Y,Z, = LOOP VARIABLES
300 REM      H(X) = HOURS ARRAY
310 REM      N$ = NAME (20)
320 REM      PN$ = EMPLOYEE NUMBER (5)
330 REM
340 REM    CONSTANTS
350 LET FR = .0613: REM                    SOC. SEC. RATE
360 LET SDR = .01: REM                     SDI RATE
370 REM
380 REM    FILES USED
390 REM           ITM = FEDL. TAX MASTER FILE
400 REM           STM = STATE TAX MASTER FILE
410 REM
```

(Notice the method used to indicate string length in lines 310 and 320.)
(Notice the use of on-line remarks in lines 350 and 360.)

The final part of the introductory module is the initialization section. In this section, dimension the size of all single and double arrays and all string arrays, even if DIMENSION is not required by your computer. This is valuable information for a reader. Any variables that need to be initialized to zero should be done here for clear communication, even if your computer initializes all variables to zero automatically. This section also includes any user-defined functions *before* they are used in the program.

```
420 REM     INITIALIZE
430 DIM H(7), R(10,3), N$(30)
440 :
450 REM
```

THE MODULES THAT FOLLOW THE INTRODUCTION

The remainder of your program consists of major function modules, subroutines, DATA statements, and PRINT USING format IMAGE statements, when they are used. Remember to separate each module from others by a blank line REMARK statement and a remark identifying the module. These modules can be further divided into user-defined program blocks, each separated by a blank line REMARK statement.

A typical second module would be for data entry. Data can be operator-entered from the keyboard or entered directly from DATA statements, a file, or other device. Chapter 3 discusses in detail how to write data entry routines with extensive error-checking procedures to ensure the accuracy and integrity of each data item entering the computer.

For now, we suggest that you write data entry routines so that even a completely inexperienced operator would have no trouble entering data to your program. This means the operator should ALWAYS be prompted as to what to enter and provided with an example when necessary.

```
240 INPUT "ENTER TODAY'S DATE (MM/DD/YY)";D$
```

If data are entered from DATA statements, place the DATA statements near the end of your program (some suggest even past the END statement) using REMARK statements to clearly identify the type of data and the order of placement of items within the DATA statements.

```
9400 REM    DATA FOR CORRECT ANSWER ARRAY IN QUESTION ORDER
9410 REM    10 ANSWERS, RANGE 1-5
9420 REM
9430 DATA 4,5,1,3,2,1,,1,4,4,5
9440 REM
9460 REM    RESPONDENTS ANSWERS TO QUESTIONS
9470 REM    RESP. ID # FOLLOWED BY 10 RESPONSES, 1-5
9480 REM
9490 DATA 17642, 4,5,1,3,2,2,1,4,4,4
9500 DATA 98126, 3,5,2,3,2,1,5,4,5,2
.
.
.
```

You can think of DATA statements as a separate program module. The "in-between" program modules might do computations, data handling, file reading and writing, and report writing. Modular programming style dictates that all printing and report generation, except error messages, be done in one program module labeled as such. This limits the use of PRINT and PRINT USING statements to one easy-to-find location within your program. (There might be more than one print module.) This makes it that much easier for you to make subsequent changes on reports when paper forms change or new reports are designed. In the print module your program should NOT perform any computations except trivial ones. Make important computations BEFORE the program executes the print module(s). This may require greater use of variables and/or arrays to "hold" data pending report printing, but your programs will be much cleaner and easier to debug, since everything will be easy to find in its own "right" place.

SUBROUTINES

Program control flows smoothly from one module to the next. A well-designed module has *one* entry point at its beginning and *one* exit point at its end. The exception to this is a mid-module exit to a subroutine.

```
290 REM
300 REM    COMPUTATION MODULE
310:
320 LET T = (V * X) / Q
330 LET T9 = T9 + T
340 GOSUB 800
350:
400 REM    REPORT PRINTING MODULE
410:
```

A subroutine exit from a module always RETURNs to the next statement in the module. The use of subroutines is desirable provided you don't overdo it. Some program stylists recommend that the entire main program consist of nothing but GOSUB statements "calling up" a series of subroutines located later in the program. Such a technique is probably guilty of overkill. Strive for a happy medium between the two extremes of no subroutines and nothing but subroutines.

Technically, you need use a subroutine only to avoid duplicating the same program statements in two or more places in your program. A subroutine should be called from MORE than one place in your program. Otherwise, why use a formal subroutine? Program stylists now agree that subroutines enhance readability and clarity and can be used at the convenience of the programmer (you!). However, again the caution – don't overdo it. Use subroutines to enhance the flow and readability of your program. Stylists also agree that subroutines should be clearly identified using REMARK statements and set off from other program sections with blank REMARK statements. Program stylists disagree, however, on where to place the subroutines. There are two schools of thought. Placement of subroutines can be either immediately past the end of the module that calls the subroutine or in one common module toward the end of the program.

EITHER

```
300 REM      COMPUTATION MODULE
310....
320....
330 GOSUB 410
340 GOSUB 460
.
.
.
.
400 REM      NUMBER CONVERSION SUBROUTINE
410 ....
.
.
.
.
450 REM      COMPUTATION SUBROUTINE
460 ....
.
.
.
```

OR

```
330 GOSUB 810
340 GOSUB 910
.
.
.
.
800 REM      NUMBER CONVERSION SUBROUTINE
810...
.
.
.
900 REM      COMPUTATION SUBROUTINE
910....
.
.
```

JUST FOR LOOKS

You can do a host of things to your programs to enhance looks and clarity. These techniques are generally called "prettyprinting." Some of these techniques may not be possible on your computer; others may be done by it automatically. Try them out. If they work, use them to make your programs look nicer.

Spacing

One way to make your programs look nicer is to use line numbers of equal length throughout the program. If your program is small, use line numbers 100 through 999. If long, start the program at 1000 and continue to 9999. When your program is listed, it will be aligned neatly. If your computer has a renumber or resequence command, it looks nice if the entire program is incremented by steps of ten (10).

Without a resequence command this is virtually impossible to do. A partial solution is to enter statements in sequence increments of ten when you first enter your program. When you have completed the program, even with changes, MOST of the program will still be in increments of ten and look nice.

Prettyprinting also includes adding spaces in statements for clarity. Add spaces so the statement is easy to read. TRS-80 BASIC and BASIC-80 permit you to add spaces whenever you wish. Whatever you type on the keyboard is EXACTLY what is entered into the computer and printed in a program listing. This is not true on many computers which disregard user-typed spaces and do their own version of prettyprinting automatically.

The following rules for spacing are suggested:

1. Use spaces to show the difference between REMARK comments and BASIC code.

GOOD

```
100 REM     SUBROUTINE TO TEST DATA ENTRY
110 REM
120 LET D$ = N$
130 LET Z = LEN(D$)
```

BETTER

```
100 REM    SUBROUTINE TO TEST DATA ENTRY
110 REM
120        LET D$ = N$
130        LET Z = LEN(D$)
```

2. Space before and after arithmetic operators and relational operators.

```
140 LET C = (A * B) / D
150 IF D$ <> C$ THEN PRINT "DATA ENTRY ERROR"
160 IF C <= D THEN 700
```

3. Space before each item in a DATA list.

```
340 DATA A, B, C$
900 DATA 36, 14, "WIDGETS"
```

4. Space between BASIC command and variables.

```
150 LET X = Y
160 FOR N = 1 TO X
170 IF R$ = "STOP" THEN 999
```

5. For NEXT loop spacing:

   a. Indent the body of a FOR NEXT loop two to three spaces.

```
100 FOR X = 1 TO 40
110       LET Y = 2 * D
120       PRINT X, Y
130 NEXT X
```

   b. Indent nested FOR NEXT loops two to three spaces, or use colons to indicate nesting.

```
100 FOR X = 1 TO 10
110     FOR Y = 1 TO 5
120        LET A(X,Y) = 0
130     NEXT Y
140 NEXT X
```

or

```
100 : FOR X = 1 TO 10
120 :: FOR Y = 1 TO 5
130       LET A(X,Y) = 0
140 :: NEXT Y
150 : NEXT X
```

6. Indent nested IF. . .THEN statements two to three spaces.

```
100 IF A$ = "STOP" THEN 999
110      IF B$ = "END" THEN 999
120           IF C = 0 THEN 999
```

7. Indent the body of IF. . .THEN loops.

```
140 IF X <> Y THEN 200
150       PRINT "INVALID ITEM ENTERED": GOTO 240
```

Other Techniques To Enhance Looks and Readability

You can do still more to make your program clearer to you and another reader. These few ideas are the "finishing touch."

Using LET, even though unnecessary, is very readable. The absence of LET can be confusing, especially in a multiple statement line.

Confusing

```
260 X=Y : C = X*Y: IF X=N THEN X=C
```

Better

```
140 LET X = 0 : Y = 0 : C = 0
```

Best

```
260 LET X = Y : LET C = X * Y : IF X = N THEN LET X = C
```

Arrange BASIC statements so that they read smoothly from left to right, just as the readers' eyes flow across the paper. This includes placing A before B and 1 before 2. Some stylists recommend that in IF. . .THEN statements, you place the least varying variable last, as shown in lines 270 and 300 below.

```
150 READ A, B, C


260 FOR X = 1 TO 8
270 IF M(X) <> N THEN 290
280 LET M9X0 = N
290 NEXT X
300 IF D$ = "STOP" THEN 999
```

If your typed statement is long, it is probably confusing, especially if it is a mathematical equation. Break it into two or more pieces so it is easy to read. Read the statements aloud to test their readability.

Confusing

```
250 LET T = (N * 3.75) + ((N -40) * 3.25) + ((N - 60) / 3)/
    ((D * N) * A)
```

Clearer

```
250 LET T = (N * 3.75) + ((N - 40) * 3.25)
255 LET T = T + ((N - 60) / 3) / ((D * N) * A)
```

To maximize the "prettiness" of any printed report, use the PRINT USING or formatted output capability available in most BASICs. For the best looking results in your screen displays, use whatever graphic display commands your BASIC includes. However, be aware that the PRINT USING and graphic display commands are very different from BASIC to BASIC. Although you should use PRINT USING and graphics to enhance output, you inhibit program portability when you do so. One possible solution to this problem is to place all graphic display routines in clearly identified subroutines so a reader is directed to the right section of your program to make changes. Formatted strings used with PRINT USING can all be placed in one location toward the end of the program, making it easy for another user to change.

UNDOING IT ALL TO SAVE SPACE AND SPEED UP RUN TIME

After reading all these rules and ways to enhance readability, you are probably wondering how you will possibly remember them all. You probably won't, but we hope we have at least sensitized you to the need for writing clear, readable programs. You will adopt your own typing style based on some of these techniques, plus others that you devise for convenience.

Nearly every technique illustrated in this chapter uses what some would consider to be unnecessary memory space. You may in fact find that your computer memory is filled before you have completely entered your program. When this happens, either rethink your entire problem-solving technique or look for ways to save memory space by making changes to your program. A well-written, readable program takes up more memory space than a poorly written, less readable program. Thus, to save memory space, you may have to undo some of the things you did to enhance readability.

To save large numbers of memory "bytes:"

1. Use multiple statements per line.
2. Delete all REMARK statements beginning with the introductory module.

For further space saving:

1. Use one-letter variable names.
2. Delete unnecessary parentheses.
3. Reuse variables when possible (normally a terrible technique).
4. Delete spaces between characters in a statement.
5. Use integer variables when possible.

```
FOR X% = 1 TO 10
```

6. Dimension arrays sparingly.
7. Use GOTO, not GOSUB, for a routine accessed from only one place in a program.

If you are concerned about the speed of your program run, you can use some techniques to shave microseconds, even seconds, off the run time. Some of these overlap with the space-saving techniques.

1. Delete all REMARKS and/or move the introductory module to the end.
2. Use multi-statement lines.
3. Use variables rather than constants (as recommended earlier).
4. Define the most commonly used variables first.
5. Use integer variables where possible.
6. Place subroutines before the main program.
7. Use FOR NEXT loops whenever possible.
8. Remove extra parentheses.
9. Limit the use of GOSUBs.

Remember, these techniques may speed up your run, but they are generally considered to be bad programming techniques and contrary to nearly everything said in this chapter.

To save space and lessen distraction we have not followed ALL the rules suggested in this chapter in the rest of this book. However, you will still find our programs easy to read and self-documenting.

CHAPTER 1 SELF-TEST

1. Will a useful program written in BASIC on one computer system also RUN on a different brand of computer that uses BASIC? Why or why not?

   ____

   ____

   ____

2. How can you be most certain that a program you write will also run on another person's computer?

   ____

   ____

   ____

3. What is meant by the portability of a computer program?

   ____

   ____

   ____

4. Name at least three types of information to include in REMARK statements in a program's introductory module.

   ____

   ____

   ____

5. Describe the "top-to-bottom format" for organizing programs.

   ____

   ____

   ____

   ____

6. When branching statements such as GOTO and GOSUB are used, what statements should not be branched to and why?

7. Define "initializing."

8. What is the most important reason for designating a segment of a program as a subroutine accessed by GOSUB?

9. When writing a self-documenting, easy to read program, what sacrifices are made?

10. In a multiple statement line with three statements, the first being a REMARK statement, how many statements will be executed?

Answer Key

1. The program might not run on a different brand of computer, because different computers use different versions of BASIC.

2. Use conservative programming techniques and the least fancy statements in your version of BASIC.

3. Portability means that the program is likely to run on many computers with few or no modifications.

4. Variables used and what they stand for, files used, descriptive name for program, description of program if necessary, author of program, last revision of program, version of BASIC and/or system used. (any three answers)

5. To the extent possible, the program is written so that it begins execution at the smallest line number and procedes towards the largest, with a minimum of confusing branching within the program.

6. REMARK statements, in case they are removed from a program to save computer memory space.

7. The first time in a program that value(s) are assigned to variables or elements in a array (often means assignment of zeros); DIMENSIONING where needed.

8. The segment would otherwise have to be repeated because it is used more than once in executing the program.

9. Amount of memory used and possibly speed of program execution.

10. None. The computer goes on to the next line numbered statement if it sees that the first statement in the line is a REMARK.

CHAPTER TWO

An Important Review of BASIC Statements

Objectives: To review important aspects of BASIC. When you finish this chapter, you will be able to write BASIC statements using: LET, READ, DATA, INPUT, LINE INPUT, IF. . .THEN, FOR NEXT, GOSUB, RETURN, ON. . .GOTO, LEN, ASC, MID$, LEFT$, RIGHT$, and INSTR.

INTRODUCTION

We assume you have used BASIC to write programs and that you can read and understand a listing of a BASIC program (are you BASICly literate?); this information serves as a review. Many of the programming techniques in this and the next chapter will be used over and over again in your programming of data files. Even masters at programming in BASIC should give the material a quick run through. This is important information and skill to have under your belt so that you can give your fullest attention to learning file-handling BASIC statements and techniques in Chapter 4.

VARIABLE NAMES

In early versions of BASIC, the names you could choose for a variable were limited to one letter, or one letter and one number only. A, A1, Z7, ZØ, B$, and B1$ were all acceptable variable names: while AA, A25, SALARY, or NAME$ were unacceptable to the computer. In contrast, BASIC-80 and other new dialects of BASIC permit the use of multi-letter variable names. The unacceptable variable names mentioned above are all acceptable in these newer versions of BASIC, as are SUBTOTAL, TOTAL, NETPAY, GRANDPRIZE, GUESS, OLDNAME$, NEWNAME$, and many others you may think of. The temptation to use long variable names may be overwhelming, but beware! *TRS-80 BASIC recognizes and identifies the variable using only the first two letters of the variable name.* Thus, the variables SALES and SALARY are not really two variables, but rather *one* – SA. PAYMENT and PAYROLL are really the same variable – PA – in TRS-80 BASIC, but are different variables in BASIC-80, which identifies up to forty characters in a variable name. Be extremely cautious selecting variable names to avoid unusual errors that are hard to detect. Also note that longer variable names take up more computer memory space, which may become a problem as the programs you write become longer and more complex.

Another limitation when using long variable names is that you cannot use a combination of letters that are also used for a BASIC statement, command, or function. A Reserved Word List in your reference manual tells you which words cannot be a part of a long variable name. Examples are:

FOR, DATA, OPEN, CLOSE, PRINT, KILL, IF, THEN

Use of simple variable names (A, T1, Y$) precludes having to debug a program when the problem is a reserved word accidentally used (embedded) in a long variable name. Notice in our examples, that even with simple variables we have selected names that are more likely to be remembered and make sense to someone reading the program. We encourage you to do the same. Use T for total, T9 for grand total, S for salary, N$ for name, etc.

The letters O and I are poor variable names since they are easily confused with the number Ø (zero), the number 1 (one), or the lower case letter l (el). Some experienced programmers reserve a few variables and use them the same way in all programs they write. X, Y, and Z are popular as control variables in FOR NEXT loops. K and C are popular for counting in statements like LET C = C + 1.

Variables, also called variable names or labels, identify for the computer a particular place in its memory where information is stored. The information may be numeric (a value) or alphanumeric (a string, discussed more fully later). A value or string is first stored by an assignment statement (LET, READ, INPUT), and subsequent references to the variable tell the computer to use the value or string assigned to (and identified by) that variable. Assignment statements are included in this review of BASIC.

(a) Give two reasons for using simple variable names such as A, X3, and Y$.

(a) 1. Conserves computer memory space.
2. No reserved words are accidentally embedded in the variable.
3. Portability of programs between different versions of BASIC.
(any two answers)

String Variables

The rules for constructing names for string variables are the same as for numeric variables, except that a string variable always has a dollar sign ($) as its last character. A is a numeric variable, whereas A$ is a string variable. A string is one or more letters, symbols, or numbers that can be used as information in a BASIC program. Strings are stored in the computer's memory with an assignment statement such as LET B$ = "EXAMPLE OF A STRING." The string variable B$ acts as a label in the computer's memory for the place where the string assigned to B$ is stored. A reference to B$ elsewhere in the program automatically tells the computer to use the string assigned to B$. The string assigned to a string variable is often referred to as the "value" of the string variable.

String variables act much like numeric variables and can generally be manipulated just like numeric variables. The crucial difference, is that you cannot use string variables in arithmetic expressions and calculations, even if numeric information is assigned to the string variable. For example, LET F$ = "8.99" does not let you use F$ in numeric calculations, even though the string is comprised of numbers.

String variables and the strings assigned to them take up space in your computer's memory. You can visualize this as a box or compartment that contains alphanumeric information identified by a string variable. For example, the assignment statement LET N$ = "ALPHA PRODUCTS COMPANY" can be thought of as creating a storage compartment in the computer's memory like this:

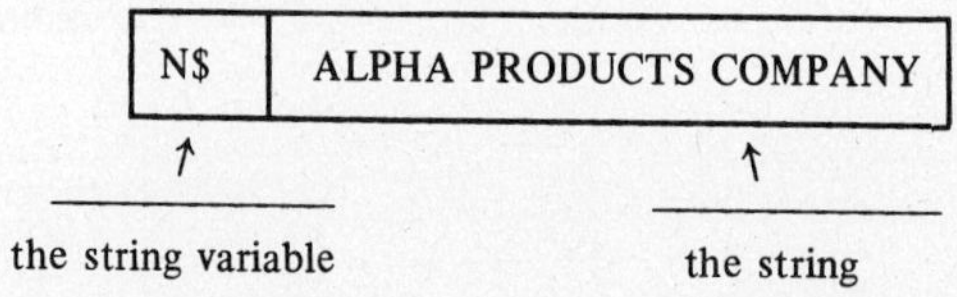

Remember that a string assigned to a string variable in this way has the string enclosed in **quotation marks.** Only the information between the quotation marks comprises the string; the quotes themselves are not part of the string.

Many, if not most, business and personal applications of data files make much greater use of alphanumeric data (strings) than numeric data (numbers or values), so we are taking this opportunity to reinforce and extend your understanding of the use of string variables. Notice the word "alphanumeric." This term comes from the data processing industry and refers to data that may consist of alphabetic characters, numeric characters, and/or special characters. For example, the product identification number FC1372 appearing in a catalog is alphanumeric data consisting of two alphabetic characters followed by four numeric characters. An address or hyphenated phone number is also alphanumeric data. To use and store such information in BASIC, assign it to a string variable (LET P$ = "FC1372") because a simple numeric variable would not accept the two alphabetic characters. If an identification number is mostly numeric, but includes a hyphen, asterisk, or even a space (e.g., 84992*, where the "*" denotes a special location, price, etc.), then it too requires the use of a string variable.

One string variable can have from zero to 255 characters, including all spaces, punctuation, and special characters. A string with no characters (zero characters) is called a *null string* or empty string. An assignment statement for a null string would be: LET Z$ = " ".

There is a crucial difference between the *maximum* length of a string (255 characters) and its *actual* length. The actual length is the number of alphanumeric characters presently assigned to the string variable and stored in the computer's memory. Remember, spaces count as characters. Consider the lengths of the following strings assigned to string variables.

N$	ALPHA PRODUCTS

Actual length: Fourteen characters

C$	MENLO PARK, CA. 94025

Actual length: Twenty-one characters (includes comma, period, and spaces)

Now you do this one:

A$	161 DAWN ST. SUITE 3

(a) What is the maximum length for a string assigned to A$?

____

(b) What is the actual length of the string shown as assigned to A$ above?

____

— — — — — — — — — — — — — — —

(a) 255 characters
(b) Twenty characters

Since TRS-80 BASIC and BASIC-80 automatically assume that a string variable can be assigned a string with up to 255 characters, there is no need to DIMENSION string variables. However, we recommend that you show a person using your program what the string size (maximum *actual* size) is for all string variables listed in the program. Do this by including REMARK statements in the introductory module, as shown:

```
4 :
140 REM    STRING VARIABLES
150 REM      N$ = CUSTOMER NAME(20)
160 REM      A$ = CUST. ADDRESS(25)
170 REM      C$ = CUST. CITY(15),STATE(2),ZIP(5)
180 REM              (26 TOTAL INCLUDING SPACES)
190 REM
```

(a) How many characters are contained in a null string assigned to a string variable?

____

(b) In the actual length of a string, how many characters does a space use?

____

(a) zero (none)
(b) one

As noted earlier, you can *assign a string to a string variable using the LET statement.* Remember to place the string inside quotation marks, or the computer will reject the statement; it will tell you that an error has been made. Example:

```
240 LET N$ = "TYPE A POSITIVE"
```

Almost all versions of BASIC allow omitting the word LET from an assignment statement. For this reason, LET statements are sometimes called *direct assignment statements* to distinguish them from INPUT and READ assignment statements. A variable (numeric or string) followed by an equal sign (=) implies LET to BASIC; thus, the "implied LET" direct assignment statement can save a bit of typing and a little memory space. We generally include LET for clarity in reading a program listing. This statement:

```
240 N$ = "TYPE A POSITIVE"
```

means the same in BASIC as the example before this paragraph.

READ-DATA ASSIGNMENT STATEMENTS

DATA statements are like data files in that they hold data to be assigned to variables and are then used in a program. The difference is that a DATA statement holds data that can only be used by the program in which the DATA statement appears, whereas a data file can be created and the data used by a variety of different programs, since it is separate from the program itself. This will be explained in greater detail later.

The READ statement, which must have one or more DATA statements in the same program to READ from, is an assignment statement. One or more data items from a DATA statement are assigned to one or more variables by a READ statement.

```
10 READ A
20 DATA 15, 76.5, 1892, -999
```

The statement READ A assigns a numeric value from the DATA statement to variable A.

```
10 READ A, B
20 DATA 15, 76.5, 1892, -999
```

The statement READ A, B assigns two consecutive values from the DATA statement; the first to variable A, the second to B.

A program can also use the READ and DATA statements to assign strings to string variables. A DATA statement can contain strings as data items, and these strings are assigned to string variables by a READ statement using the same procedure as for reading numeric values.

```
220 READ A$, B$, C$
 .
 .
 .
910 DATA BLUE, GREEN, GOLD
```

In TRS-80 BASIC and BASIC-80, the individual string items in the DATA statement do not have to be enclosed in quotation marks *unless* the string data item includes a comma, semicolon, or one or more leading spaces (blank spaces that are to be included and considered part of the string). In the latter cases, enclose the string data item in quotation marks, just as for a LET direct assignment statement. In TRS-80 BASIC and BASIC-80, any trailing spaces left between a string data item and the comma separating it from the next item in the same data statement are accepted as part of the string and duly assigned to the string variable. Note that the actual length of such a data item includes these trailing spaces, even though they seem invisible.

In the following example, quotation marks are necessary around each data item because a comma is part of the string data items themselves.

```
220 READ N$
 .
 .
 .
910 DATA "BROWN, JERALD R.", "FINKEL, LEROY P."
```

Try this test program to see how the "trailing space" rule works on your system.

```
220 READ N$, A$
230 PRINT N$; A$
910 DATA TEST    ,    ITEMS

RUN
TEST   ITEMS
```

There should be only three spaces between the words TEST and ITEMS because the leading spaces before items are not included, while the trailing spaces after TEST and before the comma are included. Now change line 910 as shown below and RUN the program segment again.

```
910 DATA "TEST   ","   ITEMS"
```

(a) How many spaces should now appear between the strings when the program is RUN? ______________________________

- - - - - - - - - - - - - - - - -

(a) six spaces

The computer uses an internal "pointer" system to keep track of items in a DATA statement that are "used up" or already assigned to variables in a program RUN. When executing READ-DATA statements, each time a data item is read and assigned to a variable the internal pointer advances one position in the DATA statement to the next data item. If the pointer is pointed at alphanumeric data (a string) and the READ statement is looking for numeric information to assign to a numeric variable, the program will terminate in an error condition. For example:

```
210 READ A
910 DATA ALPHA, NUMERIC
```

An error condition would result from executing this program segment because the statement READ A is "looking" for numeric data to assign to the numeric variable A, but the pointer is pointing at alphanumeric information.

What will happen if this program is RUN?

```
210 READ A$, B$
220 PRINT A$; B$
910 DATA 17926, NUMERIC
```

(a) Will the program RUN without an error condition? ________________

(b) What will be assigned to A$ and why? ______________________________

____

(a) Yes (in TRS-80 BASIC and BASIC-80).
(b) A$ = 17926, since a number can be assigned as a string to a string variable (but not vice versa).

UNDERSTANDING INPUT, AN IMPORTANT ASSIGNMENT STATEMENT

You can enter numeric or alphanumeric information to be assigned to a numeric variable or a string variable using the INPUT statement. A related assignment statement, the LINE INPUT statement, can accept only alphanumeric information to be assigned to one string variable, as discussed in more detail later.

When using INPUT statements, make certain that the data entry person using your program at a computer terminal knows exactly what kind of information to enter for assignment to a variable by the INPUT statement. To do so, *you* must fully understand how INPUT works in your version of BASIC.

The INPUT statement should always include a prompting string (a message that appears on the printer or display screen) to tell the user exactly what sort of information is to be entered. A typical format for an INPUT statement is:

```
160 INPUT "ENTER YOUR NAME, FIRST NAME AND THEN LAST"; N$
```

An INPUT statement without a prompting message (the part enclosed by quotes) causes the computer to print or display a question mark; the computer then waits for a response from the keyboard. There is nothing more frustrating to a computer user than an INPUT question mark with no hint as to what sort of response is requested. *Always use a prompting string in an INPUT statement.* If necessary, use PRINT statements preceding the INPUT statement to explain to the user what information to enter.

Another source of user frustration is the funny responses the computer can make when incorrect data are entered. Consider the following example:

```
360 INPUT "ENTER PRODUCT NUMBER AND QUANTITY"; N, Q

RUN
ENTER PRODUCT NUMBER AND QUANTITY?137
??
```

The user entered the number 137 after the prompting message and question mark, and then pressed the ENTER key. The computer responded with a double question mark (??), indicating that more data were expected. Notice that the INPUT statement had two variables to assign values to but only one value (137) was entered. An inexperienced user would not know that.

RUN the same program segment again and enter three items of data.

```
RUN
ENTER PRODUCT NUMBER AND QUANTITY?137,12,164
? ENTRY IGNORED
```

or

```
INPUT ERROR-RETYPE
```

or

```
? REDO FROM START
```

These general error messages don't provide any help to the user since they don't pinpoint the problem. To make matters worse, the computer may accept incorrect data and assign it to the INPUT variables!

The same error conditions and input problems can occur in string data with an additional peculiarity. Consider the following program segment:

```
180 INPUT "ENTER CUSTOMER NUMBER AND NAME"; C, N$
190 PRINT C, N$

RUN
ENTER CUSTOMER NUMBER AND NAME?13726
??
13726
```

Here the user entered the customer number (13726) and pressed ENTER, and the number was duly assigned to variable C. But when the ?? appeared, indicating that the computer expected yet another entry, the user pressed the ENTER key again without making another entry. While the computer wanted a second entry to assign to N$, it accepted "nothing" as an entry; that is, it accepted a null string and assigned it to N$. If we changed the INPUT variables to C$ and N$ (instead of C and N$), the computer would accept null strings for assignment to both string variables. In that case, the computer interprets two presses on the ENTER key as meaning that it should assign null strings to both variables.

Not all versions of BASIC, even MICROSOFT BASIC, react as we have explained for TRS-80 BASIC. MICROSOFT BASIC-80 will give you the message ? REDO FROM START if you enter for INPUT:

(1) too few values or strings.
(2) too many values or strings.
(3) the wrong type of data; that is, a string for a numeric variable.

Furthermore, pressing the ENTER or RETURN key without making an entry will assign a zero to a numeric variable and a null string to a string variable.

Our insistence on the importance of understanding INPUT should now be hitting home. So what do you do for the accidental null string entry and the other eccentricities of the INPUT statement?

Two programming techniques can help eliminate errors. First, ask the user to enter only *one* value or string per INPUT statement, period! This makes data entry (and data checking, as we will discuss in the next chapter) nice and clean. For example:

```
RUN
ENTER CUSTOMER NUMBER?137
ENTER CUSTOMER NAME?BISHOP BROTHERS
ENTER PRODUCT NUMBER?18625
ENTER QUANTITY ORDERED?106
```

Second, to have *all* input entries, whether string or numeric, assigned to string variables. This eliminates error messages for numeric variables that cannot accept alphanumeric information for assignment. In the next chapter you will learn to test for null strings (no entry made) and appropriately advise the user with explicit messages as to the proper entry to be made. Numbers (numeric values) assigned to string variables can be converted from strings to numeric values for arithmetic operations using the VAL function. If Q$ = 106 (a string), then VAL(Q$) converts 106 to a numeric value that can be assigned to a numeric variable and/or used directly as a numeric value in a BASIC expression. VAL is discussed in the next chapter.

(a) Write an INPUT statement that will result in the following RUN:

```
RUN
ENTER YOUR HOME ADDRESS?
```

____

____

____

– – – – – – – – – – – – – – – –

(a) 100 INPUT "ENTER YOUR HOME ADDRESS"; A$ (your line number and string variable may be different).

The LINE INPUT Statement

TRS-80 BASIC and BASIC-80 provide an alternate INPUT statement called the LINE INPUT statement. This statement allows you to enter data that includes commas, quotation marks, and lead blanks (spaces). LINE INPUT (LINPUT on some computers) is used only to enter data for assignment to a string variable, with only one string assignment (and string variable) per LINE INPUT statement. This parallels our emphatic recommendation that you request only one entry per INPUT statement and that all data be entered as strings, whether numeric or alphanumeric. Note that LINE INPUT allows a prompting string just as the INPUT statement does. However, it does not automatically add a question mark at the end of the prompt when the program is RUN. If you want a question mark (or a hyphen or colon) to appear at the end of the prompting string, include it inside the quotation marks as part of the prompt. If a LINE INPUT statement contains no prompt, not even a question mark will indicate to the user that the program is waiting at a LINE INPUT statement for data to be entered from the keyboard. Here is an example of a LINE INPUT statement:

```
160 LINE INPUT "ENTER MAILING ADDRESS:"; M$

RUN
ENTER MAILING ADDRESS:
```

LINE INPUT is particularly useful when entering a line of text (LINE INPUT, get it?), because it will accept all commas and quotes within the text and stops accepting data only when you press the ENTER key. However, the maximum length of a "line" is still 255 characters per string variable and, therefore, per LINE INPUT statement. We use LINE INPUT for convenience. If your computer doesn't accept a LINE INPUT statement, use INPUT.

(a) Give two reasons the authors prefer the use of LINE INPUT over the INPUT statement.

____

____

____

____

____

____

- - - - - - - - - - - - - - - -

(a) 1. LINE INPUT forces you to ask for only one entry per INPUT statement.
2. Only string assignments can be made with the LINE INPUT statement.

CONCATENATION

Strings can be joined to form longer strings; a process called *concatenation.* Strings are concatenated in BASIC using the plus (+) sign. The process, however, is one of joining, not of arithmetic addition. For example, the strings assigned to F$ and L$ can be concatenated and the new, longer string assigned to another variable N$ in an assignment statement like this:

```
110 LET N$ = F$ + L$
```

Strings assigned to variables can be concatenated with string constants, like this:

```
120 LET G$ = N$ + "CUSTOMER"
```

or

```
150 LET N$ = F$ + " " + L$
```

The statement above concatenates the strings associated with F$ and L$ and assigns them to N$, but it also places a space in the new N$ string between the parts of N$ that were assigned to F$ and L$. Look at the following program and show what will be printed when it is RUN.

(a)
```
10 LET F$ = "JANET"
20 LET L$ = "BARRINGTON"
30 LET N$ = F$ + " " + L$
40 PRINT N$

RUN
```

____

- - - - - - - - - - - - - - - - -

(a) JANET BARRINGTON

IF. . .THEN STATEMENTS

The IF. . .THEN statement in BASIC gives the language real power. Its syntax varies from one BASIC system to another. Some BASICs permit only a GOTO statement to follow and IF. . .THEN expression.

```
140 IF X<Y THEN (GOTO) 800
```

(The GOTO can be, and usually is, omitted.)

The simplest form of IF. . .THEN is a COMPARISON between two numeric values or expressions. IF the comparison is true, THEN (GOTO) a given line number and continue executing the program with the statement at that line number. Since GOTO is usually omitted, just the line number follows THEN. The possible comparisons are:

=	equals
<	less than
>	greater than
<=	less than or equal to*
>=	greater than or equal to*
<>	not equal to**

*Note: most BASICs allow you to put the equal sign either before or after the greater than or less than symbol.

**Note: some BASICs either use <> or allow the # sign as a "not equal to" symbol.

TRS-80 and BASIC-80 also include in the IF. . .THEN family of statements:

IF. . .THEN	LET. . .	(Follow rules for regular LET statements. LET can be omitted.)
IF. . .THEN	GOSUB. . .	(Line number follows GOSUB.)
IF. . .THEN	RETURN. . .	(Unusual, but possible.)
IF. . .THEN	PRINT. . .	(Follow all the rules for regular PRINT statements.)
IF. . .THEN	INPUT. . .	
IF. . .THEN	READ. . .	(These two are possible, but are not recommended because of confusion and debugging complications.)
IF. . .THEN	STOP. . .	
IF. . .THEN	END. . .	
IF. . .THEN	IF. . .THEN. . .	(Possible, but confusing and unnecessary.)

(a) What statement is implied after the THEN in the simplest form of the IF. . .THEN statement? ______________

(b) List at least five BASIC statements that can be part of an IF. . .THEN statement and that will be executed if the condition (comparison) is true.

(a) GOTO
(b) PRINT, GOTO (assuming a line number appears after THEN),
LET (direct assignment statement, with the option of omitting the word LET),
READ, INPUT, another IF. . .THEN statement (not recommended),
GOSUB, RETURN (any 5 answers)

IF. . .AND. . .THEN. . . and IF. . .OR. . .THEN. . . are called the logical AND and logical OR. They allow you to put more than one comparison in a single IF. . .THEN statement. The comparisons on both sides of an AND must be true for the entire IF. . .THEN comparison to be true. Only one comparison on either side of an OR must be true for the comparison to be true. You can use more than one AND and more than one OR between IF and THEN, and you may use both AND and OR in the same IF. . .THEN statement which allows three or more comparisons in one IF. . .THEN statement! Be certain you understand how to use the logical AND and OR to produce the results you want. We find they are useful for certain checks on user INPUT entries. If an INPUT value should be between five and twenty, then the following statement would check that the value was within these parameters.

```
150 IF F<5 OR F>20 THEN PRINT "ENTRY IS INCORRECT"
```

Alternately, the following line would check for "within bounds" parameters for the value assigned to F, instead of "out of bounds" values.

```
150 IF F>=5 AND F<=20 THEN PRINT "ENTRY WITHIN BOUNDS"
```

Note: be very careful to have your logic straight or such comparison statements will not do what you want. For some, flow charts help visualize the alternatives so you can properly construct your comparison statements. Thorough testing of programs and program segments with every conceivable mistake that you could enter is a must.

(a) Write two IF. . .THEN statements, one using a logical AND and another using a logical OR. The statement should test to see if the value assigned to variable Y is greater than, but not equal to, zero, and less than, but not equal to, one. When the comparison is true, one statement should print the message BETWEEN ZERO AND ONE, and the other should print NOT BETWEEN ZERO AND ONE.

(a)
```
IF Y > 0 AND Y < 1 THEN PRINT "BETWEEN ZERO AND ONE"
IF Y <= 0 OR Y >= 1 THEN PRINT "NOT BETWEEN ZERO AND ONE"
```

Having seen how more than one comparison can be made within a single IF. . .THEN statement, now consider the other end of the comparison statement and how to have more than one instruction executed in the case of a true IF. . .THEN comparison.

TRS-80 BASIC and BASIC-80 permit you to do nearly anything after an IF. . .THEN expression, frequently encouraging you to place multiple statements on one line.

```
150 IF X<Y THEN PRINT "TOO LOW": LET C = C + 1 : GOTO 10
160 IF X>Y THEN LET C = C + 1: LET G = 0 : GOTO 10
```

When you use this MICROSOFT BASIC feature, keep in mind that you may be hindering the portability of your program. If this doesn't concern you, forget it! We do urge you to complete your entire "activity" on one line after an IF. . .THEN statement, otherwise the program is extremely awkward to follow. If you cannot complete your activity on one line, then GOTO a section where all of the activity can be done together. Follow the acceptable example:

Bad

```
150 IF X<Y THEN LET X = X+D: LET Y = Y/N: GOTO 200
160 IF X>Y THEN LET X=X - D: Y = Y/N: GOTO 10

200 LET C=C+1 : PRINT "TOO LOW": GOTO 10
```

Acceptable

```
150 IF X<Y THEN 200
160 IF X>Y THEN 250


200  LET X = X+D
210  LET Y = Y/N
220 LET C = C + 1          . . . or all on one line
230 PRINT "TOO LOW"
240  GOTO 10
```

Most of us who program for fun ignore what is going on inside the computer because we don't have to pay attention. However, on occasion, little "bugs," inconsistencies, and our own ignorance can cause some interesting (and frustrating) problems. BASIC software sometimes does funny things, barely detectable because the problem exists at the seventh or eighth decimal location, which may be invisible to the BASIC user. We once spent hours trying to fix a "money changing" program that kept giving us 4.9999 pennies change instead of a nickel. (This points out a very important lesson: Your BASIC language interpreter does not always do things with the accuracy and consistency you might expect.) Therefore when you are comparing numeric values, especially numbers that have been computed by your computer, try to compare using less than (<), greater than (>), or not equal (< >).

Good

```
IF X<1125.75 THEN...
IF X>1125.75 THEN...
IF X <> 1125.75 THEN.....
```

Not wise

```
IF X = 1125.75 THEN....
```

(a) Why should you avoid IF. . .THEN comparisons for equality?

(a) Internal round-off errors may produce very slightly inaccurate values in calculations. Therefore, a comparison for equality might fail (be false) where you would expect the comparison to be true.

IF. . .THEN String Comparisons and the ASCII Code

So far the only comparisons used in IF. . .THEN examples have been between two numeric expressions or values. Comparing *strings* in IF. . .THEN statements begins to get a little tricky. However, comparisons for equality or inequality are fairly straightforward. Examine these statements:

```
220 LINE INPUT "ENTER YOUR LEGAL NAME:"; N$
230 IF N$ = "STOP" THEN 999
```

Notice that in line 230 a string variable (N$) is compared with a string constant ("STOP"). A string constant in a comparison must be enclosed in quotation marks. In order for a comparison for equality between two strings to be true, each and every character in the two strings must be identical (upper and lower case are different), and the length of the strings and any leading or trailing spaces must be the same. Any difference *whatsoever,* and the equality comparison will be false.

In line 230 above, the string assigned to a string variable was compared to a string constant. Likewise, the contents of two string variables can be compared.

```
310 LINE INPUT "ENTER THE OLD TITLE:"; T$
320 IF T$ <> D$ THEN PRINT "WRONG TITLE. TRY ANOTHER"
```

The difficulty in string comparisons comes with the "less than" or "greater than" comparisons. These have application in sorting strings, alphabetizing data, or inserting new information into an alphabetically organized data file. In IF. . .THEN comparisons, BASIC compares the two strings one character at a time, from left to right.

Rather than comparing within the construct of a twenty-six-character alphabet, *BASIC uses a standard code that represents every possible signal a terminal keyboard can send to the computer (and vice versa).* Each key and each permitted combination of keys, such as the shift or CONTROL key along with another key, sends a unique electronic *code* pattern to the computer. *These patterns are represented by the decimal numbers 0 through 127 in the ASCII Code chart.* Mercifully, here is one instance of standardization throughout the computer industry. ASCII stands for American Standard Code for Information Interchange. The ASCII code's 128-character set includes the upper and lower case letters of the alphabet, numbers, punctuation, and other special characters and special function keys. The ASCII code also includes 128 other special codes that are numbered 129 through 255, that do not concern us. Find the ASCII chart in the Appendix, and refer to it for your understanding of the following.

Notice that the numbers 0 through 9 have ASCII codes of 48 to 57. The alphabet has ASCII codes of 65 to 90 for upper case letters; lower case starts at 96. Therefore, the lower case equivalent of an upper case letter is the upper case letter's ASCII code number plus 31.

$$A = 65, \text{ so } a = 65 + 31 = 96$$

This fact will be of use later.

What actually happens in an IF. . .THEN string comparison? BASIC compares the ASCII code number for each character in the two strings, comparing just *one* character at a time. As soon as an inequality exists between characters, the string with the character that has the lower ASCII code number will be considered "less than" the other string. BASIC *does not* add up the ASCII code values for the two strings being compared to determine "less than" or "greater than." The following chart shows the results of comparing a series of strings assigned to A$ and B$.

A$	B$		
ABC	ABD	A$ IS LESS THAN B$	
MN!	MNO	A$ IS LESS THAN B$	
STOP	STO	B$ IS LESS THAN A$	(A$ is greater than B$)
123A	123a	A$ IS LESS THAN B$	

In the comparison process, if one string ends before the other and no other difference has been found, then the shorter string is said to be "less than" the longer one. One result is that a null string is always "less than" a non-null string, since the ASCII code for null is zero. Here are some more examples of string comparisons:

```
A$            B$

SMITH         SMITHE      A$ IS LESS THAN B$
ALCOTJONES    ALCOT       A$ IS GREATER THAN B$
JOHNSEN       JOHNSON     A$ IS LESS THAN B$
KELLOG        KELLOGG     A$ IS LESS THAN B$
EQ-8          EQ 8        B$ IS LESS THAN A$
```

(B$ is less than A$)

Now it's your turn to familiarize yourself with ASCII code comparisons. Fill in the blanks with the appropriate string variable.

	C$	D$			
(a)	JACOB	JACOBS	______	is greater than	______
(b)	LOREN	LORAN	______	is less than	______
(c)	SMITH-HILL	SMITH HILL	______	is less than	______
(d)	ABLE12	ABLE-12	______	is less than	______
(e)	Theater	THEATER	______	is less than	______
(f)	95.2	95-2	______	is less than	______

\- - - - - - - - - - - - - - -

(a) D$,C$ D$ has more characters, others being equal
(b) D$.C$ Letter A is less than letter E
(c) D$,C$ A space is less than a hyphen
(d) D$,C$ A hyphen is less than the number 1
(e) D$,C$ Uppercase letters are less than lower case letters
(f) D$, C$ A hyphen is less than a decimal point

Two string functions are used in conjunction with the ASCII code. The ASC ( ) function gives the ASCII code number for the first character of the string contained in the parentheses or for the first character of the string assigned to the string variable contained in the parentheses. The ASCII number produced by ASC ( ) may be assigned to a variable, displayed by a PRINT statement, used in arithmetic expressions, and used as a value in an IF. . .THEN comparison.

```
LET X = ASC(A$)
LET X = ASC("ANTWERP")
PRINT ASC(A$)
IF ASC(N$) = 0 THEN...
```

Give the ASCII number or value that will be printed for each of these program segments. Refer to the ASCII chart in the appendix.

(a)
```
10 LET D$ = "DOLLAR"
20 PRINT ASC(D$)
RUN
```

____

(b)
```
10 PRINT ASC("YES")
RUN
```

____

(c)
```
10 LET F$ = "FRANK"
20 LET L$ = "JONES"
30 LET N$ = L$ + "," + F$
40 PRINT ASC(F$)
50 PRINT ASC(L$)
60 PRINT ASC(N$)
RUN
```

____

____

____

(d)
```
10 PRINT ASC(" ")
RUN
```

____

- - - - - - - - - - - - - - - -

(a) 68
(b) 89
(c) 70
74
74
(d) 32

Describe the string that must be assigned to A$ in order for the following IF. . .THEN comparisons to be true.

(a) IF ASC(A$) = 53 THEN 510 ______________________________

(b) IF ASC(A$) <> 48 THEN 810 ______________________________

(c) IF ASC(A$) = Ø THEN 950 ______________________________

- - - - - - - - - - - - - - - -

(a) First character in A$ is 5
(b) First character in A$ is not zero
(c) A$ must be a null string

The opposite of the ASC( ) function is the CHR$( ) function. An ASCII number is placed in the parentheses. It causes the computer to send that ASCII code signal to the terminal, which can cause the printing of an alphanumeric character. CHR$( ) is also used to send special control signals to the CRT screen or printer (ASCII numbers 0 through 31). On the TRS-80, it can be used for graphic control codes (ASCII numbers 129 to 191 – see your reference manual). You can also use CHR$( ) in a PRINT statement to print characters corresponding to the ASCII number in the CHR$( ) parentheses.

```
840 PRINT CHR$(69); CHR$(78); CHR$(68)
```

(a) By running this program or by reference to the ASCII chart, what will this program line print? ____________

- - - - - - - - - - - - - - -

(a) END

CHR$(7) rings the bell or sounds the beeper on many terminals. CHR$(34) produces quotation marks in situations where they would not otherwise be printed around a string. Remember these possibilities. Check the ASCII codes, especially 0 through 31, in your computer reference manual. There may be some interesting capabilities to explore.

THE LEN FUNCTION

Recall that while the maximum length of a string that can be assigned to a string variable is 255 characters, the *actual* length of the string is the number of characters *currently* assigned to a string variable. BASIC provides a function to "count" and report the actual length of a string, or of a string assigned to a particular variable; a function appropriately called the LEN (for LENgth) function. LEN can be used in a print statement to print the number of characters in the string in question. Since the execution of LEN results in a numeric value, it can be assigned as a value to a numeric variable, used as a value in an IF. . .THEN comparison, or used in calculations.

For example:

```
10 LET G$ = "WHAT A GAS"
20 PRINT LEN(G$)

RUN
 10

100 PRINT LEN("NORTHERN MUSIC")

RUN
 14

10 LET H$ = "1582 ANCHORAGE DRIVE"
20 LET A = LEN(H$)
30 PRINT A

RUN
 20

150 LET R$ = "YES"
160 IF LEN(R$) = 3 THEN PRINT "GO ON TO THE NEXT QUESTION"

RUN
GO ON TO THE NEXT QUESTION

10 LET M$ = "AMERICAN"
20 LET N$ = "FOREIGN"
30 PRINT LEN(M$) + LEN(N$)

RUN
 15
```

Show the results of executing each of the following program segments:

(a)
```
10 LET C$ = " "
20 PRINT LEN(C$)

RUN
```

____

(b)
```
10 LET F$ = "FRANK"
20 LET L$ = "JONES"
30 LET N$ = L$ + ", " + F$
40 PRINT N$
50 PRINT LEN(N$)

RUN
```

____

____

\- - - - - - - - - - - - - - -

(a)
```
1
```
(b)
```
JONES, FRANK
12
```

SUBSTRING FUNCTIONS: VERSATILE TOOLS TO MANIPULATE STRING DATA

Three MICROSOFT BASIC string functions (MID$, RIGHT$, LEFT$), allow you to manipulate the parts of a string, called substrings. The MID$ function is by far the most useful substring manipulating function. It works for two different processes. It allows you to *select* substrings from within a larger string. The MID$ selection function has the following forms:

(1) `MID$("CHARGE IT", 1,6)`

(2) `MID$(T$, 3, 15)`

(3) `MID$(D$, 10)`

(4) `MID$(W$, A, C*D)`

In example (1), the MID$ function selects characters 1 through 6 inclusive as the substring within the string constant CHARGE IT, with the substring starting at character position 1 (the C) and including six characters total, making the substring CHARGE. Example (2) assumes that a string has been assigned to T$, and the substring comprises fifteen characters of the T$ string, starting with the third character in the string and continuing on to the 15th character after the third one. In example (3), the "last character position" notation (the last value inside the MID$ parentheses) has been omitted, which tells the computer that the substring will start at character position 10, and will include all the rest of the string to the right of the character at position 10. Example (4) shows that the starting position for the substring, as well as the number of characters to be included in the substring, can be represented by variables or expressions that evaluate to a numeric value. Of course, these variables must have been previously assigned values, just as the string variable must have previously been assigned a string. So in general, the MID$ function has the form

MID$(string variable or constant, substring starting position, how many characters in the substring from the start position).

Note that the three parameters in the MID$ function are separated by commas. The first is usually a string variable to which a string has previously been assigned. The second parameter is the starting position for the substring. The third parameter *does not* tell the last character position number in the substring, but rather tells how many characters total to include in the substring – a point that sometimes confuses people.

In addition to the *selection* function, MID$ is also used as a *replacement* function.

For example:

```
LET MID$(N$,2,6) = B$  where N$ = "SSSSSSSSSS" and B$ = "XXXXXX"
```

This statement tells the computer to replace (or substitute) six characters of the string assigned to N$ with the characters in B$. If B$ contains less than six characters, only those assigned to B$ will be replaced in N$. If the substitution would overlap the end of the string currently assigned to B$, then the new N$ (after substring substitution) could have a longer actual length than it did originally (before the execution of the statement). After execution of the example replacement statement above, N$ = SXXXXXXSSS.

On the other hand, if B$ in our example above actually contained only three characters (B$ = XXX), then only those three characters would end up in the new string assigned to N$, like this: N$ = SXXXSSSSSS. Another example:

```
LET MID$(D$,8,12) = "1046 ELM ST."
```

This instructs the computer to replace twelve characters, starting with character position 8 and going to position 19 of the string assigned to D$, with the string constant 1Ø46 ELM ST. Yet another example:

```
LET MID$(G$,5,5) = MID$(B$,8,5)
```

This tells the computer to replace characters 5 to 9 (five characters starting at position 5) of the string assigned to G$, with characters 8 through 12 of the B$ string. Notice that the string *into which* the replacement is to be made always appears to the *left* of the equal sign in the assignment statement. In the last example above, the string assigned to G$ is changed, while the string assigned to B$ remains unchanged. You try it: Fill in the blanks for Z$ after the execution of the statement(s).

	Z$ BEFORE	Z$ AFTER
(a) 160 LET MID$(Z$,8,6) = "SMITHE"	JOANNE JAYSON	____________
(b) 190 LET N$ = "12879" 200 LET MID$(Z$,1,5) = N$	21879 CORNER ST.	____________
(c) 300 LET X = 8 : LET Y = 6 310 LET D$ = "CANCEL" 320 LET MID$(Z$,X,Y) = D$	0794025072279	____________
(d) 420 LET Y$ = "NY 08106" 430 LET MID$(Z$,14,5) = MID$(Y$,5,5)	NEW YORK NY 01202	____________

- - - - - - - - - - - - - - - -

(a) JOANNE SMITHE
(b) 12879 CORNER ST.
(c) 0794025CANCEL
(d) NEW YORK NY 08106

Note that MID$ is a *selection* or *replacement* function. Therefore, it requires something to be there already, that is, the string variable referred to inside the parentheses must have previously been assigned a string. You cannot use MID$ to place data into a null string or a string variable with no string previously assigned to it. The example below, if executed, would result in an error condition because the actual length of X$ is zero.

Illegal example:

```
210 LET X$ = ""
220 LET MID$(X$,1,6) = "TRS-80"
```

No replacement could take place because a six-character string cannot replace a zero-character (null) string.

Examine this next program segment carefully, and then answer the question below. Assume that you wish to change the last name of Mariam Martinson to Jones. (Say that Mariam got married and took a new last name.) It's tricky.

```
120 LET N$ = "MIRIAM MARTINSON"
130 LET T$ = "JONES"
140 LET MID$(N$,8,9) = T$
150 PRINT N$
```

(a) What string ends up assigned to N$? ______________________

(a) MARIAM JONESNSON

But that's not what we wanted. We were trying to replace MARTINSON with JONES. Instead, we got the new name combined with part of the old name in a strange way.

What happened? Even though the MID$ function said to replace nine characters starting with position 8, only five characters in N$ were replaced because that was the entire LENGTH of T$. The point is that the remainder of the characters in N$ were not replaced with blanks, as we had hoped (and you may have assumed in answering the question above.)

Notice the use of the MID$ selection function in PRINT statements in the program below. This is different than using MID$ as a replacement function. Remember, it allows you to select and print any part or substring of the string assigned to the string variable in the MID$ parentheses. The other two values or parameters inside the parentheses still indicate where the substring to be printed starts and how many characters it includes.

```
150 LET N$ = "FOGHORNE WHILDEFLOWER"
160 PRINT MID$(N$,1,8)
170 PRINT MID$(N$,10,12)
180 PRINT N$

RUN
FOGHORNE
WHILDEFLOWER
FOGHORNE WHILDEFLOWER
```

Notice the use of MID$ as a *selection* function in lines 160 and 170 above. In contrast to the replacement function of MID$, the selection function in no way changes the string assigned to N$, as demonstrated by the execution of line 180, even after substrings from N$ have been selected and printed by lines 160 and 170. This same selection function can be used to assign a substring from a string assigned to a string variable without changing the original string from which the substring was selected. Notice in the program segment below that a substring from an existing string can be assigned to a new variable without changing the string from which it was selected. F$ (for first name) and L$ (for last name) are selected from the entire name (N$) without changing N$.

```
150 LET N$ = "FOGHORNE WHILDEFLOWER"
160 LET F$ = MID$(N$,1,8)
170 LET L$ = MID$(N$,10,12)
180 PRINT N$
190 PRINT "FIRST NAME IS "; F$
200 PRINT "LAST NAME IS "; L$
```

(a) Show the RUN for the program segment above.

____

____

____

(b) Which character in N$ is not selected for inclusion in either F$ or L$?

____

- - - - - - - - - - - - - - - -

(a) RUN
FOGHORNE WHILDEFLOWER
FIRST NAME IS FOGHORNE
LAST NAME IS WHILDEFLOWER

(b) The space at character position 9 of N$

The LEFT$ and RIGHT$ string functions are not as versatile as MID$ and are not used as much in our programming. They both work the same way, however, as shown in these program segments:

```
160 PRINT LEFT$(A$,8)
```

means print the leftmost eight characters of A$ (the first eight characters in the string assigned to A$);

```
170 LET R = 12
180 LET B$ = RIGHT$(A$,R)
```

means assign to B$ the twelve rightmost characters of A$ (the last twelve characters in the string assigned to A$).

These examples demonstrate the substring selection capabilities of LEFT$ and RIGHT$. These two functions *cannot* be used for replacing information in an existing string as we were able to do with the MID$ function. They are strictly *selection* functions, selecting one or more characters from one end or the other of an existing string to treat as a substring.

We often use LEFT$ for convenience to check for a user's YES or NO response to an INPUT prompting question. Using an IF. . .THEN statement, we have the computer look at the first character of the response string to determine whether or not the answer was YES, as shown in the following program segment:

```
240 LINE INPUT "DO YOU NEED INSTRUCTIONS (YES OR NO)?"; R$
250 IF LEFT$(R$,1) = "Y" THEN 600
```

(a) What responses could a user make to the INPUT prompt above in order for the IF. . .THEN comparison to be true?

____

- - - - - - - - - - - - - - - -

(a) Could type YES or Y or any string that started with the letter Y.

We have found less use for the RIGHT$ function than for MID$ or for LEFT$, but here is an example. Remember, the numeric value inside the RIGHT$ function's parentheses means to start counting the characters for the substring at the right-most end of the string from which the substring is being selected, counting toward the beginning of the string.

```
240 LINE INPUT "WHICH HIGH SCHOOL CLASS DID YOU GRADUATE FROM?"; Y$
250 PRINT "YOU GRADUATED IN 19"; RIGHT$(Y$,2)
```

Assume that several people responded to the INPUT prompting question when the above program segment was RUN. Show what the computer will print for each user's response.

(a) User responds: CLASS OF 1938

Line 250 prints: ______________________

(b) User responds: CLASS OF '64

Line 250 prints: ______________________

(c) User responds: 1958 ____

Line 250 prints. ______________________

(d) User responds: FORTY EIGHT

Line 250 prints: ______________________

(a) YOU GRADUATED IN 1938
(b) YOU GRADUATED IN 1964
(c) YOU GRADUATED IN 1958
(d) YOU GRADUATED IN 19HT

String Searches With INSTR

Another useful string function is INSTR, the INSTRing searching function. The INSTR function is used to pinpoint the location of a substring of one or more characters within a longer string. In effect, the string is checked character by character until the substring is found. The value produced by the INSTR search indicates the character position of the *first* character of the substring within the string being searched. An example or two will clear up the mystery.

```
250 LET X = INSTR("JOEJEFF", "JEFF")
```

The first string inside the parentheses is the string being search. The second string is the string being searched *for.* In this case, X = 4 since JEFF, the string we are searching for, begins at character position 4 of the string being searched, JOEJEFF.

The INSTR function can also look like this:

```
INSTR(A$,B$)
```

where A$ is the string being searched, and B$ is the substring being looked for. The string variables A$ and B$ must have previously been assigned strings, of course. Note that the string, substring, or both can be string constants or string variables. Examples:

```
INSTR(A$, "TON")
INSTR("WASHINGTON", B$)
INSTR("WASHINGTON", "TON")
```

An INSTR value of Ø (zero) results if the substring is *not* found. If the substring *is* found, the *character position* of the *first* character of the substring within the string being searched is pinpointed by the INSTR value. Example:

```
10 LET A$ = "WASHINGTON"
20 LET B$ = "ASH"
30 LET C$ = "TON"
40 LET X = INSTR(A$,B$)
50 PRINT X
60 LET Y = INSTR(A$,C$)
70 PRINT Y

RUN
 2
 8
```

Note that the INSTR function can search for a substring as short as one character. INSTR only reports the first character position of the first occurrence it encounters of the substring being searched for.

(a) In the program above, the substrings being searched for in lines 40 and 60 are three characters long. Then how can the value of X be 2 for lines 40 and 50?

(a) The INSTR value corresponds to the character position of the first character in the substring ASH that is found *starting* at character position 2 in WASHINGTON.

The following program shows more about how INSTR( ) works and some pointers about its use.

```
250 LET M$ = "JANFEBMARAPRMAYJUNJULAUGSEPOCTNOVDEC"
260 LINE INPUT "WHICH MONTH?"; M1$
270 LET L = INSTR(M$, M1$)
280 PRINT "POSITION: "; L
290 GOTO 260

RUN
WHICH MONTH?MAR
POSITION:   7
WHICH MONTH?AP
POSITION:   10
WHICH MONTH?JU
POSITION:   16
WHICH MONTH?JULY
POSITION:   0
WHICH MONTH?A
POSITION:   2
```

Note that with only two letters entered, INSTR finds JU in JUN, even though JUL would also qualify. INSTR responds with the first occurrence of the string being searched for. But when we entered JULY, INSTR responded with Ø, indicating that the string could not be found. When we entered A, the first occurrence was in JAN. For this demo you need to enter at least the first two letters, and three letters to ensure an accurate match.

Related techniques can be used to search for wanted and unwanted characters in a string without using INSTR. Find the clever use of the FOR variable to locate the end of a substring where you know a space separates the substring.

```
740 LET F$ = "JANE FONDA"
750 FOR S = 1 TO LEN(F$)
760 IF MID$(F$,S,1) = " " THEN 780
770 NEXT S
780 PRINT MID$(F$,1,S-1)
```

(a) What is the upper limit for S (the FOR control variable)? ______________

(b) What is the length of the substring selected by the MID$ function in line 760?

____

(c) What is the length of the first name substring in F$? ______________

(d) In what character position in F$ is the space? ______________

(e) Why doesn't S-1 in the MID$ function in line 780 cause one character in the name to be lost? ______________

____

(f) What is printed by line 780? ______________

(a) LEN(F$) = 10
(b) one character
(c) four characters
(d) character position 5
(e) Because S gives the character position of the first space, not the last letter, in the F$ "first name" substring.
(f) JANE

MULTI-BRANCHING WITH ON. . .GOTO

The ON. . .GOTO statement allows the computer to branch to a number of different statements throughout a program. The format for the statement is a list of line numbers:

```
ON X GOTO 310, 450, 660, 660, 660, 720, 830, 910
```

Note: X = any variable or expression from which a value will result.

If the value of X is 1 when the ON. . .GOTO statement is encountered and executed, the computer branches (goes to) the first line number in the list of line numbers (in our example, line 310). If the value of X is 2, the second line number in the list is branched to. As many line numbers can follow GOTO as will fit in a statement line. Notice also in our example that if X = 3, 4, or 5, the same line number (660) will be branched to.

If the value of X is a zero, a negative number, or larger than the number of line numbers in the list, then:

(1) either the ON. . .GOTO statement will be skipped without execution and the next statement executed, or
(2) in some BASICs, the computer will stop execution and give an error message.

Run some tests to see how your BASIC reacts for negative, zero, fractional, and "too large" values for the ON. . .GOTO variable.

Here is a technique using ON. . .GOTO and the INSTR function to determine which choice has been made by a user. The situation could be a "menu" of choices from which the user must select one, or a multiple choice question where the user selects one response.

```
250 REM MENU PROGRAM DEMO
260 LINE INPUT "DO YOU NEED INSTRUCTIONS?"; R$
270 IF R$ <> "YES" THEN 500
280 :
290 :
300 REM MENU SET
310 CLS
320 PRINT "THESE ARE THE THINGS THIS PROGRAM WILL DO:"
330 PRINT "A. BEGIN WRITING TO A NEW FILE"
340 PRINT "B. ADD TO EXISTING FILE"
350 PRINT "C. CHANGE EXISTING FILE"
360 PRINT "D. PRINT CONTENTS OF EXISTING FILE"
370 PRINT "E. SELECT DATA FROM FILE AT OPERATORS REQUEST"
380 :
390 LINE INPUT "ENTER YOUR REQUEST (A-E):"; R$
400 ON INSTR("ABCDE", R$) GOTO 500,600,700,800,900
410 PRINT "ENTRY ERROR. PLEASE ENTER AS DIRECTED": GOTO 390
420 :
430 :
```

Here is an alternate method to arrive at an ON. . .GOTO value in a "menu" selection situation. In the following program segment, the ASC( ) function is used to convert a letter entered by the user to an ASCII value that is used to determine the value for an ON. . .GOTO statement. The ON. . .GOTO is a multi-branching instruction. In line 260, if the value of R is 1, then the program goes to the first line number given after GOTO. If R = 2, then the program branches to the second line number given, and so on. The value of R must be greater than 1 and no higher than the number of line numbers that follow GOTO.

```
200 :
210 :
220 :
230 LINE INPUT "ENTER YOUR CHOICE, A-E :"; R$
240 LET R = ASC(R$) - 64
250 IF R < 1 OR R > 5 THEN 270
260 ON R GOTO 300,400,500,600,700
270 PRINT "ENTRY ERROR. PLEASE REENTER AS REQUESTED": GOTO 230
280 :
290 :
```

(a) In the program above, why is line 250 included?

_ _ _ _ _ _ _ _ _ _ _ _ _ _ _ _

(a) If R evaluates to less than 1 due to a data entry error or larger than 5, an error would occur; so the checking is done by line 250.

FOR NEXT STATEMENTS

It is preferable to use a FOR NEXT loop when you have a controlled, repeating sequence of instructions.

Preferred

```
100 FOR X = 1 TO N
110 PRINT X, X↑2
120 NEXT X
```

Undesirable

```
100 LET K = 1
110 PRINT X, X↑2
120 LET X = X+1
130 IF X>N THEN 200
140 GOTO 110
```

As you can see, the FOR NEXT loop is more space efficient (it could even have been done in one line), it looks better, and it is easier to read.

A general rule when using FOR NEXT loops is: DO NOT EXIT from the middle of a FOR NEXT loop, except to GOSUB to a subroutine. Leaving the controlled loop makes the program difficult to read and hard to understand. Further, internally your computer wants to complete the entire FOR NEXT sequence. If you exit prematurely, there is no certainty that your computer will behave "normally" the next time it encounters the loop variable (X in the example above). This uncertainty can cause some very serious program errors that are extremely hard to detect. An exit to a subroutine is acceptable because a subroutine will RETURN the program to the *inside* of the FOR NEXT loop to continue in sequence, as if there was no exit at all.

Never

```
100 FOR X = 1 TO N
110 IF A(X) = B(X) THEN 200
120 NEXT X
```

Not desireable

```
100 FOR X = 1 TO N
110 IF A(X) = B(X) THEN 130
120 NEXT X
130 LET S = S + 1
140 GOTO 120
```

Preferred

```
100 FOR X = 1 TO N
110 IF A(X) <>B(X) THEN 130
120 LET S = S + 1
130 NEXT X
```

You can usually write your program to include everything you need to do *inside* the loop, rather than leaving the loop. (There will be exceptions.)

(a) Write a program segment using nested FOR NEXT loops that will print the word HELLO three times, but will print the word GOODBY four times after each appearance of the word HELLO.

(a)
```
10 FOR X = 1 TO 3
20 PRINT "HELLO"
30 FOR Y = 1 TO 4
40 PRINT "GOODBY"
50 NEXT Y
60 NEXT X
```

MULTIPLE STATEMENT LINES

Many language features in MICROSOFT BASIC are *not* available on other computer systems. Some of these features speed up the program's run time, others save memory space, and some do both. Some features enhance program readability while others confuse the reader. A popular feature is the ability to place multiple BASIC statements on one line separated by a colon, as we showed earlier in discussing IF. . .THEN.

```
140 FOR X = 1 TO 10: PRINT X, X↑2: NEXT X
```

or

```
200 IF X=Y THEN PRINT "YOU WON! ": GOTO 10
210 PRINT "SORRY, WRONG NUMBER": GOTO 60
```

A few cautions and suggestions are applicable as you use multiple statement lines:

1. Multiple statement lines are often hard to read and sometimes hard to understand. If you later change a program, readability may be a problem. It is more clear to use one statement to a line.
2. If you must use multiple statement lines, carry out a complete procedure or action on *one* line, whenever possible. Carryover to other lines makes reading more difficult and less clear.
3. Finding program errors buried in multiple statement lines is difficult.
4. Understand completely how IF. . .THEN statements work in a multiple statement line. In line 200 above, if X *does* equal Y, then "You won" will be printed and the program will branch to line 10. If the X=Y condition is false, line 210 will be executed next. Some people incorrectly presume that GOTO 10 will be executed whether the condition is true or false.
5. REMARK statements must be the *last* statement on a multiple statement line. Any executable statement after a remark will *not* be executed.

Special consideration of the GOSUB statement in multiple statement lines is warranted. Remember that each GOSUB statement must have a corresponding RETURN statement, that appears as the last statement in the subroutine the GOSUB branches to.

Say, a GOSUB is executed when an IF. . .THEN condition is true. After completing the subroutine, the computer must always be instructed to RETURN. The statement it returns to will be:

(1) the next statement after GOSUB if it is a multiple statement line, or
(2) the next lined numbered statement in normal line number order.

(a) Assume that the comparison in line 120 below is true and the GOSUB statement is executed. Which statement will be executed next after the RETURN from subroutine execution? ____________________

```
120 IF X = 2 THEN GOSUB 510 : GOTO 360
130 PRINT "X IS LESS THAN TWO"
```

- - - - - - - - - - - - - - -

(a) GOTO 360 is the next statement executed after the RETURN.

CHAPTER 2 SELF-TEST

1. Why do the authors recommend using "greater than" and "less than" comparisons in IF. . .THEN numeric comparisons, rather than comparisons for equality?

2. When must quotation marks be placed around string data items in a DATA statement?

3. How can a null string be assigned to an INPUT or LINE INPUT string variable?

4. Show the results of a RUN of the following program:

```
10 LET A$ = "ALFRED"
20 LET B$ = "CONTRACT"
30 LET C$ = "32C"
40 PRINT ASC(A$), ASC(B$), ASC(C$)
RUN
```

5. Describe the string that must have been assigned to D$ for each of these comparisons to be true:

(a) `IF ASC(D$) < 48 OR ASC(D$) > 57 THEN 660`
(b) `IF ASC(D$) > 64 AND ASC(D$) < 91 THEN GOSUB 1520`

6. What value will the LEN function show for a string to which fifteen spaces have been assigned?

7. Show the RUN for the following program:

```
10 LET M$ = "STAR TREK"
20 LET N$ = "WARS"
30 LET G$ = MID$(M$,1,5) + N$
40 LET MID$(M$,6,4) = MID$(N$,1,4)
50 PRINT G$
60 PRINT M$
RUN
```

8. Give an example of a simple numeric variable and a simple string variable.

9. Give a reason for avoiding multiple statements in one program line.

10. Examine the following statement:

```
120 IF X > 10 THEN GOSUB 810 : GOTO 110
```

After executing the subroutine starting at like 810, to which statement will the computer return?

11. If a variable name has more than two alphanumeric characters, how many of those characters does the computer use to identify the value assigned to that variable?

Answer Key

1. Round-off error in the computer's computational process may introduce tiny errors that make expected values slightly more or less. Therefore, an equality comparison may fail where you would expect it to succeed.

2. When the string data item includes a comma as part of the string or leading spaces are to be included as part of the string.

3. By pressing the ENTER key without entering anything else from the keyboard.

4.
```
65          67          51
```

5. (a) First character of D$ must *not* be a number (Ø to 9).
   (b) First character of D$ must be a capital letter (A to Z).

6. 15 (Spaces count as characters in a string.)

7.
```
RUN
STAR WARS
STAR WARS
```

8. Numeric variable: A (or any letter of the alphabet); string variable: A$ or any letter of the alphabet followed by a dollar sign.

9. May make it harder to read the program; may make errors in programming harder to detect. (either answer)

10. GOTO 110

11. In TRS-80 BASIC, only the first two characters; in MICROSOFT BASIC-80, up to forty characters.

CHAPTER THREE

Building Data Entry and Error Checking Routines

Objectives: When you finish this chapter, you will be able to write statements in a data entry program module to check the following aspects of data items:

- Proper length
- Non-response (null strings)
- Type of data (numeric or alphanumeric)
- Inadvertant inclusion of wrong characters
- Parameters for numeric data

In addition, you will be able to write data entry modules that:

- Have clearly stated prompts
- Use reasonable data fields
- Concatenate data items into a single field
- Check and "pad" entries, as necessary, for proper field length
- Remove excess spaces from data taken from data fields
- Replace data items contained in a data field
- Provide complete explanations of a data entry error to the user

INTRODUCTION

If you are wondering when you are going to get into data files themselves, be patient. Experience has shown that you need a good background in some special techniques associated with data file programming which use BASIC statements you already know. This will make it much easier and faster to learn the new BASIC statements and functions specifically applied to data file handling. You shouldn't have to struggle to understand a new use for a familiar BASIC statement while trying to absorb the data file statements and techniques, so please don't gloss over this material.

Concern for data entry procedures was introduced in the section on INPUT and LINE INPUT in the previous chapter. For our purposes *data* are defined as any information that is or will be stored in a data file on disk or cassette. Common examples of data include mailing, subscription, or billing lists; inventories of retail merchandise; accounting information; files of books, recordings, journal articles, or notes for a book; statistical information. *Data entry* includes the process of getting such information into the computer so that it can be stored in a data file. *Data files* usually contain large amounts of data, which, to be useful, must be accurate, valid, and error-free in content and format. The accuracy and usefulness of your program output depends entirely on the accuracy of the data in these files. Furthermore, inaccurate or invalid data in a data file (or any place in a program) can cause your program to interrupt, halt, or abort in an error condition in the middle of its run. If your program terminates unexpectedly, there may be no telling what is happening inside the computer. Printed reports can be only partially completed, entered data can be lost or destroyed, data in files can be half processed; the list goes on.

The result of an unexpected program interruption can be catastrophic, though it may not always be so. It is almost impossible to predict exactly what will happen. Therefore, always do everything you can in your programming to avoid errors that can precipitate program interruptions.

Unfortunately most errors occur at data entry time. That is why we emphasize the use of data entry checking procedures in this chapter – procedures to guarantee that data are entered as clean, valid, and accurate in content and format as your ingenuity and knowledge of programming techniques can make it. Throughout the remainder of this book "error-traps" and places where programming errors are likely to occur are illustrated.

This chapter focuses on constructing the data entry module of a program. This is where, usually with INPUT statements, the computer user is instructed to type in information that is going to be placed in a new data file, or to tell the computer to locate information in an already existing data file. After each response to an INPUT statement, we will use one or more statements to check the response for possible errors. These error-checking statements comprise the largest part of a data entry program module.

DATA FIELD LENGTH

In an earlier chapter, the following example program appeared:

```
120 LET N$ = "MIRIAM MARTINSON"
130 LET T$ = "JONES"
140 LET MID$(N$,8,9) = T$
150 PRINT N$
```

When asked the question, "What string ends up assigned to N$?" the answer was MIRIAM JONESNSON. The problem was that the new last name was shorter than the old last name, resulting in a combination of the two last names.

This problem, and many like it, are avoided by establishing a certain amount of space; a certain number of character positions into which a given element of data or data item is placed. Establish strings, or defined substring positions within one string, where data must be located (data fields). *A data field can be thought of as a string that contains more than one data item. These data items always fit between two defined character positions within the string.* A simple example would be one string variable to which both a customer's first and last names are assigned like this:

```
N$ = "VIVIAN VANCE"
```

The first name field is a six-character field in N$, occupying the first six character positions of that string (1 through 6). The separator field is a one-character field, located at character position 7. To be sure you understand, fill in the blanks in this sentence.

The last name field has (a) ________ characters and occupies character positions

(b) ________________ in the string assigned to (c) ____________ .

\- - - - - - - - - - - - - - - - -

(a) five
(b) 8 to 12
(c) N$

Below is a graphic look at the fields in N$ with a slash (/) marking the field designation:

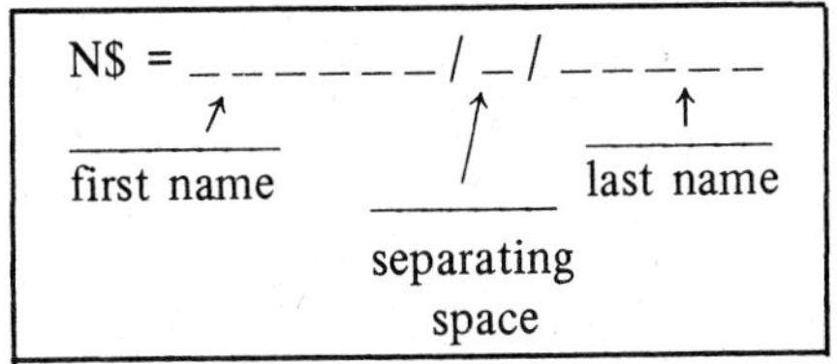

This particular data field works for the name in the example. However, the goal is to establish *reasonable* data fields. In this case, a reasonable data field should hold ANY first or last name that might be assigned to N$. Certainly, many names contain more than six letters for the first name and five letters for the last. On one hand, you want to provide reasonably sized fields for the data. On the other hand, much storage space will be wasted if you try to cover all possibilities. There really may be someone named *John Jacobjingleheimerschmidt,* but reserving twenty-four character positions for a last name data field could be wasteful of storage space; if 95 percent of the last names in a data file have twelve letters or less, then half or more of the last name data field goes unused 95 percent of the time. In a file of 1,000, 10,000, or 100,000 names, such as a mailing list, this can amount to a vast amount of unused string and disk storage space.

Data field lengths must be adequate and reasonable. If all the catalog numbers in an inventory data file are five characters, then obviously a five-character data field is sufficient.

To review, use a slash(/) to mark off the fields in a twenty-six character string assigned to A$, where the data fields hold the city, state, and zip code (the last line in a mailing address). Place a number in each field indicating which of the following data items are to occupy that field.

1. City name (fifteen characters maximum)
2. Two separator spaces
3. State code (two-letter standard postal abbreviation)
4. Two separator spaces
5. Zip code (five characters)

(a) A$ = _

(a) A$ = _ _ _ _ _ _ _ _ _ _ _ _ _ _ _(1)/ _ _(2)/ _ _(3)/ _ _(4)/ _ _ _ _ _(5)

Next, consider the following data entry module to enter the city, state, and zip code. These data items are to be placed into the data fields you just defined above.

```
100 LINE INPUT "ENTER NAME OF CITY:"; C$
110 LINE INPUT "ENTER STATE CODE:"; S$
120 LINE INPUT "ENTER ZIP CODE:"; Z$
130 LET A$ = C$ + "  " + S$ + "  " + Z$
140 PRINT A$
```

Notice the concatenating statement in line 130 – an attempt to get the data items into data fields. But these two RUNs demonstrate a serious problem that relates to the length of the city name.

(a)
```
RUN
ENTER CITY NAME:IOWA CITY
ENTER STATE CODE:IA
ENTER ZIP CODE:52240
IOWA CITY  IA  52240
```

(b)
```
RUN
ENTER CITY NAME:SOUTH SAN FRANCISCO
ENTER STATE CODE:CA
ENTER ZIP CODE:94080
SOUTH SAN FRANCISCO  CA  94080
```

Fill in the spaces to show the results of line 130 in the program for each of the sample RUNs:

(a) A$ = _ _ _ _ _ _ _ _ _ _ _ _ _ _ _/ _ _/ _ _/ _ _/ _ _ _ _ _

(b) A$ = _ _ _ _ _ _ _ _ _ _ _ _ _ _ _/ _ _/ _ _/ _ _/ _ _ _ _ _

(a) A$ = IOWA_CITY__IA__|52|24|0_|_____

(b) A$ = SOUTH_SAN_FRANC|15|CO|__|CA__94080

The fact that all cities don't have fifteen letters means that simple concatenation of this data does not place it into the defined character positions for the data fields. One approach is to assign a string of twenty-six spaces to A$ and then use the MID$ function to place each data item into its data field in the string. But SOUTH SAN FRANCISCO would end up being truncated to SOUTH SAN FRANC, and even with the fifteen-character limit, a more intelligent and preferable city name entry would be S. SAN FRANCISCO, SO. SAN FRAN., or even SOUTH S. F.

Checking Data Entries for Acceptable Length

One programming technique to check data entries for acceptable length uses the LEN function in an IF. . .THEN comparison. If the data requested always have a defined number of characters, then an important check for mistakes in data entry would be to see whether the entry has the exact length it should. A U. S. zip code always has five characters, so a check for that data item would look like line 170:

```
160 LINE INPUT "ENTER ZIP CODE:"; Z$
170 IF LEN(Z$) <> 5 THEN PRINT "REENTER AS 5 DIGIT CODE" :
    GOTO 160

RUN
ENTER ZIP CODE:9543
REENTER AS 5 DIGIT CODE
ENTER ZIP CODE:954316
REENTER AS 5 DIGIT CODE
ENTER ZIP CODE:
```

If the entry for the zip code does not have exactly five characters, then a mistake has been made, the user is so advised, and the computer repeats the prompting message and waits for another entry. With new zip code formats, abit of reprogramming will be necessary.

Now you write a statement to check for proper length of the entry for the LINE INPUT statement below:

(a)
```
140 LINE INPUT "ENTER STATE CODE:"; S$
```

150 ______________________________

\- - - - - - - - - - - - - - - -

(a)
```
150 IF LEN(S$) <> 2 THEN PRINT "REENTER AS STANDARD 2 LETTER
    CODE" : GOTO 140
```

How can you check something like a city name, which is allowed fifteen characters or less? The city name could have less than fifteen characters, exactly fifteen, or more than fifteen. If it has more, you could settle for having the data entry truncated (cut off) after fifteen characters. Remember SOUTH SAN FRANC? A better option is to advise the user that a shorter entry is needed and allow the user to reenter the data item with an intelligent abbreviation.

```
120 LINE INPUT "ENTER CITY NAME:"; C$
130 IF LEN(C$) > 15 THEN PRINT "REENTER AS 15 CHARACTERS OR
    LESS" : GOTO 120

RUN
ENTER CITY NAME:SOUTH SAN FRANCISCO
REENTER AS 15 CHARACTERS OR LESS
ENTER CITY NAME:
```

Write a statement (similar to line 130 above) to check the entry for the LINE INPUT statement below, where the data field for the entry is twenty characters maximum;

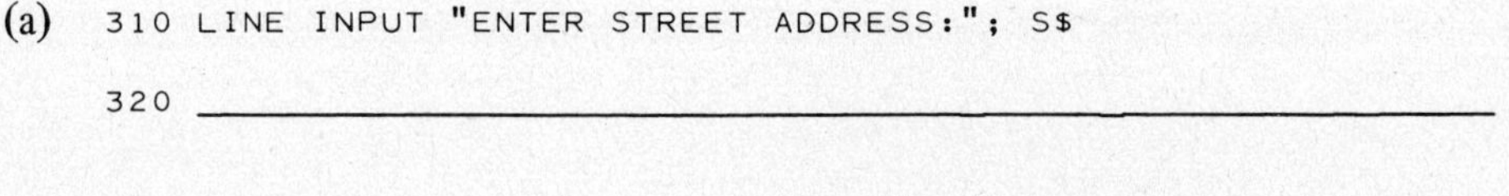

(a) `310 LINE INPUT "ENTER STREET ADDRESS:"; S$`

`320` ______________________________

(a)
```
320 IF LEN(S$) > 20 THEN PRINT "REENTER AS 20 CHARACTERS OR
    LESS" : GOTO 310
```

"Padding" Entries With Spaces to Correct Field Lengths

You are probably wondering how to *increase* the length of a data entry that has fewer characters than its data field. The solution involves automating the addition of spaces to "pad" the short entry (say, a short city name) with trailing spaces, so that the resulting city name *string*, which includes the padding spaces, exactly fits the data field. Remember, spaces occupy character positions and count as characters in the length of the string. Line 140 shows how to pad with spaces:

```
120 LINE INPUT "ENTER CITY NAME:"; C$
130 IF LEN(C$) > 15 THEN PRINT "REENTER AS 15 CHARACTERS OR
    LESS" : GOTO 120
140 IF LEN(C$) < 15 THEN LET C$ = C$ + " " : GOTO 140
```

In line 140, if the city name entered and assigned to C$ has less than fifteen characters, then a space is concatenated on to the end of the string. The new string assigned to C$ is the old string plus a space. The statement "goes back to itself" (GOTO 140) and keeps adding another space to the end of the C$ string until the string contains exactly fifteen characters including the spaces. Clever?

You write a statement to pad an entry with spaces if it has less than the eight characters required to fit in its data field.

(a)
```
120 LINE INPUT "ENTER YOUR FIRST NAME:"; F$
130 IF LEN(F$) > 8 THEN PRINT "SHORTEN ENTRY TO 8 CHARACTERS OR
    LESS" : GOTO 120

140 ______________________________________________
```

(a)
```
140 IF LEN(F$) < 8 THEN LET F$ = F$ + " " : GOTO 140
```

Now apply the techniques you have been using in a data entry module.

(a) Write a program routine to request that a user enter an alphanumeric product identification code with three characters, plus a product description with up to twenty characters maximum, followed by a two-character code identifying the person making the entries, using their first and last name initials. Once these three data items have been entered and tested, combine the data into one string of twenty-five characters assigned to a single string variable.

(a)

```
110 CLEAR 300
120 INPUT "ENTER A THREE CHARACTER CODE"; C$
130 IF LEN(C$) <> 3 THEN PRINT "ENTRY MUST BE 3 CHARACTERS.
    PLEASE REENTER": GOTO 120
140 INPUT "ENTER DESCRIPTION"; D$
150 IF LEN(D$) > 20 THEN PRINT "ENTRY TOO LONG. PLEASE
    REENTER": GOTO 140
160 IF LEN(D$) < 20 THEN LET D$ = D$ + " ": GOTO 160
170 INPUT "ENTER YOUR TWO INITIALS"; N$
180 IF LEN(N$) <> 2 THEN PRINT "PLEASE REENTER AS REQUESTED":
    GOTO 170
190 LET R$ = C$ + D$ + N$
200 :
210 :
```

What's the advantage in setting up data fields in a single string and putting more than one data item into it? The reasons will become clear in later chapters. For now, the answer has to do with how data files can store information using some automated data entry procedures and equipment and with the ease with which BASIC allows the manipulation of substrings using MID$ for particular applications.

Examine the program below and answer the questions that follow it.

```
120 INPUT "ENTER CITY NAME"; T$
130 IF LEN(T$) > 15 THEN PRINT "REENTER AS 15 CHARACTERS OR LESS
    PLEASE": GOTO 120
140 IF LEN(T$) < 15 THEN T$ = T$ + " ": GOTO 140
150 INPUT "ENTER STATE CODE"; S$
160 IF LEN(S$) <> 2 THEN PRINT "PLEASE REENTER AS 2 CHARACTERS":
    GOTO 150
170 INPUT "ENTER ZIP CODE"; Z$
180 IF LEN(Z$) <> 5 THEN PRINT "REENTER AS 5 DIGIT CODE": GOTO 170
190 LET C$ = T$ + " " + S$ + " " + Z$
200 :
210 REM  FOR DEMONSTRATION PURPOSES ONLY WE PRINT C$
220 PRINT C$
```

(a) What is the purpose of line 130?

(b) What does T$ = T$ + " " in line 140 do?

(c) In line 190, what is the purpose of " " in the concatenation?

(a) Tests to be sure user has not entered more than the acceptable number of characters (fifteen) for the city name field.
(b) Fills in, adds on, or concatenates spaces from the last character of the T$ string up to and including character field position 15. Changes T$ to a fifteen-character string if there were fewer than fifteen characters in the string entered for T$.
(c) Places two spaces in the C$ string, one between the fields for city and state and another between state code and zip code.

Stripping the Padding Spaces From Substrings in Fields

You know how to pad a string with extra spaces to arrive at the proper field length for that data item. Now let's explore a way to eliminate the extra blank spaces when you extract data packed into a string. In the example where we wanted to change a person's last name, it was necessary to pad names with spaces to the proper field length so that corrections could be made, if necessary, and so the first and last names could be found separately. But for name printing purposes, you want to eliminate all the extra blank spaces. The method shown below uses the INSTR function combined with the MID$ function. In our example, N$ really consists of the eight characters for F$, one space separating the two fields, and twelve characters for L$. If the name concatenated into N$ is Jenny Smiles, then N$ = "JENNY   SMILES   ", including the field-separating space at character position 9.

The example program below shows how to use first and last names separately, without extra spaces, in a computer-printed "thank you" letter.

```
3 LET F$="JOHN     "
4 LET L$="ROBERTS     "
200 LET N$ = F$ + " " + L$: REM CONCATENATES ENTIRE NAME INTO N$
210 :
220 :
230 :
700 REM   ROUTINE TO ELIMINATE EXTRA SPACES AND PRINT
710 REM   UNCONCATENATE N$
720 :
730 LET F$ = MID$(N$,1,9)
740 LET L$ = MID$(N$,10,12)
750 LET S = INSTR(F$," "): REM  S CONTAINS THE FIRST SPACE IN
    FIRST NAME
760 PRINT "DEAR"; MID$(F$,1,S-1): REM  PRINTS THE FIRST NAME IN
    SALUTATION
770 :
780 LET S1 = INSTR(L$," "): REM S1 CONTAINS THE FIRST SPACE IN
    LAST NAME
790 PRINT "IT WAS SURE NICE TO SEE YOU AND MRS."; MID$(L$,1,S1-1);
    "AT THE GET TOGETHER THE OTHER EVENING"
800 :

RUN
DEAR ROSEMARY
IT WAS SURE NICE TO SEE YOU AND MRS. ROBERTS AT THE GET TOGETHER
THE OTHER EVENING
```

Notice in lines 730 and 740 how MID$ was used to make new string assignments out of substrings contained in N$.

(a) In lines 750 and 780, what does the INSTR function search for?

____

(b) What value is assigned to S in the same lines? ____________________

____

(a) Looks for first space in string
(b) Assigns character position number of first space to S

CHECKING ENTRIES FOR NULL STRINGS

One idiosyncracy of the INPUT statement already pointed out is that if the user merely presses the ENTER key when the computer is waiting for a response to an INPUT (or LINE INPUT) statement, a null string is assigned to the string variable. If the computer then encounters a checking statement that pads the entry with spaces to the proper field length, the entire entry would end up as a string of spaces and be duly included in the data field for that entry. So checking data entries for null string assignments is a must and should be part of your data entry program modules.

You can use two different techniques to test whether a string variable has been assigned a null value. They work equally well.

```
IF A$ = "" THEN...
```

or

```
IF LEN(A$) = 0 THEN...
```

The decision the programmer must make (and it will vary with each situation) is what to do after the THEN when the IF. . .THEN condition is true and a null assignment has been mistakenly made. Whatever you do, do *not* have the computer merely repeat the INPUT prompt, as in the "what-not-to-do" example below.

```
170 INPUT "ENTER CUSTOMER NUMBER"; C$
180 IF LEN(C$) = 0 THEN    170

RUN
ENTER CUSTOMER NUMBER?
ENTER CUSTOMER NUMBER?
ENTER CUSTOMER NUMBER?
```

A user who persists in not entering the customer number gets no information as to what is wrong. Always provide a helpful error message, perhaps even a beep, bell, or other sound if available on the terminal, so the user knows something is amiss with the present response or entry.

```
170 INPUT "ENTER CUSTOMER NUMBER"; C$
180 IF LEN(C$) = 0 THEN GOSUB 1010
 .
 .
 .
1010 PRINT "PLEASE, WE MUST HAVE THE CUSTOMER NUMBER TO CONTINUE."
 .
 .
 .
```

With this information in mind, write the data entry routine that will produce the prompts shown below. Test each data item for null response immediately after it is entered.

(a)
```
ENTER CUSTOMER NUMBER:
ENTER CUSTOMER NAME:
ENTER PRODUCT NUMBER:
ENTER QUANTITY ORDERED:
```

(a)
```
210 :
220 LINE INPUT "ENTER CUSTOMER NUMBER:"; C$
230 IF LEN(C$) = 0 THEN PRINT "ENTRY ERROR. PLEASE REENTER";:
    GOTO 220
240 LINE INPUT "ENTER CUSTOMER NAME:"; N$
250 IF LEN(N$) = 0 THEN PRINT "PLEASE RESPOND AS REQUESTED":
    GOTO 240
260 LINE INPUT "ENTER PRODUCT NUMBER:"; P$
270 IF LEN(P$) = 0 THEN PRINT "WE CANNOT CONTINUE WITHOUT THIS
    DATA": GOTO 260
280 LINE INPUT "ENTER QUANTITY ORDERED:"; Q$
290 IF LEN(Q$) = 0 THEN PRINT "PLEASE ENTER THE CORRECT VALUE":
    GOTO 280
```

(or some similar messages)

Depending upon the program user's sophistication, even more detailed error messages for problems like the null string entry and others may be necessary. Our examples have given minimum messages to keep the examples short, uncluttered, and easy to understand, but they may not be adequate to ensure a proper response. Return to this example:

```
170 LINE INPUT "ENTER CUSTOMER NUMBER:"; C$
180 IF LEN(C$) = 0 THEN GOSUB 1010 : GOTO 170
 .
 .
 .
1010 PRINT "YOU APPARENTLY PRESSED THE 'ENTER' KEY WITHOUT MAKING
     AN ENTRY."
1020 PRINT "WE NEED A CUSTOMER NUMBER THAT LOOKS LIKE THIS: A-121."
1030 RETURN
```

Another example:

```
230 LINE INPUT "ENTER COMPANY NAME:"; C$
240 IF LEN(C$) > 12 THEN GOSUB 1010 : GOTO 230
 .
 .
 .
1010 PRINT "YOU ENTERED: "; C$
1020 PRINT "PLEASE ABBREVIATE THE COMPANY NAME TO 12 CHARACTERS
     OR LESS."
1030 PRINT "EXAMPLE: ALPHA PRODUCTS COMPANY COULD BE SHORTENED
     TO 'ALPHA PRO CO'"
1040 RETURN
```

Subroutines need to be protected from the main program that calls or branches to them. Depending on how a program is constructed, a subroutine could be encountered and executed as if it were part of the main program, especially if the subroutine section is one of the program's last modules. *Use a STOP or END statement between the main program and the module(s) containing the subroutines.* This protects the first subroutine in the subroutine module from being executed in normal line number order. If the first subroutine is executed, the computer will stop executing the program and give an error message when it encounters a RETURN statement for which the program has no matching GOSUB statement that sent it to the subroutine.

(a) Write an error message subroutine, accessed by a GOSUB statement executed after a true IF. . .THEN comparison, that displays an INPUT entry and describes how to comply with the limit of twenty characters (because of data field length) for entries to the following statement:

```
320 LINE INPUT "ENTER PRODUCT DESCRIPTION:"; P$
```

Sample entry to above statement:

```
RUN
ENTER PRODUCT DESCRIPTION:LEFT HANDED MONKEY WRENCH
```

- - - - - - - - - - - - - - - -

(a) Your solution should be similar to this:

```
330 IF LEN(P$) > 20 THEN GOSUB 1120 : GOTO 320
•
 •
  •
1110 STOP
1120 PRINT "YOU ENTERED "; P$; "FOR PRODUCT DESCRIPTION."
1130 PRINT "PLEASE REENTER, BUT SHORTEN YOUR ENTRY BY USING
     ABBREVIATIONS"
1140 PRINT "SO THAT THE PRODUCT DESCRIPTION IS LESS THAN 20
     CHARACTERS LONG,"
1150 PRINT "INCLUDING THE SPACES AND PUNCTUATION."
1160 RETURN
```

REPLACEMENT OF DATA ITEMS CONTAINED IN A DATA FIELD

The first example program at the beginning of this chapter illustrated the problem of changing part of an existing string; attempting to change MIRIAM MARTINSON to MIRIAM JONES by substituting the new last name for the old using MID$ as a replacement function. The attempt to substitute JONES for MARTINSON resulted in MIRIAM JONESNSON. The most practical solution is to *always use data fields of predefined lengths for each data item in a string.* That way any changes or replacements with MID$ will be complete, rather than partial, as happened above.

Now design program modules to accomplish assignments and replacements of fields within strings, using first and last names as examples.

Step 1. Define the field for the first name to have eight characters and that for the last name, twelve characters, with a space separating the name fields.
Step 2. Create the data entry routine.

```
100 LINE INPUT "ENTER FIRST NAME:"; F$
110 IF LEN(F$) = 0 THEN PRINT "PLEASE, WE MUST HAVE THE NAME":GOTO 100
120 IF LEN(F$) > 8 THEN PRINT "FIRST NAME IS TOO LARGE. 8 CHAR. MAX.":
    GOTO 100
130 IF LEN(F$) < 8 THEN LET F$ = F$ + " ": GOTO 130
140 LINE INPUT "ENTER LAST NAME:"; L$
150 IF LEN(L$) = 0 THEN PRINT "PLEASE, WE MUST HAVE THE LAST NAME":
    GOTO 140
160 IF LEN(L$) > 12 THEN PRINT "LAST NAME IS TOO LONG 12 CHAR. MAX.":
    GOTO 140
170 IF LEN(L$) < 12 THEN LET L$ = L$ + " ": GOTO 170
180 LET N$ = F$ + " " + L$
190 :
200 :
```

Step 3. Replacement routine for last name field.

```
—400 LINE INPUT "ENTER NEW LAST NAME:"; L1$
 405 IF LEN(L1$) = 0 THEN PRINT "PLEASE, WE MUST HAVE A LAST
     NAME": GOTO 400
 410 IF LEN(L1$) > 12 THEN PRINT "LAST NAME TOO LONG. 12 CHAR.
     MAX.": GOTO 400
 420 IF LEN(L1$) < 12 THEN LET L1$ = L1$ + " ": GOTO 420
 430 :
 440 LET MID$(N$,10,12) = L1$
```

Step 4. Name printing routines.

```
600 REM*** TO PRINT FIRST NAME ONLY
610 PRINT MID$(N$,1,8)
620 REM
630 REM*** TO PRINT LAST NAME ONLY
640 PRINT MID$(N$,10,12)
650 REM*** TO PRINT COMPLETE NAME
660 PRINT N$
```

Check your understanding of the routines above by answering the following questions.

(a) In line 170, what is the purpose of L$ = L$ + " "?

(b) What does line 180 do? ______________________________

____

____

(c) In line 440, what does the MID$ function do? ______________________________

____

____

____

____

____

(d) If F$ = "VAL" and L$ = "JEANS", how will N$ appear when printed or displayed by line 660? ______________________________

____

____

- - - - - - - - - - - - - - - -

(a) Fills in unused character positions with blanks to the correct field length (same technique used in lines 160 and 420).
(b) Packs first and last names into N$, separated by a space.
(c) Replaces twelve characters of N$ string beginning at character position 10 with the string assigned to L1$.
(d) VAL JEANS
(All "padding" spaces are included when N$ is printed.)

THE VAL FUNCTION IN DATA ENTRY CHECKS

If the product number and quantity ordered in a program must be numeric quantities, VAL( ) can easily convert these numbers stored as strings to numeric values.

```
330 A$ = "128.95"
340 PRINT VAL(A$)
350 A = VAL(A$)
360 PRINT A

RUN
 128.95
 128.95
```

In the conversion, either a leading space is added for the implied plus sign, or a minus sign is provided if the quantities were negative.

But the VAL( ) function does not completely solve the problem of converting string numbers to numeric values. For example, alphabetic information included in a string you wish to convert to a numeric value presents a very real problem that can range from accidentally using the letter O (oh) for a zero, to a quantity that includes the units that measure that quantity (12 quarts). Therefore, always test to be sure that if numeric values are needed, that is what was entered.

Following are some sample values run on our TRS-80 computer. Try them on your computer before you continue. (Hints for other computers are given below.)

```
5 REM*** VAL TEST #1
10 LET A$ = "ABC"
20 PRINT A$, VAL(A$)
25 REM*** VAL TEST #2 - NULL STRING
30 LET A$ = ""
40 PRINT A$, VAL(A$)
45 REM*** VAL TEST #3
50 LET A$ = "123ABC"
60 PRINT A$, VAL(A$)
65 REM*** VAL TEST #4
70 LET A$ = "ABC123"
80 PRINT A$, VAL(A$)
```

The TRS-80 run:

```
RUN
ABC          0
             0
123ABC       123
ABC123       0
```

If you get an error at line 20, start your next RUN at line 30 by typing RUN3Ø (a RUN starting at line 30). This is a useful debugging technique when part of a program is giving you problems. If your BASIC doesn't support this type of RUN (line number), then eliminate lines 10 and 20 and do a regular RUN. Continue this technique through the test program to see how your BASIC responds to these four tests. The discussion below assumes that your VAL( ) function responds like the RUN above. Alternate means to the same ends are discussed in the section on ASCII codes.

Notice in the RUN above that alphabetic characters result in a value of Ø, as do a null string and the mixed alphanumeric data where the alpha information *precedes* the numeric (ABC123). Notice also that the mixed data 123ABC results in a value of 123. The MICROSOFT BASIC's VAL function disregards the alphabetic information that *follows* numeric information in the same string. This is convenient if you wish to enter the quantity and the units, such as 14 gallons, but inconvenient if you wish to check for the validity of the data entered. Here, you want to ascertain that the data entered are numeric, so when the VAL function is used you get valid numeric values. At this point, for mixed numbers and letters, assume that the user did enter the correct value.

The test to validate numeric information would be:

```
IF VAL(A$) = 0 THEN PRINT "ENTER NUMERIC VALUES ONLY"
```

Place this data test *after* the statement that tests for a null string, because on some computers the VAL function encountering a null string results in an error condition and program execution stops.

(a) Now do some programming. For the data entry problem on page 66, you wrote a program to produce a data entry sequence with null string checks added. Now add data checks that ensure that the product number and quantity ordered are numeric values. Also include a data check to be certain that the product number is a four-digit number.

(a)
```
210 :
220 LINE INPUT "ENTER CUSTOMER NUMBER:"; C$
230 IF LEN(C$) = 0 THEN PRINT "ENTRY ERROR. PLEASE REENTER" :
    GOTO 220
240 LINE INPUT "ENTER CUSTOMER NAME:"; N$
250 IF LEN(N$) = 0 THEN PRINT "PLEASE RESPOND AS REQUESTED":
    GOTO 240
260 LINE INPUT "ENTER PRODUCT NUMBER:"; P$
270 IF LEN(P$) = 0 THEN PRINT "WE CANNOT CONTINUE WITHOUT THIS
    DATA": GOTO 260
272 IF VAL(P$) = 0 THEN PRINT "PLEASE ENTER NUMBERS ONLY": GOTO 260
274 IF LEN(P$) <> 4 THEN PRINT "PLEASE BE SURE TO ENTER A 4
    DIGIT NUMBER": GOTO 260
280 LINE INPUT "ENTER QUANTITY ORDERED:"; Q$
290 IF LEN(Q$) = 0 THEN PRINT "PLEASE ENTER THE CORRECT VALUE":
    GOTO 280
295 IF VAL(Q$) = 0 THEN PRINT "ENTER NUMBERS ONLY, PLEASE":
    GOTO 280
```

USING STR$ TO CONVERT VALUES TO STRINGS

The STR$( ) function serves the opposite purpose of the VAL( ) function. It converts numeric values into strings. This allows you to manipulate numbers with string functions. You can use it to convert numeric values to strings assigned to variables, in concatenating several small strings into a string variable, as done earlier in this chapter. For example, you may have combined product number, product description, and quantity in inventory into one long string. You may then need the quantity in inventory for an accounting procedure or another calculation. Such operations require a *numeric* value. You would convert the string to a numeric value by using the VAL( ) of the entry string. When the quantity is stored, you can convert back to a string by taking the STR$( ) of the numeric value to place it into the P$ string.

P$	17633	BOOK TITLE	144

```
P$ = P$ + STR$(Q)
```

or

```
Q$ = STR$(Q)
P$ = P$ + Q$
```

When the computer converts a numeric value to a string with STR$( ), a leading space is included if the numeric value is positive. A minus sign is included in the string if the value is negative.

Try this demonstration program:

```
140 LET X = 847.25
150 LET X$ = STR$(X)
160 PRINT "X ="; X
170 PRINT "X$ ="; X$

RUN
X = 847.25
X$ = 847.25
```

Notice that the leading space is still there after the value has been converted to a string.

In the example above, the LEN(X$) is seven – five numeric characters, the decimal point, and the leading space in a positive value converted to a string. (Remember, blank spaces, decimal points, and other punctuation marks are characters.) If you fail to provide enough string length or field space, you will inadvertently lose significant digits or characters due to computer truncation. A six-digit number with a leading space does *not* fit in a six-character field.

How many characters will the following data items have if they are converted from values to strings with the STR$ function?

(a) 171.83 __________

(b) 2001 __________

(c) -999 __________

- - - - - - - - - - - - - - - -

(a) 7
(b) 5
(c) 4

CHECKING FOR ILLEGAL CHARACTERS

Using the ASC function in a data entry checking statement is a powerful tool to determine whether illegal or unlikely characters have been included in an INPUT string. Checking is done by a combination of the ASC function, the MID$ function, an IF. . .THEN statement, and a FOR NEXT loop. First the length of the entry is determined by the LEN function, which is used as the upper limit of the FOR control variable, like this:

```
350 LINE INPUT "ENTER 6 CHARACTER CATALOG CODE:"; C$
360 FOR X = 1 TO LEN(C$)
```

Then the MID$ function, using the FOR control variable (value of X for any iteration) to determine which character to examine, selects each character in the string for comparison to an ASCII number, like this:

```
370 IF ASC(MID$(C$,X,1)) = 32 THEN PRINT "REENTER BUT DO NOT USE
    SPACES": GOTO 350
380 NEXT X
```

(Note: Here is one of those exceptions when you "leave" a FOR NEXT loop.)

Notice that any character that can be entered as part of a string can be checked to see that legal characters that should be there are there, or that illegal characters are not included. Notice, too, that the error message could be located in a subroutine outside of the FOR NEXT loop. In addition, you can use the logical AND and OR, to check for more than one character or group of characters in the same IF. . .THEN statement.

What if a user made the following response to line 350 in the example above? Answer the questions based on this response and this program segment:

```
RUN
ENTER 6 CHARACTER CATALOG CODE:A - 1314
```

(a) What is the length of the substring selected by the MID$ function in line 370?

____

(b) What ASCII value is compared to 32 the first time through the FOR NEXT loop? __________

(c) The second time through? __________

(d) On which iteration (time through) of the FOR NEXT loop is the comparison in line 370 true? __________

(e) What value does the FOR statement control variable have as an upper limit for this user's response? __________

(a) 1
(b) 64 (for A)
(c) 32 (for a space)
(d) second iteration
(e) LEN(C$) = 8

(a) Write a data entry checking routine similar to the one before that prints an error message if an illegal character is encountered. Use more than one IF. . . THEN statement with the ASC function in the comparison, or a single IF. . . THEN statement that uses the logical AND and OR. The only *legal* characters for the entry are the digits Ø (zero) through 9 inclusive and the decimal point, such as would be entered for a dollar and cents entry without a dollar sign.

(a)
```
100 LINE INPUT "ENTER A VALUE:"; V$
110 FOR X = 1 TO LEN(V$)
120 IF ASC(MID$(V$,X,1)) > = 48 AND ASC(MID$(V$,X,1)) < = 57 OR
    ASC(MID$(V$,X,1)) = 46 THEN 140
130 PRINT "INVALID ENTRY. ENTER NUMBERS AND DECIMAL PT. ONLY":
    GOTO 100
140 NEXT X
150 :
```

A DISCUSSION OF DATA ENTRY AND CHECKING PROCEDURES

This chapter has included recommendations, hints, and techniques for dealing with and checking data. This section describes and summarizes procedures used to check and validate all data entries.

There are two schools of thought regarding at what point incoming data should be checked for errors. One states that since the data entry operator's time is costly, the operator should merely enter data using the fastest possible procedures, with no checks for accuracy at the time data are entered. This position requires that more time be spent training the data-entry operator in fast, accurate computer entry techniques. Then, later, another program does the error checking on the data at fast computer speeds. Whenever a data error is encountered, the computer "kicks out" or rejects the entire data entry transaction for that set of data and prints the rejected information in a special report. The rejected data set is then reprocessed or reentered by the data-entry staff. This procedure works well if the number of rejects is low.

In contrast, we prefer the second approach – checking data on the way in. As each item is entered, it is error-checked immediately. If an error is detected, the computer operator is advised to reenter the data. One advantage is that the person making the entry error is responsible for correcting it. This method also gives management a better measure of an operator's work flow since only accurate, accepted information is completed during a work day. In the alternate method, data entry rates may seem high, but so may be the reject rate, and special procedures are needed to verify who is making the entry errors. A less subtle technique is to signal an entry error with a terminal beeper or bell. Each time faulty data are detected, the sound signals the operator (and the manager, if present) that an error was made and draws attention to the "culprit." But these are concerns in a business environment. The immediate error check is more in keeping with the small business or personal nature of most programming applications presented here. And since all the error checking routines follow the data entry immediately, you can easily read the program to see what kinds of error checks are being made.

Two general data entry techniques are universally accepted. One uses a graphic reproduction on the video screen of the paper form from which data are entered. It makes sense to reproduce that form on the screen and have the computer prompt the operator to "fill in the blanks" just as they appear on the paper form or data source sheet. Of course, this technique assumes you are using a video terminal as a data input device and that your BASIC has graphic programming capabilities. Since graphic instructions vary so widely from one version of BASIC to the next, we do not show you a program to reproduce a data entry form.

A second generally accepted technique is one that repeats back to the operator one or more sets of data entered. The operator is then given the chance to reenter any incorrect items, even after the entry checking has been performed by the computer. This is the "last chance" to pick up spelling errors, number transpositions, typographical errors, and anything else for which entry error checks cannot be designed into the program itself. An example of such a post-data entry display appears below:

```
THANK YOU. HERE IS THE DATA YOU ENTERED.

      CUST. #           PROD. #           QUANTITY

1 - 98213               17892             18
2 - 98213               24618             12
3 - 98213               81811             144

ARE THERE ANY CHANGES (YES OR NO)? YES
ENTER THE NUMBER OF THE LINE IN WHICH A CHANGE IS NECESSARY:
```

Before a summary report such as the above is displayed, clear the screen of previously displayed information. If fact, clearing the screen before each new entry or after the entry of a data set is important in the entire concept of avoiding errors. If the graphic display of a data source form is used, then the screen should be cleared and the form redisplayed with the just-entered data. The operator can then double check with the option to make any corrections directly on the new form.

Many error-checking procedures depend on personal preference or company policy. Either way, plan ahead. Look carefully at the complete problem or job for which you are using your computer. In what form and format should the data be entered? Are there subtle limits or tests that you can apply to data to detect operator errors? For instance, if you are entering addresses with zip codes and a large percentage of your business is in California, then you know that most zip codes should start with the number 9. It would be appropriate to test whether the entered zip code value begins with a 9, and if not, to inform the operator of a *possible* error.

```
140 LINE INPUT "ENTER ZIP CODE:"; Z$
150 IF LEN(Z$) <> 5 THEN PRINT "ZIP CODE MUST BE 5 CHARACTERS.
    PLEASE REENTER": GOTO 140
160 IF LEFT$(Z$,1) = "9" THEN 200
170 PRINT "THE ZIP CODE YOU ENTERED, "; Z$; " IS NOT FOR
    CALIFORNIA"
180 LINE INPUT "IS IT CORRECT ANYWAY?"; R$
190 IF LEFT$(R$,1) <> "Y" THEN PRINT "PLEASE REENTER": GOTO 140
200 REM    PROGRAM CONTINUES
```

We also strongly recommend consistency in your data entry formats, especially for such things as data field lengths. Don't confuse yourself or others who use your programs. If you write several programs that use personal names, use the same size delimiters or data fields. This also allows you to have compatible data files for various uses. The same goes for address sizes and formats, product descriptions, and other alphanumeric data. Remember, your company may have already made the decision for you, so be sure you know the policies!

For numeric values, quantities, and entries involving monetary values, you may have to dig a little to discover the limits for which the data should be tested. Company policy, common sense, and actual experience may give you the logical limits for a "not less than" or "not to exceed" data entry check. And you can always use the operator override procedure for possibly erroneous data, as shown below:

```
330 LINE INPUT "ENTER QUANTITY ORDERED:"; Q$
340 IF VAL(Q$) <= 96 THEN 400
350 PRINT "THE QUANTITY ENTERED EXCEEDS NORMAL LIMITS OF 96 UNITS.
    PLEASE REENTER": GOTO 330
360 :
370 :
399 REM    ANOTHER PROCEDURE
400 LINE INPUT "ENTER PRICE QUOTED:"; P$
410 IF VAL(P$) < 75.00 THEN 450
420 PRINT "THE PRICE YOU QUOTED EXCEEDS NORMAL LIMITS OF $75.00"
430 LINE INPUT "IS IT CORRECT, ANYWAY?"; R$
440 IF LEFT$(R$,1) <> "Y" THEN PRINT "PLEASE REENTER": GOTO 400
450 :
```

Let's review the general data entry error-checking procedures for alphabetic and numeric information.

1. Enter all data into string variables after a clearly stated prompt request from the computer.
2. Enter only one data item per prompt.

3. If you are going to pack a number of data items (a data set) into one string, enter the data into separate string variables and then concatenate after all checking has been accomplished. Do *not* enter data directly into a substring position.
4. Checking should include a test for nonresponse (a null string) of the type IF LEN(R$) = Ø. . .
5. When an error is discovered, include a message not only to tell the operator that an error was made, but also to describe as completely as possible what the error was. Do not merely request a reentry.
6. Check alphabetic data for field length using the LEN function.
7. It may be necessary to pad the entry with spaces to the proper field length, especially for alphabetic data.
8. Thoroughly test numeric data (which we recommend be entered into a string variable) in this order:
   (a) for non-response (a null string)
   (b) for excess string length, if applicable
   (c) for the inadvertent inclusion of alphabetic characters in numeric values, using VAL or ASC
   (d) for any company policy tests or size limit
   (e) if the datum is an integer value, use the integer declaration (a percent sign following a variable in many BASICs) or test the value to see if it is an integer with a statement like IF X <> INT(X). . .
   (f) test for negative values if they are not acceptable. If this sounds like a lot of work, remember that your otherwise excellent program must have valid and accurate data to do its job. Don't skimp. Be complete. For example, the capability of the IF. . .THEN statement to PRINT a message may lull you into trying to oversimplify an error message in order to fit it into the same programming line as the IF. . .THEN statement. Don't fall into this trap. Use GOSUBs and provide complete, clear messages to the operator.

You may want to place all error tests and messages in subroutines. This gives your program neatness and clarity. Various entries may be put to the same tests, allowing the check statements to work for various entries if variables and other factors are compatable.

Be alert to other occasions throughout your programs where data errors may occur. While we encourage sensitivity to errors at data entry time, always check for data errors later in your program, especially if the data are subject to various manipulations after the entry routines. Watch for strange results from functions such as VAL. Get to know the version of BASIC you are using inside and out by thoroughly exploring the reactions of statements and functions in various circumstances. The error conditions you encounter will depend largely on your programming skills and the kinds of applications you program. Be alert to the errors that occur and include tests for them. Don't get psychologically locked in to your first, second, or third version of a program or programming technique.

Finally, be aware that many programmers test their programs with only sensible data, neglecting the ridiculous mistakes that can, and without a doubt will, be made. When you think you have covered every possibility, let a child with no computer experience try it out. If the program survives, you've checked it all out!

CHAPTER 3 SELF-TEST

1. Write an IF. . .THEN comparison that will be true if:
   (a) the entry has exactly seven characters.
   (b) the entry does not have exactly seven characters.
   (c) the first character in an entry is not a number.
   (d) the first character in an entry is a number other than zero.
   (e) the entry is not a null string.

2. Write a statement line that checks to see if an entry has less than twelve characters, and if so, pads the entry with spaces so that the resulting string has exactly twelve characters.

3. Write a data entry checking routine that checks to see that no numbers have been included in a string entry. Write an accompanying subroutine to be called when a number is found that tells the user what was entered, and to reenter without including numbers in the entry.

4. You now have the background to write a data entry module for most kinds of data to be later placed into a data file (covered in the next chapter). Write the data entry module and complete it with data entry error checks, as described below:

   (a) Write a data entry routine that prompts the use to enter:
      (1) a five-character alphanumeric product code (must always have five characters)
      (2) a product name with a twelve character maximum length
      (3) the quantity ordered into a three-digit field with a limit of 288 per order
      (4) the price, into a five-digit field, with no price exceeding $99.99

   (b) Pack the information entered into one long string (M$) with the following fields:

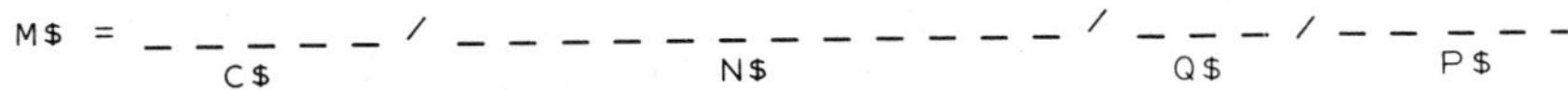

   Note: do not include slashes in the data field string.

   (c) Print parts of M$ in a "report" with the format shown below:

   PRICE QUANTITY PROD. CODE

   Refer back through this chapter for ideas, and try debugging your solution program before looking at our way of doing it. Our solutions are not the only ones possible. The real test is whether the program works, and how fool proof it is.

Answer Key

1. (a) `IF LEN(A$) = 7 THEN...`

   (b) `IF LEN(A$) <> 7 THEN...`

   (c) `IF ASC(A$) < 48 AND ASC(A$) > 57 THEN...`

   (d) `IF VAL(A$) <> 0 THEN...`

   (e) `IF LEN(A$) <> 0 THEN...`

2.
```
120 IF LEN(A$) < 12 THEN LET A$ = A$ + " ": GOTO 120
```

(Your string variable and line number may be different, of course.)

3.
```
310 LINE INPUT "ENTER YOUR NAME:"; A$
320 FOR X = 1 TO LEN(A$)
330 IF ASC(MID$(A$,X,1)) > 47 AND ASC(MID$(A$,X,1)) < 58 THEN
    GOSUB 1100 : GOTO 310
340 NEXT X

1100 PRINT "YOU ENTERED: "; A$
1120 PRINT "PLEASE REENTER, BUT DO NOT INCLUDE ANY NUMBERS."
1130 RETURN
```

4.
```
110 REM  SOLUTION FOR #3, PROBLEM 4, SELF-TEST
115 :
119 CLEAR 1000
120 :
130 LINE INPUT "ENTER PRODUCT CODE(5):"; C$
140 IF LEN(C$) <> 5 THEN PRINT "CODE MUST BE 5 CHARACTERS.
    REENTER": GOTO 130
150 LINE INPUT "ENTER PRODUCT NAME(12):"; N$
160 IF LEN(N$) > 12 THEN PRINT "ENTRY TOO LONG. PLEASE REDUCE TO
    12 CHAR.": GOTO 150
170 IF LEN(N$) < 12 THEN LET N$ = N$ + " ": GOTO 170
180 LINE INPUT "ENTER QUANTITY ORDERED:"; Q$
200 IF LEN(Q$) > 3 THEN PRINT "TOO MANY DIGITS. 3 MAX.": GOTO180
210 IF LEN(Q$) < 3 THEN LET Q$ = Q$ + " " : GOTO 210
190 IF VAL(Q$) = 0 THEN PRINT "ENTRY ERROR. NUMBERS ONLY":
    GOTO 180
220 IF VAL(Q$) > 288 THEN PRINT "TOO MANY UNITS ORDERED.
    REENTER": GOTO 180
230 LINE INPUT "ENTER UNIT PRICE:"; P$
240 IF LEN(P$) > 5 THEN PRINT "PRICING ERROR. 5 DIGIT MAX.":
    GOTO 230
250 IF LEN(P$) < 5 THEN LET P$ = P$ + " " : GOTO 250
260 IF VAL(P$) = 0 THEN PRINT "PRICING ERROR. NUMBERS ONLY":
    GOTO 230
270 IF VAL(P$) > 99.99 THEN PRINT "PRICING ERROR. 99.99 MAX.":
    GOTO 230
280 :
290 LET M$ = C$ + N$ + Q$ + P$
300 :
310 CLS
320 PRINT "PRICE", "QUANTITY", "PROD. CODE"
330 PRINT RIGHT$(M$,5),
340 PRINT MID$(M$,18,3),
350 PRINT LEFT$(M$,5) : REM 330,340,350 COULD BE ON ONE LINE
360 :
```

CHAPTER FOUR

Creating and Reading Back Sequential Data Files

Objectives: When you complete this chapter, you will be able to store and retrieve numeric and/or alphanumeric data in sequential disk data files, using the following BASIC data file statements in their special formats: OPEN, CLOSE, INPUT, PRINT, KILL.

INTRODUCTION

A data file is stored alphanumeric information that is separate and distinct from any particular BASIC program. It is located (recorded) on either a magnetic disk, diskette, or cassette tape. This chapter discusses using sequential (also called serial) data files on disks and diskettes. Such files are very similar to cassette tape files, and the working concepts are the same. Therefore, even if your computer system uses a cassette recorder to store information, read these next two chapters to learn about sequential files, as well as Chapter 6, which deals specifically with cassette tape files.

In your previous BASIC programming experiences you probably hand-entered all data needed by your programs using INPUT statements. You did this each time you ran your programs. Or, if you had larger amounts of data, you might have entered the data with DATA statements and used the READ statement to access and manipulate the data. In either case, the data were program-dependent; that is, they were part of that one program and not usable by other programs.

A data file is *program-independent.* It is *separate* from any one program and can be accessed and used by many different programs. In most cases, you will use only one program to load a data file with information. But once your data file is loaded (entered and recorded) on disk or cassette tape, you can read the information from that file using many different programs, each performing a different activity with that file's data.

For example, perhaps you have computerized your personal telephone and address directory using data files stored on a disk. You may need just one program to originally load information into that file and add names to it. (This chapter will show you how.) Another program allows you to select phone numbers from the file using NAME as the selection criterion. You can use still another program to change addresses or phone numbers for entries previously made in the file. Another program could print gummed mailing labels in zip code order using the same data file. You could design yet another program to print names and phone numbers by phone number area code. The possibilities go on and on. Notice that one data file can be accessed by many different computer programs.. The data file is located separately on the disk in a defined place. Each program mentioned above copies the information from the disk into the electronic memory of the computer as it is needed by that particular program. Alternatively, the program could transfer information from the computer's memory to be recorded onto the disk.

If you already use your disk to SAVE and/or LOAD BASIC programs, then you have some experience with disk files. When you SAVE a BASIC program, it is recorded on this disk in a file. Such files containing BASIC programs are called *program files.* In contrast, the files discussed in this chapter contain data and are therefore called *data files.* The two types of files are different and are used differently. A BASIC program file contains a copy of a BASIC program that you can LOAD, RUN, LIST, and SAVE. A data file contains information only. You access this information using a BASIC program that includes special BASIC statements that access data files; that is, transfer all or part of the data from the magnetic recording on disk or cassette into the computer's electronic memory so the program can use it. You *cannot* LOAD, RUN, LIST, or SAVE a data file. You can access the information only by using a BASIC program.

(a) Describe in general terms how you can access data in a data file.

\- - - - - - - - - - - - - - - -

(a) Using a BASIC program that includes special file accessing BASIC statements.

DATA STORAGE ON DISKS

A magnetic disk has limited data storage capacity that varies from one computer to another, from one size disk to another, and from one recording system to another. For our TRS-80, the file capacity of the first disk drive is approximately 55,000 bytes of information, while the capacity of the second and any additional disk drive units is 83,000 bytes of information. The term "byte" will be explained shortly.

A "disk" refers to several styles of magnetic storage. Floppy disks are made of a flexible, magnetic-coated plastic, and come in two sizes – 8 inch and 5¼ inch. The smaller is often called a diskette. Hard disks are also available for microcomputers.

Although more expensive, they have larger data storage capacities. Fortunately, these physical variations do not affect the BASIC statements used to store and access data files.

Other variations occur in the way data are recorded on disks. A disk can be recorded on one or both sides and in more or less space, depending on the disk drive system. A double-density system records twice as much data in the same space as a single-density system. A quad-density system is double-density recording on a system that can record both sides of a disk without "turning it over." Again, such variations do not affect the BASIC statements used to store and access data files.

A closer look at a single-density 5¼-inch diskette provides an example. As you see in Figure 4–1, the disk is divided into thirty-five concentric circles called tracks. Each track, in turn, is divided into ten sectors, each of which can accept one *record* of recorded data. Each record has the capacity to store 256 bytes of information. This TRS-80 Model 1-style disk in a single disk drive system has approximately 215 records available to store data. Other disk drive systems may have different patterns of tracks or number of sectors per track.

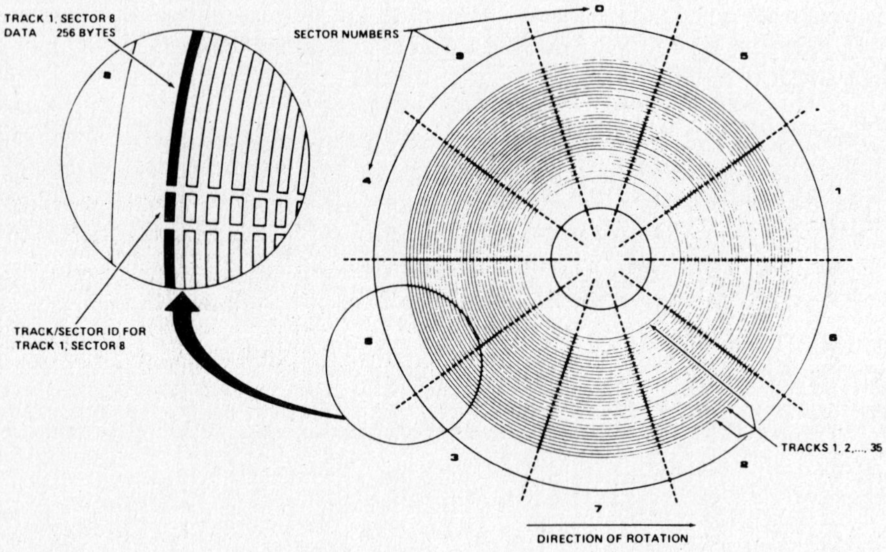

Figure 4–1. A single-density 5¼ inch diskette. Copyright 1979, Tandy Corporation. Reproduced by permission.

What is this thing called a byte? A *byte* is computer jargon for both a unit of computer memory and a unit of disk storage. Each byte has an electronic pattern that corresponds to one alphanumeric character of information. One letter of the alphabet, one special character, or one numeric character entered as a string (such as LET B$ = "3") takes up one byte of storage space. A twenty-character name takes twenty bytes of disk storage space. The general rule for storing strings in data files is that the amount of storage needed for each string is equal to the actual length of the string (plus one or two bytes for "overhead," depending on which computer and disk system you use).

(a) How many bytes of disk storage are required by the string assigned to N$?

____

```
N$ = "BASIC DATA FILES ARE FUN"
```

- - - - - - - - - - - - - - - -

(a) Twenty-four, plus two for "overhead." (Spaces also take one byte.)

Keeping track of disk storage space requirements for alphanumeric data in strings is easy, since one character equals one byte. The storage requirements for numeric values *not* entered as strings are much more difficult to count and vary from one version of BASIC to another. Even within one version of BASIC the number of bytes to hold a numeric value differs, depending on the value's precision. Precision refers to the actual number of digits in the value that the computer keeps track of. For our TRS-80 computer, numeric values use storage space as follows:†

Integer numbers (%) = 2 bytes (whole numbers in the range of ± 32768)
Single precision numbers (!) = 4 bytes (up to six significant digits, i.e., 123456, 354798)
Double precision numbers (#) = 8 bytes (up to sixteen significant digits)

For a personal telephone and address directory application, let's see how much disk storage space is required for each person on file. Each data item has a defined field length.

Name	20 characters	
Address (street)	25	
City	10	
State	2	
Zip code	5	
Phone (xxx-xxx-xxxx)	12	
Age	2	(Entered as an integer number)
Birthdate (xx/xx/xx)	8	
Subtotal	84	
Overhead	7	
Total	91	

Note that string character values are used for the zip code. Filing the zip code as an integer number instead of a five-character string would have saved disk storage space.

(a) How many bytes would be required to store the zip code as an integer value instead of a string? ______________________

(b) Why was a twelve-character string rather than a numeric value used for the phone number? ______________________

____

(c) How many records would 150 entries in the address and phone directory take up in storage? ______________________

____

(d) What is the maximum number of people you could file in your directory on one disk with a capacity of 55,000 bytes? ______________________

____

- - - - - - - - - - - - - - - - -

(a) Two, plus "overhead."

(b) Could not have included hyphens, which make number easier to read. (Note that if the telephone number had been entered without hyphens as a numeric value, the precision would have had to be at least ten in order not to lose significant digits from the number.)

(c) 91 times 150 = 13650 bytes. 13650 divided by 256 = 53.32, or 54 records. (Note that if you placed all eight data items into one long string, you could save six bytes of overhead, leaving eighty-five bytes per entry for a total of fifty records. This technique can save bytes per entry and, therefore, valuable storage space.)

(d) 55000 divided by 91 = 604.

The eight items in each entry in the personal directory are called a *dataset.* A dataset consists of all data that are included in one complete transaction or entry into a data file. Grouping information by dataset and then accessing or otherwise manipulating the dataset as a group of data items makes programming and reading programs much easier.

Sequential data files can be visualized as one long, continuous stream of information, with datasets recorded one after the other. Imagine datasets recorded continuously on a magnetic tape cassette (a single, long ribbon of tape) and you have a fairly accurate image of how a sequential file looks in theory. That is how you as a file user should think of it. The truth is, a file can be partially located on one track or one sector, and partially on another, depending on the computer system and how the file was filled. Fortunately, the physical location of the file on a disk is "invisible" to the user. All you need remember is the long, continuous stream of information.

SEQUENTIAL VS RANDOM ACCESS DATA FILES

Data filing systems can use sequential data files or random access data files. The latter are explained fully in Chapters 7 and 8. Sequential data files use disk storage space more efficiently than random access data files. It will quickly become clear to you that a disk is very easy to fill to capacity, despite the seemingly large number of bytes that can be stored on it. Thus, sequential files are *space-efficient.* However, it is somewhat difficult to change data stored in a sequential file. *Sequential files are designed for "permanent" information* that changes infrequently. You can change data in sequential files, but it is not as easy or efficient as in random access files. Thus, another criterion for choosing between sequential and random access data files is how often changes in data can be expected.

A third consideration is the time it takes to access information stored on a disk. When you have a large data file with loads of information, it takes more computer time to find or access a particular dataset at the end of a sequential file than it would in a random access file. To access the 450th data set in a sequential file of 475 data sets, the computer must sequentially search through 449 datasets before coming upon the 450th dataset. Using random access files, the computer can immediately access the 450th dataset without having to search through the other 449 datasets. Therefore access time is another factor in selection of sequential or random access data files.

(a) What are three factors to consider when choosing to use sequential or random access data files? ______________________________

____

- - - - - - - - - - - - - - - -

(a) Storage space efficiency, changing data, and time for accessing data.

INITIALIZING SEQUENTIAL DATA FILES

To use a data file, you must first OPEN the file on your disk. This is done as part of the program's initialization module. The procedure varies from one version of BASIC to another. MICROSOFT BASIC-80 and TRS-80 BASIC are used in our examples.

When you load the disk operating system (DOS) from your disk, TRS-80 asks you, "HOW MANY FILES?" Your response determines how many files you can use at once (a non-response allows three at once). In MICROSOFT BASIC 80 and TRS-80 BASIC, a record is automatically added to the file *as needed* for incoming data. Therefore, users need not concern themselves with file size, as you might have on another computer, except to use disk space efficiently and to avoid having a large collection of disks.

The OPEN statement tells the computer which file (or files) your program will use. It also provides the computer with other information. The OPEN statement creates a new file if none exists for the file name specified. It also sets the access mode for using the file, as input ("I"), output ("O"), or random access ("R"). For sequential files, use the "I" mode for files from which information will be read into the computer's electronic memory, and "O" mode for files that will take information "out" of the computer and store into the data file. The OPEN file will either be input or output. It can*not* be both at the same time.

OPEN also assigns a buffer to the file referred to in the OPEN statement. A *buffer* is a 256 byte section of the computer's memory that is created to act as a go-between for the computer and the disk data file (see Figure 4-2). Input information accessed from a disk file is first copied into a buffer, 256 bytes at a time. It is then available for manipulation by the program. Likewise, data to be output from the computer for recording onto the disk are first accumulated in the buffer. When the buffer is full, the information is copied onto the disk. The buffer is a *holding area* for all data coming to or from a data file. The OPEN statement assigns a buffer and buffer number to each file to be used by your program. A buffer is needed for each file that is OPEN at the same time in the program. TRS-80 BASIC and BASIC-80 provide buffer numbers from one to fifteen. You can choose any numbers in that range. Allocate the number of buffers when you respond to the initializing question "HOW MANY FILES?"

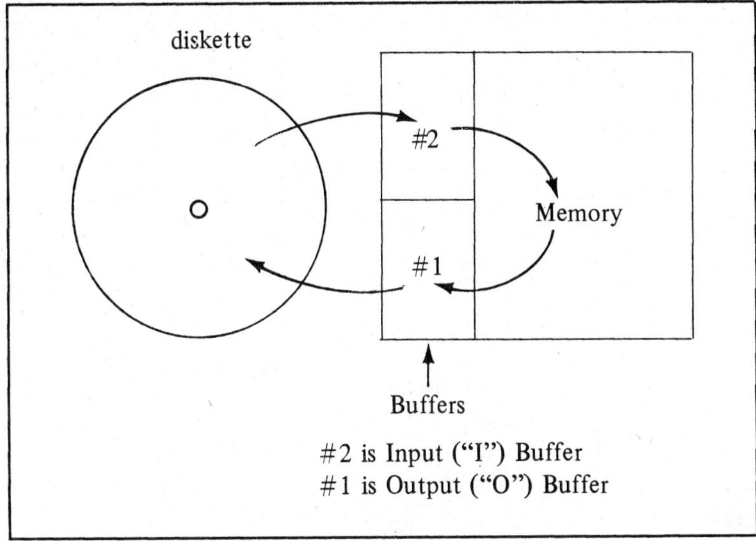

Figure 4-2. Data flow through buffers.

Let's now examine various OPEN statements and then practice writing OPEN statements that include all the information needed by the computer to deal with data files in a program.

The OPEN statement has the following form:

```
140 OPEN "I", 1, "NAMES1"
```

This statement opens the file with the name NAMES1 as a sequential input ("I") file assigned to buffer number 1. If the file with the name NAMES1 does not exist on the disk, an error message will indicate that the file cannot be found. (It is an error condition, since you cannot input or read data into the computer from a nonexistent file.) Remember, input and output, in the context of a data file OPEN statement, refer to input from the disk to the computer, and output from the computer onto the disk. If you think of the disk as a peripheral device, like a computer terminal, this way of using "input" and "output" makes sense, like input from the keyboard and output to the CRT.

Another example:

```
140 LINE INPUT "ENTER FILE NAME:"; F$
150 OPEN "I", 4, F$
```

This shows that the file name can be assigned with a string variable. Line 150 opens the file designated by the user in F$, as an input ("I") sequential file assigned to buffer number 4.

One important point about using the OPEN statement to open an output ("O") file is illustrated by the following statement:

```
180 OPEN "O", 2, "TEMPFIL"
```

This statement opens the file TEMPFIL as a sequential output file assigned to buffer number 2. If no file by that name exists on the disk, it will be created. But here is the tricky part: *If TEMPFIL already exists, all of that file's previous contents will be lost!* Be sure you understand that. If you attempt to reopen an existing file in output mode, you destroy all data previously recorded in the file – a lesson you do not want to learn the hard way!

You can even allow the user to enter all of the information needed for the OPEN statement, as in this example:

```
140 LINE INPUT "ENTER FILE MODE:"; M$
150 INPUT "ENTER BUFFER NUMBER"; B%
160 LINE INPUT "ENTER FILE NAME:"; N$
170 OPEN M$, B%, N$
```

In a "real" program, you would undoubtedly include error checking statements for all user inputs. The percent sign in B% indicates that only an integer will be assigned to the numeric variable B% (no fractional value).

Check your understanding by writing three statements or program segments according to the following specifications.

(a) Open an input file named PHONES, assigned to buffer 6.

(b) Open an output file with a user-designated name, assigned to buffer 2.

(c) Open an input file with a user-designated name and buffer number.

– – – – – – – – – – – – – – –

(a)
```
110 OPEN "I",6, "PHONES"
```

(b)
```
140 LINE INPUT "ENTER FILE NAME:"; N$
150 OPEN "O", 2, N$
```

(c)
```
210 LINE INPUT "ENTER FILE NAME"; N$
220 INPUT "ENTER BUFFER NUMBER"; B%
230 OPEN "I", B%, N$
```

Every file that is opened with an OPEN statement must also be closed with a CLOSE statement before the program finishes executing. As soon as the program is through using a file, and always before the program terminates, include a CLOSE statement to unassign the buffer from that file. This also completes any transaction inside the computer system that the buffer was involved in, as explained in more detail in the next section. Once a file has been closed and the buffer unassigned, the same buffer number can be reused for any other file you open. Here are some sample CLOSE statements:

800 CLOSE 1	unassigns buffer number 1
820 CLOSE 1, 4, 3	unassigns the three buffers indicated
860 CLOSE	unassigns any and all open buffers from their files

The Buffer Problem

CLOSE is a vitally important statement and, in most cases, is used to maintain the integrity and accuracy of your data files. Recall that the buffer acts as a go-between for the computer and the disk system. When you *output* data from the computer to the disk file, the data go first to the buffer. Then, when the buffer is full (256 bytes), the data are output and recorded onto the disk. This is often referred to as *updating the disk file.*

What happens if the buffer is only partly full of data and there is no more data to finish filling it? You might expect the half-full buffer to simply transfer its contents to the disk for recording when the program finishes execution. But it won't do that. The data in the half-filled buffer will not necessarily be recorded into the file. Your file may not contain all the information you expected. One important purpose of the CLOSE statement is to force the buffer to transfer its contents to the data file even though the buffer is not full. As a rule of thumb, any program with an OPEN statement should have a CLOSE statement that is always executed before the program terminates. If you get trapped with a program that aborts or terminates and the buffer still contains some data, CLOSE can be executed in direct mode, forcing the buffer to transfer its contents to the disk file. However, to have to do so indicates poor programming technique and would be completely unacceptable in a work environment. Further instructions on writing your programs to include a CLOSE statement that is always executed are given later in the chapter.

(a) What are two purposes of the CLOSE statement?

____

____

- - - - - - - - - - - - - - - -

(a) To unassign the buffer and to force the buffer to transfer its contents to the disk data file.

Our TRS-80 reference manual states that the buffer will automatically "flush" (transfer its contents to the disk data file) under normal conditions if the program terminates at an END or STOP statement, because of a disk error, or when the user types RUN, NEW, or CLEAR, and even when a program line is added or deleted. Check your reference manual to see what happens with your computer but don't count on what is said! To repeat: Always include a CLOSE statement that is executed before the program terminates, so that buffer-flushing is automatic. You should only force buffer-flushing under emergency conditions, and then you should use the CLOSE statement in direct mode.

The buffer-flushing problem – and it is a real problem – makes it imperative that you *never* remove a disk from the disk drive if the disk contains an open file. Be certain all files are closed before you remove the disk from the drive, or you may find yourself with data from a half-filled buffer placed in the wrong file on the wrong disk, which can create some nasty errors. Be cautious, and remember that data go first to the buffer. They then transfer to the disk file once the buffer is full. If the buffer is not full, force it to transfer the data to the disk file with the CLOSE statement.

(a) If you are outputting data in a program to a data file and the program accidentally terminates without executing a CLOSE statement, what should you do?

____

____

- - - - - - - - - - - - - - - -

(a) Close the file with a CLOSE statement in direct mode.

PRINTING OR WRITING DATA INTO A SEQUENTIAL DATA FILE

You have learned to set up communication between the computer and the disk system with the OPEN statement and CLOSE statement. Now you will learn how to place data into a file; that is, actually record onto the disk. TRS-80 BASIC does this with a special form of the PRINT statement, distinguished from a regular print statement by using a # sign followed by the buffer number of the file into which the data is to be recorded. BASIC-80 uses WRITE # as well as PRINT #.

```
240 PRINT #1, A, B, C
```

This statement tells the computer to print or write into buffer #1 (and then, of course, into the file assigned to buffer #1) the values assigned to numeric variables A, B, and C.

```
270 LET X = 3                    or
280 PRINT #X, A, B, C                     280 WRITE #X, A, B, C
```

The buffer number can be a variable, but be sure the variable has an assigned value before the PRINT # or WRITE # statement is executed!

Look at the next example carefully. The program prints or writes data into a file starting at the very beginning of the file. Remember, when you OPEN a file for *output,* any previous data in that file is destroyed.

```
100 REM    FILE PRINT DEMO #1
110 :
120 OPEN "O",1, "DEMO1"
130 :
200 REM    READ DATA AND PRINT TO FILE
210 :
220 READ A, B, C
230 IF A = -1 THEN 990: REM    CHECK FOR END OF DATA FLAG
240 PRINT #1,A;B;C
250 GOTO 220
260 :
900 REM    DATA FOR DEMO
910 DATA 23, 26, 18, 19, 22, 20
920 :
930 REM    END OF DATA FLAG
940 DATA -1, -1, -1
950 :
980 REM    CLOSE FILE
990 CLOSE 1
999 END
```

The resulting sequential data file has recorded information that looks like this:

```
23 26 18
19 22 20
```

Commas and semicolons have a different effect on the data in the file. You could change line 240 as follows:

```
240 PRINT #1, A, B, C
```

using commas between the variables instead of semicolons. The resulting file includes many more spaces between the values. Therefore more disk space is used and actually wasted. It would look like this:

```
23        26        18
19        20        22
```

The file "image" is similar to the image you would get on a CRT display screen had you executed a regular PRINT statement. *To save disk space, use semicolons between variables in the PRINT list.* But notice that you must use a comma after the buffer number, before the variable list. (See line 240 above.)

(a) Write a statement that prints variables J, K, and L to buffer number 3.

(a)
```
160 PRINT #3, J; K; L
160 WRITE #3, J, K, L          (BASIC-80 only)
```

How you print data into a file becomes very important when you try to read (input) the data already in the file back into the computer. The print "image" for numeric data has already been described. Use semicolons between variables in your PRINT # statements, and you will save file space and have no trouble reading numeric data from the file. The following discussion applies only to potential problems with string data being printed into a data file.

Printing alphanumeric data into a file can cause the TRS-80 BASIC user some problems, depending on the type of data being written into the file. If you use a separate PRINT # statement for *each* string assigned to a string variable that you wish to place into the file, you should have no trouble later reading the data back from the file. In the file a carriage return will be placed after each string variable, separating one string from another. Consider the following example:

```
220 LINE INPUT "ENTER YOUR NAME:"; N$
230 PRINT #1, N$
240 LINE INPUT "ENTER YOUR PHONE NUMBER:"; P$
250 PRINT #1, P$
260 INPUT "ENTER YOUR AGE"; A
270 PRINT #1, A
```

This inefficient, incomplete solution to a small problem is inconsistent with the desire to work with the entire dataset together. If your data are simple alphanumeric strings that include *no* delimiters or separators, such as commas or carriage returns, and you wish to print the entire dataset into a file with one PRINT # statement, then follow the format shown below, with a "forced" comma between the variables. The comma acts as a separator, but you must "force" it between the variables by enclosing it in quotation marks.

```
270 PRINT #1, N$; ","; P$; ","; A
```

Notice the comma after the buffer number, the semicolon following each variable, *and* each of the commas in quotation marks.

For the record, we found that the semicolons are optional to accomplish the same purpose. Nonetheless, we use semicolons in case your system requires it.

A caution: If your program reads data from DATA statements, a carriage return can become a part of the string when the string is placed into the data file. This inclusion of a carriage return as part of the string itself can later cause problems, for instance, if you are reading data from the data file and then using it to print a report.

```
920 DATA THUMB TACKS, BATTERIES, PENCILS
```

A carriage return can be included at the end of the string PENCILS, the last item in that DATA statement. To avoid that surreptitious carriage return, include that DATA statement item inside quotation marks: "PENCILS."

(a) Write a program segment that will READ all of the strings from line 920 above and then print the strings to file buffer number 2.

- - - - - - - - - - - - - - - -

(a)
```
240 READ N1$, N2$, N3$
250 PRINT #2, N1$; ","; N2$; ","; N3$
```

The hard-to-remember part of printing strings to a file is when you want your strings to include commas or to purposely include carriage returns.

```
LET B$ = "PUBLIC, JOHN Q."
```

You would expect that the statement,

```
PRINT #1, B$
```

executed after the B$ assignment statement, would take the entire string enclosed by quotation marks and place it into the file as one string. But it doesn't! The quotation marks are essentially ignored. The comma actually separates PUBLIC from JOHN Q. in the file, breaking the one name into two separate data items! The solution is to "force" quotation marks on either side of the entire name string by using the CHR$( ) function. CHR$(34) is the ASCII code for the quote (") symbol. Notice how that is done in this program segment.

```
240 LET B$ = "PUBLIC, JOHN Q."
250 PRINT #1, CHR$(34); B$; CHR$(34)
```

We found that if we were printing a complete dataset into a file and had to force the inclusion of quotation marks, we also had to force commas between the variables.

```
250 PRINT #1, CHR$(34); N$; CHR$(34); ","; CHR$(34); P$; CHR$(34)
```

The typing alone in the above statement may cause you anxiety. However, you only need to worry about forcing quotation marks when your string will also include commas or a carriage return. That should not happen very often, and with careful planning, it may never be necessary.

Following are some file printing samples and problems. Review the samples.

```
150 INPUT "ENTER PRODUCT NUMBER:"; P
160 INPUT "ENTER PRICE:"; P1
170 INPUT "ENTER QUANTITY:"; Q
210 PRINT #3, P; P1; Q
```

Remember to use semicolons between numeric variables.

```
430 LINE INPUT "ENTER CUSTOMER NUMBER:"; C$
440 LINE INPUT "ENTER DATE:"; D$
450 PRINT #3, C$; ","; D$
```

Use "forced" commas between string variables to separate them.

```
600 LINE INPUT "ENTER NAME, LAST NAME FIRST:"; N$
610 LINE INPUT "ENTER SUN SIGN:"; S$
620 PRINT #3, CHR$(34); N$; CHR$(34); ","; S$
```

Force quotes where needed.

```
700 LINE INPUT "ENTER SOCIAL SECURITY NUMBER:"; S$
710 INPUT "ENTER NUMBER OF DEPENDENTS:"; D
720 INPUT "ENTER ANNUAL EARNINGS:"; E
730 PRINT #3, S$; ","; D; E
```

With mixed data (numeric and string), always follow the string variables with forced commas. Although not always necessary, it is certainly always safe.

BASIC-80 has an alternate statement to the PRINT # statement, called WRITE #, for output to data files. With WRITE #, all variables are separated with a comma and with no forced commas or quotation marks that PRINT # requires in TRS-80 BASIC. This improvement will undoubtedly be available in all MICROSOFT BASICs eventually. Test your BASIC to see if it has this form of PRINT #. For compatibility with earlier MICROSOFT BASICs, BASIC-80 also accepts PRINT #.

The equivalent WRITE # statements to the PRINT # examples above are:

```
250 WRITE #1, N$, P$
210 WRITE #3, P, P1, Q
450 WRITE #3, C$, D$
730 WRITE #3, S$, D, E
```

(a) Now it is your turn. Print all data to the file assigned to buffer number 3.

```
300 INPUT "HOW MANY SAMPLES"; S
310 INPUT "HOW MANY WERE GREEN"; G

320 PRINT ____________________________________

500 LINE INPUT "ENTER TODAY'S DATE:"; D$
510 LINE INPUT "ENTER CITY NAME:"; C$
520 LINE INPUT "ENTER STATE CODE:"; S$

530 PRINT ____________________________________

800 LINE INPUT "ENTER TITLE, INCLUDE PUNCTUATION:"; T$
810 LINE INPUT "ENTER FIRST LINE OF TEXT:"; F$

820 PRINT ____________________________________

900 LINE INPUT "ENTER TITLE OF BOOK:"; T$
910 LINE INPUT "ENTER AUTHOR'S NAME, LAST NAME FIRST:"; A$
920 INPUT "NUMBER OF PAGES"; P

930 PRINT ____________________________________
```

(a) TRS-80 BASIC:

```
320 PRINT #3, S; G

530 PRINT #3, D$; ","; C$; ","; S$

820 PRINT #3, CHR$(34); T$; CHR$(34); ","; CHR$(34); F$; CHR$(34)

930 PRINT #3, T$; ","; CHR$(34); A$; CHR$(34); ","; P
```

BASIC-80:

```
320 WRITE #3, S, G

530 WRITE #3, D$, C$, S$

820 WRITE #3, T$, F$

930 WRITE #3, T$, A$, P
```

As noted earlier, using files requires planning. Your plan should consider:

1. What to include in each dataset.
2. How large each data item or dataset will be.
3. Whether technical points, such as imbedded commas in strings, must be handled with special techniques.
4. How to test each data item in the dataset as completely as possible for accuracy and validity.

With these considerations in mind, here is a program to help you place a simple inventory from your home or business into a disk file. The introductory module and possible checks for data validity are included.

```
100 REM    PROPERTY INVENTORY FILE LOAD PROGRAM
110 :
120 REM    VARIABLES USED
130 REM      D$ = DESCRIPTION (20)
140 REM      N = NUMBER OF ITEMS
150 REM      V = DOLLAR VALUE
160 :
170 REM    FILES USED
180 REM      PROPERTY = SEQUENTIAL FILE
190 :
200 REM    INITIALIZE
210   OPEN "O", 1, "PROPERTY"
220 :
230 REM    DATA ENTRY ROUTINES
240 LINE INPUT "ENTER ITEM DESCRIPTION:"; D$
250 IF LEN(D$) > 20 THEN PRINT "PLEASE ABBREVIATE TO 20 CHAR. AND
    REENTER": GOTO 240
260 IF LEN(D$) = 0 THEN PRINT "PLEASE ENTER A DESCRIPTION OR WE CANNOT
    CONTINUE": GOTO 240
270 INPUT "HOW MANY ITEMS"; N
280 IF N <> INT(N) THEN PRINT "ENTER INTEGER NUMBERS ONLY.": GOTO 270
290 IF N =< 0 THEN PRINT "THERE MUST BE SOME UNITS. PLEASE ENTER A
    QUANTITY": GOTO 270
300 INPUT "WHAT IS THE DOLLAR VALUE OF EACH"; V
310 IF V = <0 THEN 350
320 PRINT #1, D$; ","; N, V
330 GOTO 240
```

```
340 :
350 LINE INPUT "DID YOU REALLY MEAN ZERO VALUE, YES OR NO:"; R$
360 IF LEFT$(R$,1) = "N" THEN PRINT "THEN REENTER THE CORRECT VALUE":
    GOTO 300
370 GOTO 320
380 :
400 REM    FILE CLOSE ROUTINE
410 CLOSE 1
420 :
499 END
```

(a) The above program has one small but important "bug." Find and describe the error.

(a) The program never executes the file closing routine at line 400; the CLOSE statement is needed to assure flushing the last data items from the buffer to the file.

The problem of how to indicate to the program when to close the file is part of preplanning. The program should include a way for the user to indicate to the computer that the user is done with the program for now, or that all data have been entered. Either of the two procedures shown below could be included in the previous program for this purpose. The choice is yours.

```
238 PRINT "TYPE STOP OR";
245 IF D$ = "STOP" THEN 410
```

or

```
325 LINE INPUT "IS THERE MORE DATA TO ENTER (YES OR NO)?; R$
326 IF LEFT$(R$,1) = "N" THEN 410
```

This procedure works for terminating a program and closing files, containing discrete datasets as have been described. But that is not always the case. What about a variable length dataset – one with no predefined field lengths, such as a data file of recipes or a file of letters? How do you indicate to the program when one recipe or letter ends and another begins? And then, how can the computer "sense" the end of such data when inputting or reading back from the recorded data file?

One popular procedure is to place a flag or "dummy" character at the end of each dataset as a separator. The dummy character could be any character that would never be part of or found in the data itself. An asterisk (*) is often used as a dummy separator. Here is one way to insert such markers into the data file, using our inventory program.

```
322 LINE INPUT "IS THIS THE END OF ONE DATASET?"; R$
324 IF LEFT$(R$,1) = "Y" THEN PRINT #1, "*"
```

Two reminders: First, when you open a file for output you also destroy all previous data in that data file. You cannot easily add data to an existing file. This will be explored in Chapter 5. Second, when you write file programs (or any program), prepare some written documentation for yourself or other users. At the least, some description of the file layout is needed. Even you may have trouble seeing how the program works without some time and effort, six months or more down the line. One good procedure is to include such information in REMARK statements in the program itself.

(a) Why is it important to inform the computer that all data to be included in the data file have been entered?

____

\- - - - - - - - - - - - - - - -

(a) So that a CLOSE statement can be executed.

READING DATA FROM A FILE

Now that you can output data from the computer to the data file, let's learn to input or read data from an existing file. To do this, the most important thing to know is how the data were placed in the file. After that, reading from a file is simple and straightforward, with none of the complications that can accompany writing to a file.

To read from a file, you first OPEN the file as an input ("I") file, and then use the INPUT # statement.

```
350 OPEN "I", 2, "TEMPFIL"
360 INPUT #2, A, B$, C
```

Line 360 will copy three data items from the file into buffer #2 and assign those first three data items to variables A, B$, and C. On most computer systems, you must have the correct type of variable (numeric or string) in the INPUT # statement to match the data that are being input from the data file. If the next data item in the file is a numeric value, then the next variable in the INPUT # statement should be a numeric variable. If it isn't, the program may abort and stop in an error condition, or some other complication may ensue. Notice that use of commas to separate variables.

Actually, whether the data were placed into the file as a numeric value or a string does not matter. However, if your program attempts to assign a numeric value from the file to a string variable in the INPUT # statement, it will be assigned to the string variable as a string with an error condition. On the other hand, if the next data item is a string and the INPUT # has a numeric variable waiting for assignment, the value assigned will be zero, and the program does not abort or terminate.

Is that good or bad? While the problem of having an open file and the program stopped in an error condition is avoided, the new problem of invalid data takes its place – and after all that error checking at data entry time to place accurate data into the file in the first place! To avoid such hassels, be sure you know how the data were initially placed into the file, whether numeric or string data, and if strings, how long.

Going back to the simple inventory program described earlier in this chapter, recall that the alphanumeric description (D$), followed by quantity (N), followed by dollar value (V) were placed into the file in that order. The variable names D$, N, and V were used in the program when the data were printed to the file. The variable names themselves were separate from the data items. Therefore, you can use any appropriate string or numeric variable name in INPUT # statements when data are read out of the file into the buffer.

(a) Which of the following statements is appropriate to input data from the property data file?

(1) 270 INPUT #1, A, B, C
(2) 270 INPUT #1, A$, B, C
(3) 270 INPUT #1, A, B$, C$

(a) Statement (2)

Below is the companion program to the property inventory program, to read the property file and print a simple report with the data.

```
100 REM    READ DATA FROM PROPERTY FILE
110 :
120 REM    VARIABLES USED
130 REM      N$ = DESCRIPTION(20)
140 REM      Q = QUANTITY
150 REM      D = DOLLAR VALUE
160 :
170 REM    FILES USED
180 REM      PROPERTY = SEQUENTIAL FILE
190 :
200 OPEN "I", 1, "PROPERTY"
210 :
220 REM    PRINT HEADINGS
230 PRINT "DESCRIPTION"; TAB(22); "QUANTITY"; "VALUE EACH"
```

continued on next page

```
240 :
250 REM    FILE READ ROUTINE/REPORT GENERATION ROUTINE
260 INPUT #1, N$, Q, D
270 PRINT N$; TAB(22); Q, D
280 GOTO 260
290 :
300 REM    FILE CLOSE ROUTINE
310 CLOSE
320 END
```

```
DESCRIPTION         QUANTITY        VALUE EACH
FILES                2               49
COMPUTERS            1               4500
GLASSES              24              .5
SDISKS               15              4.25
STOP                 15              0

INPUT PAST END IN 260
```

This RUN terminated in an error condition with the message INPUT PAST END IN 260. (You will get a similar message in all systems.) This was an aborted end to the program execution. What if you wanted to do more with the data and did not want the program to terminate when the end of the data file was reached? A technique exists that allows the program to read to the end of the file without the program stopping at that point. To understand the technique, recall how the data file "pointer" works.

Just as with regular READ and DATA statements in BASIC, the data file uses a pointer to point "at" the next data item available in the buffer holding data from the disk file. When a file is opened, the pointer is positioned at the beginning of the file and points at the first data item. Each execution of INPUT # or PRINT # pushes the pointer forward as many places as there are variables the the statement's variable list.

`PRINT #1, A$`	moves the pointer one position to the second data item.
`INPUT #1, N, N$`	moves the pointer past data items 1 and 2 to item 3. The pointer is always looking at the next position.
`PRINT #1, W, X, Y, Z`	moves the pointer 4 places, so the next data item added by a PRINT # statement will be at position 5.

When your program uses PRINT # to add data to a file, each PRINT # statement moves the pointer and an end-of-file (EOF) marker ahead. When all data have been entered, the end-of-file marker is located just past the last data item. The end-of-file marker is automatically put in place by the computer.

When you INPUT # data from the file, the file pointer is always looking at the *next* data item available in the file (or in the buffer, to be more exact). A special end-of-file statement can be used to detect whether or not the next item is the end-of-file marker. Here is how you might use it in MICROSOFT BASIC.

```
IF EOF(1) THEN CLOSE 1 : GOTO 800
```

The number in the EOF( ) parentheses is the buffer number. Notice that no explicit comparison follows IF in the IF. . .THEN statement; just the EOF( ). So the IF. . . THEN statement says that if the next data item is the end-of-file marker, then close the file and go to line 800. If the next data item is not the EOF marker, then continue executing the program with the next line numbered statement.

Now you can modify the previous program so it does not terminate with an end-of-file error condition. Add line 255 and modify line 280 as shown below.

```
255 IF EOF(1) THEN 310
280 GOTO 255 <———— Don't forget this!
```

An alternate modification would be as follows:

```
255 IF EOF(1) THEN CLOSE 1 : STOP
```

With either "fix," the file will be properly closed.

Reference manuals for various computer systems show considerable variation in explanations on how the pointer and end-of-file marker work. However, the ideas expressed here should work on any system.

(a) What does EOF stand for? ______________________________

(b) What does the number of the EOF function parentheses indicate?

(a) end-of-file (marker)
(b) the buffer number for the data file being examined for an end of file marker

PERMANENTLY REMOVING FILES FROM DISKS

Situations will arise when you want to erase a data file from a disk. It may be a temporary file such as those created for demonstration programs in this book or a file that is of no further use to you for other reasons. The ubiquitously named command in MICROSOFT BASIC is KILL. Using this command deletes the file named after the command from the disk, destroying the file's contents and deleting all reference to the file from the disk file directory. KILL is a system command that is entered and executed like RUN or LIST. KILL can also be used in an executable statement in MICROSOFT BASIC, but we discourage this use except, perhaps, for very temporary files. Here is the form:

```
KILL "TEMPFIL"
```

Notice that the file name is enclosed by quotation marks. Use the file destroying command very carefully, as the action is irreversible. Once the file has been killed or destroyed, there is no going back. Accidentally destroying the wrong file, especially if you have not made a backup copy, can mean that you wasted hours or days entering data into a file. Think carefully before using KILL.

Be sure you understand the difference between KILL and CLOSE. CLOSE merely disassociated a buffer from the file it was assigned to and flushes the buffer contents onto the disk if you are outputting data. After a CLOSE statement, the data file is still recorded on the disk. KILL eliminates the file entirely from the disk, as well as all reference to it in the file directory. *It is very important that a file be already closed before it is KILLed.* Failure to CLOSE a file before you KILL it can create irreversable errors on other disk data. which can cause trouble when you use the disk again.

We have used the word "copy" to describe how the INPUT # statement works when data are transferred from the disk data file into the computer's memory. Copy implies that the data in the file do not change when they are input into the part of the computer's electronic memory designated as the buffer. The data in the file are unaffected and unchanged and remain in the file for another use. The only way to change data in a data file is with a PRINT # statement or WRITE #.

You can fill a file with data and read from the same file in the same program.† But you must always CLOSE a file after outputting or recording information into it *before* you can reopen the file for input or copying data back into the computer memory. You must OPEN "O" to output, then close and OPEN "I" to read back the data.

The following program illustrates the procedure to open and close the files at the appropriate times. Quality assurance data are entered from a manufacturing process into a file. The program will read the QA values from the file and accumulate the number of responses in each category (1 through 6) in an array, and then print the results. The program is self-documented by REMARK statements.

```
RESULTS OF QUALITY CONTROL DATA
QA NUMBER           QUANTITY
 1                   4
 2                   7
 3                   7
 4                   7
 5                   5
 6                   4
```

```
140 REM    FILE INPUT/OUTPUT DEMO
150 :
160 REM    ENTER QUALITY CONTROL RESULTS INTO FILE
170 REM    PREPARE SIMPLE REPORT FROM FILE
180 :
190 REM    VARIABLES USED
200 REM     F$ = FILE
210 REM     N% = QA MEASURE
220 REM     V = QA MEASURE
230 REM     C() = COUNTING ARRAY
240 REM    FILES USED = USER DEFINED
250 :
260 REM    INITIALIZE ARRAY
270 FOR X = 1 TO 6: LET C(X) = 0: NEXT X
280 :
290 REM    INITIALIZE FILE
300 LINE INPUT "ENTER FILE NAME:"; F$
310 OPEN "O", 1, F$
320 :
330 REM    DATA ENTRY ROUTINE
340 PRINT "ENTER INTEGER NUMBERS 1-6 ONLY. ENTER 99 TO STOP"
350 :
360 INPUT "QA NUMBER:"; N%
370 IF N% = 99 THEN 430
380 IF N% < 1 OR N% > 6 THEN PRINT "PLEASE REENTER AS 1-6 ONLY": GOTO 360
390 PRINT #1, N%
400 GOTO 360
410 :
420 REM    FILE CLOSE
430 CLOSE 1
440 :
450 REM    OPEN FILE TO READ
460 OPEN "I", 1, F$
470 :
480 REM    READ FILE AND ACCUMULATE DATA IN ARRAY
490 IF EOF(1) THEN 550
500 INPUT #1, V
510 LET C(V) = C(V) + 1
520 GOTO 490
530 :
540 REM    PRINT REPORT FROM ARRAY
550 CLS
560 PRINT "RESULTS OF QUALITY CONTROL DATA"
570 PRINT
580 PRINT "QA NUMBER", "QUANTITY"
590 FOR V = 1 TO 6
600 PRINT V, C(V)
610 NEXT V
620 :
630 REM    CLOSE FILE ROUTINE
640 CLOSE 1
650 :
660 END
```

Refer to the program above to answer the following questions:

(a) Through which statement does the computer obtain the name of the data file?

____

(b) Which statement checks the parameters for the quality control numbers?

____

(c) How does the computer know that all data have been entered? ______________

____

(d) Why are two CLOSE 1 statements used in the same program? ______________

____

(e) What does line 490 do? ______________________________________

____

(f) In line 510, how many different values can V have? ______________________

\- - - - - - - - - - - - - - - - -

(a) line 300
(b) line 380
(c) user enters 99 as input value
(d) the data file must be closed after output and after input
(e) checks each file input data item to see if it is the end of file marker
(f) six (1 to 6)

Help us write another program that first creates a data file called DEMO1, and then displays the contents of that data file. Complete lines 200, 240, 270, 310, 360, 370, and 400. (Read the REMs and comments.)

```
    100 REM** DATAFILE DEMONSTRATION
    110 REM
    120 REM   VARIABLES USED:
    130 REM    D$ = DATA ITEM OUTPUT VARIABLE
    140 REM    R$ = DATA ITEM INPUT VARIABLE
    150 REM    X = FOR-NEXT LOOP CONTROL VARIABLE
    160 REM
    170 REM    FILE NAME: DEMO1
    180 REM    FILE DATA FORMAT: ONE STRING DATA ITEM
    190 REM

(a) 200 ________________________________________ : REM  OPEN THE FILE
    210 REM** USING A FOR-NEXT LOOP, PLACE 8 STRINGS (DATA ITEMS) INTO
        THE DATAFILE
    220 FOR X = 1 TO 8
    230 LET D$ = "TEST" + STR$(X)

(b) 240 ________________________________ : REM  PRINT TO THE FILE
    250 NEXT X
    260 REM*** NOW CLOSE THE FILE
```

____

(c)
```
270 ____________________
280 REM** A PRINT STATEMENT TELLS US SO FAR SO GOOD...
290 PRINT "FILE WRITTEN AND CLOSED"
300 REM** RE-OPEN THE FILE FOR INPUT. WE NEED NOT USE THE SAME
    BUFFER NUMBER.
```

(d)
```
310 ________________________________________
320 REM** NOW INPUT FROM THE FILE AND PRINT THE DATA ITEMS.
330 REM** USE EOF TO CHECK FOR ENDMARK OF FILE TO AVOID AN ERROR
340 REM** MESSAGE IF ALL DATA HAS BEEN INPUT FROM THE DATAFILE.
350 REM** USE CURRENT BUFFER NUMBER IN EOF PARENTHESES.
```

(e)
```
360 ________________________________________
```

(f)
```
370 ______________________________
380 PRINT R$
390 GOTO 360
```

(g)
```
400 ____________________
410 PRINT "FILE CLOSED"
```

(a) `200 OPEN "O", 1, "DEMO1"`

(b) `240 PRINT #1, D$`

(c) `270 CLOSE 1`

(d) `310 OPEN "I", 2, "DEMO1"`

(e) `360 IF EOF(2) THEN 400`

(f) `370 INPUT #2, R$`

(g) `400 CLOSE 2`

you could have used Buffer #1, again.

(a) Now show everything that will be printed or displayed when this program is RUN.

(a)
```
RUN
FILE WRITTEN AND CLOSED
TEST 1
TEST 2
TEST 3
TEST 4
TEST 5
TEST 6
TEST 7
TEST 8
FILE CLOSED

READY
```

One unique feature of file programs is that sometimes nothing appears to be happening when the program is RUN. There may be no printed report or any CRT display other than RUN and READY. To the novice, this seeming lack of activity may be alarming. Be forewarned.

And again BEWARE of reopening an existing data file as an output with OPEN "O" in MICROSOFT BASIC. You will destroy all the data in that data file; data cannot be recovered. Having made that tragic mistake ourselves, we feel obligated to keep warning you.

(a) Which statements in the previous program help assure the user that "invisible" data file activity has taken place? ____________________

(a) lines 290 and 410

CHAPTER 4 SELF-TEST

The problems in this self-test require you to write programs to store data in data files and then to write companion programs to display the data in those data files. All data files that you create in this self-test will be used in Chapter 5, *so don't skip this section.* You will need a system with a disk drive to actually store the programs. If you have only a cassette data storage system, write the programs anyway, as only minor modification will be needed in most cases to adapt the programs to cassette data file application, covered in Chapter 6. The introductory module is given so your solutions will look something like the solution provided. Save the programs and files for later use, modification, and reference. Try out your solutions and try to debug the programs before looking at the solutions provided. Good luck and keep on hackin'.

1. (a) Write a program to fill a data file with the information and format specified below:

   Four data items per dataset.
   First two data items are strings.
   Second two data items are numeric values entered as strings.
   Include data entry checks for null strings.
   For the numeric values assigned to strings, include data entry tests to see that only numeric values were entered. Then convert these strings to numeric values assigned to numeric variables before storing them in the data file.
   Place at least five datasets in the data file.

```
110 :
120 REM     VARIABLE LIST
130 REM        A$,B$ = ALPHA DATA
140 REM        C$(C), D$(D) = NUMERIC DATA
150 :
160 REM     FILES USED = PROB1
170 :
180 OPEN "O", 1, "PROB1"
190 :
```

   (b) Write a companion program to display the contents of the data file you created in 1(a).

2. (a) Write a program to make a data file called GROCERY that stores your grocery shopping list. include the description or name of each grocery item (maximum of twenty characters) and a numeric value telling the quantity of that item to buy. Store at least six datasets in the file.

```
100 REM    GROCERY LIST FILE APPLICATION
110 REM    INTRODUCTORY MODULE
120 :
130 REM    VARIABLES USED
140 REM      D$ = ITEM DESCRIPTION
150 REM      Q = QUANTITY TO ORDER
160 :
170 :
180 :
190 REM    FILES USED
200 REM      F$ = USER ENTERED INPUT FILE
```

(b) Write a companion program to display the contents of GROCERY.

3. (a) Write a program to enter the following data in a data file for a customer credit file maintained by a small business. Each dataset consists of three items:
   1. five-digit customer number (must have exactly five digits)
   2. customer name (twenty characters maximum)
   3. customer credit rating (a single digit number 1, 2, 3, 4, or 5)

   Include data entry checks for null entries and for the parameters set forth in the list above. Enter at least twelve datasets in the data file. Remember, the customer numbers must be different for each customer and should be in *ascending* order, i.e., each larger than the previous one, such as 19652, 19653, 19654, etc.

```
110 :
120 REM    VARIABLES USED
130 REM       F$ = FILE NAME
140 REM       C$ = CUST. #
160 REM       N$ = CUST. NAME
180 REM       R$ AND R = CREDIT RATING VALUE
190 :         Q$ = USER RESPONSE
```

(b) Write a companion program to display the contents of the file.

4. (a) Write a program to enter data into a transaction data file. A transaction file is the data on a business transaction, such as that of a bank, a retail store, or a mail order business. For our example, each transaction produces a dataset stored as one, fourteen character string with three fields, as shown below:

```
       1 ___ 5/67/8 ______ 14
        ↗        ↑          ↖
   Account #    Transaction code   Amount
(five characters) (two characters) (seven characters)
```

Account number = five-character field
Transaction code = two-character field (for a bank, 1 = check, 2 = deposit, etc.)
Amount = seven-character field

Your program should allow the user to select (input) a name for the data file. Create two different data files with your program, with seven datasets (transactions) in each data file. Use the account numbers given below for the two files.

File #1	File #2
10762	10761
18102	18203
43611	43611
43611	80111
43611	80772
80223	80772
98702	89012

(Note: only the account numbers are shown here; the complete datasets also include transaction codes and amounts.)

```
110 :
120 REM    VARIABLES USED
130 REM     F1$ = FILE NAMES
140 REM     D1$ = DATASETS FROM FILE 1,2
150 REM     A$ = ACCOUNT NUMBER
160 REM     T$ = TRANSACTION CODE
170 REM     C$ = CASH AMOUNT
180 REM     X = FOR-NEXT LOOP CONTROL VARIABLE
190 :
200 REM    FILES USED
210 REM     ONE OUTPUT FILE - USER DEFINED
220 :
```

(b) Write a companion program to display the contents of a data file with the above dataset format. Again, the file name should be user entered.

5. (a) Write a program to load a data file named ADDRESS with (surprise!) names and addresses. The data has the format shown below, with each dataset containing five items in fields within one string

```
                                                55
/1                  20/21              40/41   50/12/53    57/
-------------------   ----------------   -------  --  -----
        name              address          city   state  zip code
```

Include appropriate data entry checks and field padding routines. Enter at least six addresses in the data file.

```
100 REM   PROB 45 SOLUTION
110 :
120 REM   VARIABLES USED
130 REM     N$(20) = NAME
140 REM     A$(20) = ADDRESS
150 REM     C$(10) = CITY
160 REM     S$(2)  = STATE
170 REM     Z$(5)  = ZIP CODE
180 REM     D$(57) = ENTIRE DATASET
190 :
200 REM   FILE USED = ADDRESS
```

(b) Write a companion program to display the contents of ADDRESS.

6. (a) Write one program and use it to create three different data files called LETTER1, LETTER2, and LETTER3. Each file should contain the text of a form letter with at least three lines of text per letter. Each line of text in the letters is to be entered and stored as one dataset.

```
110 :
120 REM   VARIABLES USED
130 REM    R$ = TEXT LINE
140 REM    F$ = FILE NAME VARIABLE
150 :
160 REM   FILES USED
170 REM    LETTER (PLUS F$ WHICH IS USER SELECTED)
180 :
```

(b) Write a companion program to display the data file above selected by the user.

Answer Key

1 a.

```
100 REM    PROB 4-1A SOLUTION
110 :
120 REM    VARIABLE LIST
130 REM      A$, B$ = ALPHA DATA
140 REM      C$(C), D$(D) = NUMERIC DATA
150 :
160 REM    FILES USED = PROB1
170 :
180 OPEN "O", 1, "PROB1"
190 :
200 REM    DATA ENTRY ROUTINE
210 LINE INPUT "ENTER DATA ITEM:"; A$
220 IF LEN(A$) = 0 THEN PRINT "PLEASE ENTER SOMETHING": GOTO 210
230 LINE INPUT "ENTER DATA ITEM 2:"; B$
240 IF LEN(B$) = 0 THEN PRINT "PLEASE ENTER SOME DATA": GOTO 230
250 LINE INPUT "ENTER NUMERIC DATA:"; C$
260 IF LEN(C$) = 0 THEN PRINT "PLEASE ENTER SOMETHING": GOTO 250
270 IF VAL(C$) = 0 THEN PRINT "PLEASE ENTER NUMBERS ONLY": GOTO 250
280 LET C = VAL(C$)
290 LINE INPUT "ENTER NUMERIC ITEM 2:"; D$
300 IF LEN(D$) = 0 THEN PRINT "PLEASE ENTER SOMETHING": GOTO 290
310 IF VAL(D$) = 0 THEN PRINT "PLEASE ENTER NUMBERS ONLY": GOTO 290
320 LET D = VAL(D$)
330 :
340 PRINT #1, A$;",";B$;",";C; D
350 :
360 LINE INPUT "MORE DATA?"; R$
370 IF LEFT$(R$,1) = "Y" THEN 210
380 :
390 CLOSE
400 PRINT "FILE CLOSED."
410 END
```

1 b.

```
100 REM    PROB 4-1B SOLUTION
110 :
120 REM    VARIABLE LIST
130 REM      A$,B$ = ALPHA DATA
140 REM      C,D = NUMERIC DATA
150 :
160 REM    FILES USED = PROB1
170 :
180 OPEN "I", 1, "PROB1"
190 :
200 REM    DATA ENTRY FROM FILE
210 :
220 IF EOF (1) THEN 270
230 INPUT #1, A$, B$, C, D
240 PRINT A$, B$, C, D
250 GOTO 220
260 :
270 CLOSE
280 PRINT: PRINT "ALL DATA DISPLAYED AND FILE CLOSED."
290 END
```

2 a.

```
110 REM    PROB 4-2A SOLUTION (GROCERY LIST)
120 :
130 REM    INTRODUCTORY MODULE
140 REM     VARIABLES USED
150 REM        D$ = ITEM DESCRIPTION
160 REM        Q = QUANTITY TO ORDER
170 :
180 REM     FILES USED
190 REM        F$ = USER ENTERED INPUT FILE
200 :
210 REM     FILE INITIALIZATION
220 :
230 LINE INPUT "ENTER NAME OF INPUT FILE"; F$
240 OPEN "I", 1, F$
250 OPEN "O", 2, "TEMPFIL"
260 :
270 :
280 REM     DATA ENTRY ROUTINE
290 :
300 PRINT "ENTER 'STOP' WHEN FINISHED"
310 PRINT
320 LINE INPUT "ENTER ITEM DESCRIPTION:"; D$
330 IF D$ = "STOP" THEN 480
340 IF LEN(D$) = 0 THEN PRINT "PLEASE ENTER A DESCRIPTION OR 'STOP'":
    GOTO 320
350 IF LEN(D$) > 20 THEN PRINT "PLEASE LIMIT DESCRIPTION TO 20 CHARS.
    AND REENTER": GOTO 320
360 INPUT "ENTER QUANTITY:"; Q
370 IF Q >= 1 AND Q < 10 THEN 440
380 PRINT "YOU ENTERED A QUANTITY OF"; Q
390 LINE INPUT "IS THAT WHAT YOU WANTED?"; R$
400 IF LEFT$(R$,1) = "N" THEN 360
410 :
420 REM      WRITE TO FILE ROUTINE
430 :
440 PRINT #2, D$; "," ; Q
450 GOTO 320
460 :
470 REM      FILE CLOSE
480 CLOSE 1, 2
490 PRINT "FILES CLOSED."
500 END
```

2 b.

```
100 REM     GROCERY LIST FILE APPLICATION (PROB 4-2B)
110 :
120 REM    VARIABLES USED
130 REM      D$ = ITEM DESCRIPTION
140 REM      Q = QUANTITY TO ORDFR
150 :
160 REM    FILES USED
170 REM      F$ = USER ENTERED INPUT FILE
180 :
190 REM    FILE INITIALIZATION
200 LINE INPUT "ENTER NAME OF INPUT FILE:"; F$
210 OPEN "I", 1, F$
220 :
230 REM    READ AND PRINT FILE
```

```
240 :
250 PRINT "ITEM", "QUANTITY": PRINT
260 IF EOF(1) THEN 320
270 INPUT #1, D$, Q
280 PRINT D$, Q
290 GOTO 260
300 :
310 REM   CLOSE ROUTINE
320 CLOSE
330 END
```

3 a.

```
100 REM   SELF TEST PROB 4-3A SOLUTION
110 REM  CREDIT FILE LOADER
120 :
130 REM    VARIABLES USED
140 REM      F$ = FILE NAME
150 REM      C$ = CUST. #
160 REM      N$ = CUST. NAME
170 REM      R$ AND R = CREDIT RATING VALUE
175 REM      Q$ = USER RESPONSE TO CONTINUE DATA ENTRY
180 :
190 REM    FILES USED
200 REM     INPUT FILE = USER DEFINED
210 :
220 REM    INITIALIZE FILES
230 CLS
240 LINE INPUT "ENTER FILE NAME:"; F$
250 OPEN "O", 1, F$
260 :
270 REM  DATA ENTRY ROUTINE
280 PRINT "ENTER 'STOP' TO FINISH"
290 PRINT
300 LINE INPUT "ENTER CUSTOMER NUMBER:"; C$
310 IF C$ = "STOP" THEN 560
320 IF LEN(C$) = 0 THEN PRINT "ENTER NUMBERS OR 'STOP'": GOTO 290
330 IF LEN(C$) = <> 5 THEN PRINT "ENTRY ERROR. REENTER WITH 5 DIGITS.":
    GOTO 290
340 IF VAL(C$) = 0 THEN PRINT "ENTRY ERROR. NUMBERS ONLY.": GOTO 290
350 :
360 LINE INPUT "ENTER CUSTOMER NAME:"; N$
370 IF LEN(N$) = 0 THEN PRINT "PLEASE ENTER A NAME, NOW.": GOTO 360
380 IF LEN(N$) > 20 THEN PRINT "PLEASE LIMIT NAME TO 20 CHARACTERS AND
    REENTER": GOTO 360
390 :
400 PRINT
410 LINE INPUT "CREDIT RATING:"; R$
420 IF LEN(R$) <> 1 THEN PRINT "ONLY A ONE DIGIT NUMBER IS ACCEPTABLE.":
    GOTO 410
430 IF VAL(R$) < 1 OR VAL(R$) > 5 THEN PRINT "NUMBERS 1-5 ONLY, PLEASE."
    : GOTO 410
440 LET R = VAL(R$)
450 :
460 REM    PRINT NEW DATA TO FILE
470 PRINT #1, C$; ","; N$; ","; R
480 :
490 :
500 REM    REQUEST TO CONTINUE DATA ENTRY
```

continued on next page

```
510 CLS
520 LINE INPUT "DO YOU HAVE MORE DATA TO ENTER?"; Q$
530 IF LEFT$(Q$,1) = "Y" THEN 250
540 :
550 REM      CLOSE FILES
560 CLOSE
570 PRINT "JOB COMPLETED"
580 END
```

3 b.

```
100 REM   SELF TEST PROB 4-3B SOLUTION
110 REM  CREDIT FILE DISPLAY
120 :
130 REM   VARIABLES USED
140 REM     F$ = FILE NAME
150 REM     C$ = CUST. #
160 REM     N$ = CUST. NAME
170 REM     R = CREDIT RATING VALUE
180 :
190 REM   FILES USED
200 REM    INPUT FILE = USER DEFINED
210 :
220 REM   INITIALIZE FILES
230 CLS
240 LINE INPUT "ENTER FILE NAME:"; F$
250 OPEN "I", 1, F$
260 :
270 REM   READ/PRINT FILE
280 PRINT "CUST #", "CUST NAME", "CREDIT RATING"
290 IF EOF(1) THEN 350
300 INPUT #1, C$, N$, R
310 PRINT C$, N$, R
320 GOTO 290
330 :
340 REM   CLOSE FILE
350 CLOSE
360 PRINT: PRINT "ALL DATA DISPLAYED AND FILE CLOSED."
370 END
```

4 a.

```
100 REM  PROB 4-4A SOLUTION
110 :
120 REM    VARIABLES USED
130 REM     F1$ = FILE NAMES
140 REM     D1$ = DATASETS FROM FILE 1,2
150 REM     A$ = ACCOUNT NUMBER
160 REM     T$ = TRANSACTION CODE
170 REM     C$ = CASH AMOUNT
180 REM     X = FOR-NEXT LOOP CONTROL VARIABLE
190 :
200 REM     FILES USED
210 REM      ONE OUTPUT FILE - USER DEFINED
220 :
230 CLEAR 500
240 REM    FILE INITIALIZATION
250 LINE INPUT "ENTER OUTPUT FILE NAME:"; F1$
260 OPEN "O", 1, F1$
270 CLS
280 :
290 REM    DATA ENTRY/ TESTS
```

```
300 PRINT "ENTER '-1' TO END DATA ENTRY."
310 LINE INPUT "ENTER ACCOUNT NUMBER (5 DIGITS)"; A$
320 IF A$ = "-1" THEN 550
330 IF VAL(A$) = 0 THEN PRINT "PLEASE MAKE AN ENTRY.": GOTO 300
340 IF LEN(A$) <> 5 THEN PRINT "YOU ENTERED "; A$; ". PLEASE REENTER.":
    GOTO 300
350 LINE INPUT "ENTER TRANSACTION CODE (1 DIGIT):"; T$
360 REM     DATA TEST
370 IF VAL(T$) = 0 THEN PRINT "PLEASE MAKE AN ENTRY.": GOTO 350
380 IF LEN(T$) <> 1 THEN PRINT "YOU ENTERED "; T$; ". PLEASE REENTER.":
    GOTO 350
390 LINE INPUT "ENTER THE AMOUNT (DO NOT INCLUDE A '$'):"; C$
400 REM     DATA TESTS
410 IF VAL(C$) = 0 THEN PRINT "PLEASE MAKE AN ENTRY.": GOTO 390
420 IF VAL(C$) > 999.99 THEN PRINT "MAXIMUM AMOUNT IS 999.99. YOU
    ENTERED "; C$; ". PLEASE REENTER.": GOTO 390
430 FOR X = 1 TO LEN(C$)
440 IF ASC(MID$(C$,X,1)) >= 48 AND ASC(MID$(C$,X,1)) <= 57 OR ASC(MID$
    (C$,X,1)) = 46 THEN 460
450 PRINT "INVALID ENTRY. ONLY NUMBERS AND DECIMAL POINT ALLOWED.":
    GOTO 390
460 NEXT X
470 IF LEN(C$) < 6 THEN LET C$ = " " + C$; GOTO 470
480 LET D1$ = A$ + T$ + C$
490 :
500 PRINT #1, D1$
510 CLS
520 GOTO 300
530 :
540 REM    CLOSE FILE
550 CLOSE
560 PRINT "FILE CLOSED"
570 END
```

4 b.

```
100 REM   PROB 4-4B SOLUTION
110 :
120 REM     VARIABLES USED
130 REM      F1$ = FILE NAMES
140 REM      D1$ = DATASETS FROM FILE 1,2
150 :
160 REM      FILES USED
170 REM       ONE INPUT FILE - USER DEFINED
180 :
190 CLEAR 500
200 REM     FILE INITIALIZATION
210 LINE INPUT "ENTER INPUT FILE NAME:"; F1$
220 OPEN "I", 1, F1$
230 :
240 REM    FILE READ AND PRINT
250 PRINT "ACCOUNT #", "CODE", "AMOUNT"
260 IF EOF(1) THEN 320
270 INPUT #1, D1$
280 PRINT LEFT$(D1$,5), MID$(D1$,6,1), RIGHT$(D1$,6)
290 GOTO 260
300 :
310 REM    CLOSE
320 CLOSE
330 PRINT : PRINT "ALL DATA DISPLAYED AND FILE CLOSED."
340 END
```

5 a.

```
100 REM     PROB 4-5A
110 :
120 REM     VARIABLES USED
130 REM     N$(20) = NAME
140 REM     A$(20) = ADDRESS
150 REM     C$(10) = CITY
160 REM     S$(2) = STATE
170 REM     Z$(5) = ZIP CODE
180 REM     D$(57) = ENTIRE DATASET
190 :
200 REM     FILES USED = ADDRESS
210 :
220 REM     INITIALIZE
230 CLEAR 1000
240 OPEN "O", 1, "ADDRESS"
250 :
260 REM      DATA ENTRY/TESTS
270 LINE INPUT "ENTER NAME:"; N$
280 REM   DATA TESTS
290 IF LEN(N$) < 20 THEN LET N$ = N$ + " " : GOTO 290
300 LINE INPUT "ENTER ADDRESS:"; A$
310 REM    DATA TEST
320 IF LEN(A$) < 20 THEN LET A$ = A$ + " " : GOTO 320
330 LINE INPUT "ENTER CITY NAME:"; C$
340 REM   DATA TESTS
350 IF LEN(C$) < 10 THEN LET C$ = C$ + " " : GOTO 350
360 LINE INPUT "ENTER STATE CODE:"; S$
370 REM   DATA TEST
380 IF LEN(S$) <> 2 THEN PRINT "PLEASE ENTER 2 CHARACTER CODE": GOTO
    360
390 LINE INPUT "ENTER ZIP CODE:"; Z$
400 IF LEN(Z$) <> 5 THEN PRINT "PLEASE ENTER 5-DIGIT CODE": GOTO 390
410 :
420 LET D$ = N$ + A$ + C$ + S$ + Z$
430 :
440 PRINT #1, D$
450 :
460 LINE INPUT "MORE ENTRIES?"; R$
470 IF LEFT$(R$,1) = "Y" THEN 270
480 :
490 CLOSE
500 PRINT "FILE CLOSED."
510 END
```

5 b.

```
100 REM   PROB 4-5B SOLUTION
110 :
120 REM    VARIABLES USED
130 REM    N$(20) = NAME
140 REM    A$(20) = ADDRESS
150 REM    C$(10) = CITY
160 REM    S$(2) = STATE
170 REM    Z$(5) = ZIP CODE
180 REM    D$(57) = ENTIRE DATASET
190 :
200 REM    FILES USED = ADDRESS
210 :
220 REM    INITIALIZE
230 OPEN "I", 1, "ADDRESS"
```

```
240 :
250 REM    READ/PRINT FILE
260 IF EOF(1) THEN 360
270 INPUT #1, D$
280 PRINT LEFT$(D$,20)
290 PRINT MID$(D$,21,20)
300 PRINT MID$(D$,41,10), MID$(D$,51,2), MID$(D$,53,5)
310 PRINT
320 LINE INPUT "PRESS ENTER TO CONTINUE"; R$
330 GOTO 260
340 :
350 REM    CLOSE FILE
360 CLOSE
370 PRINT : PRINT "FILE CLOSED"
380 END
```

6 a.

```
100 REM    PROB 4-6A SOLUTION
110 :
120 REM    VARIABLES USED
130 REM     R$ = TEXT LINE
140 REM     F$ = FILE NAME VARIABLE
150 :
160 REM    FILES USED
170 REM      LETTER (PLUS F$ WHICH IS USER SELECTED)
180 :
190 REM    INITIALIZE
200 :
210 CLEAR 1000
220 LINE INPUT "ENTER FILE NUMBER:"; F$
230 LET F$ = "LETTER" + F$
240 OPEN "O", 1, F$
250 :
260 PRINT "ENTER TEXT LINE OR STOP"
270 LINE INPUT R$
280 IF R$ = "STOP" THEN 330
290 PRINT #1, R$
300 GOTO 260
320 REM    CLOSE FILE
330 CLOSE
340 PRINT "FILE "; F$: " CLOSED."
350 END
```

6 b.

```
100 REM   PROB 4-6B SOLUTION
110 :
120 REM   VARIABLES USED
130 REM    R$ = TEXT LINE
140 REM    F$ = FILE NAME VARIABLE
150 :
160 REM   FILES USED
170 REM     LETTER (PLUS F$ WHICH IS USER SELECTED)
180 :
190 REM   INITIALIZE
200 :
210 LINE INPUT "ENTER FILE NUMBER:"; F$
```

continued on next page

```
220 LET F$ = "LETTER" + F$
230 OPEN "I", 1, F$
240 :
250 REM   READ/PRINT FILE CONTENTS
260 IF EOF(1) THEN 320
270 INPUT #1, R$
280 PRINT R$
290 GOTO 260
300 :
310 REM   CLOSE FILES
320 CLOSE
330 :
```

CHAPTER FIVE

Sequential Data File Utility Programs

Objectives: When you finish this chapter you will be able to:

1. Write a program to make a copy of a sequential data file.
2. Write a program to add data to an existing sequential file.
3. Write a program to change the data in an existing sequential file.
4. Write a program to examine the contents in a sequential file and to change, add, or delete data.
5. Write a program to merge the contents of two sequential files into one file, maintaining the numeric or alphabetic order of the data.
6. Write a program that uses or combines selected data from more than one sequential file.

Now that you understand the BASIC statements to create and use sequential data files, let's build on this with more advanced techniques, including writing some file utility programs that help in your overall programming using data files. You will also develop embryonic file applications to practice what you have learned and provide a basis from which to develop personally useful programs. Most of the data files used in this chapter are created with programs you should have written for the Chapter 4 Self-Test, so if you skipped that, go back and write those programs before starting this chapter.

MAKING A DATA FILE COPY

A very useful file utility program is one that makes a duplicate copy of your data file. Your computer system may be equipped with a copy program, written in machine language, as part of the system software. Check the reference manual to see if it is. If so, you can make back-up copies of data files or copy a file from the disk in one disk drive to another. A file copy utility program in BASIC not only allows you to make backup copies of data files, it can also be incorporated into programs to add data to existing data files.

You have the background to write a file copying program; follow these steps:

(1) Open the input file (the one you want to copy).
(2) Open the output file (the one you are making the copy into).
(3) Test the input file for EOF. If found, go to step (7).

(4) Input the next dataset from the input file.
(5) Print the dataset to the new file (the copy).
(6) Repeat steps (3) to (5) until the EOF for the input file is encountered.
(7) Close both files.

Assume that you are going to copy a file that contains an unknown number of datasets, each containing two twenty-five character strings, followed by two numeric values. Using the on-line REMARKS as a guide, fill in the blanks in lines 240, 250, 320, 330, 340, and 410.

(a)
```
100 REM     COPY FILE PROGRAM
110 :
120 REM     VARIABLES USED
130 REM     A$, B$    25 CHAR, STRINGS
140 REM     C, D = NUMERIC DATA
150 REM     F$, F1$ = USER SELECTED FILE NAMES
160 :
170 REM     FILES USED
180 REM     SEQUENTIAL FILE NAMES ARE USER SELECTED
190 :
200 REM     FILE INITIALIZATION
210 :
220 LINE INPUT "ENTER NAME OF INPUT FILE"; F$
230 LINE INPUT "ENTER NAME OF OUTPUT FILE"; F1$
240                          :REM    OPEN INPUT FILE
250                          :REM    OPEN OUTPUT FILE
260 :
300 REM     READ/PRINT FILE TO FILE
310 :
320                          :REM    TEST EOF(1)
330                              :REM    INPUT FROM FILE #1
340                                    :REM    PRINT TO FILE #2
350 GOTO 320
360 :
400 REM     CLOSE FILE ROUTINE
410                     :REM    CLOSE FILES
420 :
499 END
```

(a)
```
100 REM    COPY FILE PROGRAM
110 :
120 REM    VARIABLES USED
130 REM     A$, B$    25 CHAR, STRINGS
140 REM     C, D = NUMERIC DATA
150 REM     F$, F1$ = USER SELECTED FILE NAMES
160 :
170 REM     FILES USED
180 REM     SEQUENTIAL FILE NAMES ARE USER SELECTED
190 :
200 REM     FILE INITIALIZATION
210 :
220 LINE INPUT "ENTER NAME OF INPUT FILE:"; F$
230 LINE INPUT "ENTER NAME OF OUTPUT FILE:"; F1$
240 OPEN "I", 1, F$
```

```
250 OPEN "O", 2, F1$
260 :
300 REM     READ/PRINT FILE TO FILE
310 :
320 IF EOF(1) THEN 410
330 INPUT #1, A$, B$, A, B
340 PRINT #2, A$;  ","  ; B$; ","; A; B
350 GOTO 320
360 :
400 REM     CLOSE FILE ROUTINE
410 CLOSE 1, 2
420 :
499 END
```

(Note: Did you remember to force the commas? If not, your file copy will not be exact.)

(a) To review the steps for this kind of program, write the corresponding line number(s) for each step in the outline.

1. Open the input file. ________________
2. Open the output file. ________________
3. Test the input file for EOF. If found, go to step 7. ________________
4. Input the next dataset from the input file. ________________
5. Print the dataset to the new file. ________________
6. Repeat steps (3) and (5) until the EOF for the input file is encountered.

   ____
7. Close both files. ________________

(b) When you RUN this program, what appears on your screen?

(a)
1. 240
2. 250
3. 320
4. 330
5. 340
6. 320, 330, 340
7. 410

(b)
```
RUN

ENTER NAME OF INPUT FILE:
ENTER NAME OF OUTPUT FILE:

READY
```

It can be unsettling to get no more than that from a program when so much internal activity is supposed to be taking place. The final READY is your only clue that your program completed its task. But you don't know for sure. We have two suggestions.

Add a statement at line 420 that prints a message indicating the job is complete – for example, 420 PRINT "COPY COMPLETED." A statement such as that lets you know the program did execute past the CLOSE statement at line 410. (That's why we chose line 420.)

A second suggestion is to OPEN the copied data file as input, read one or more datasets from it, and print them on the screen. This will verify that at least that much was done.

```
430 OPEN "I", 1, F1$
440 FOR X = 1 TO 3
450 INPUT #1, A$, B$, A, B
460 PRINT A$, B$, A, B : REM*** PRINT DATA ON SCREEN
470 NEXT X
480 CLOSE 1
```

You now have a complete file copying utility program. You can use it to copy any data file by simply changing the INPUT # and PRINT # statements at 330 and 340 to conform to the data format or datasets in the particular data file you want to copy.

Adding Data to the End of a Sequential File

Chapter 4 indicated that it is not easy to add data to an existing sequential data file. Here's why: In TRS-80 BASIC and BASIC-80, you cannot add data to an existing sequential file at all because when you open a data file as output, you destroy its previous contents. The way around this problem (there's always a way) is to follow these steps.

1. Copy the existing file into a temporary file.
2. Make the additions of data to the temporary file.
3. Copy the temporary file back to the original file with the new data.

Let's try an easy application. Assume you are using your personal computer to prepare a grocery list for your twice-monthly shopping trip. (See problem 2 of the Chapter 4 Self-Test.) Every few days you think of new items to be added to the list. Each dataset consists of one twenty-character string for the description and one numeric value for the quantity of the item needed. You can develop a program to enter the first datasets into the file, as well as all items to be added later.

Use the following procedure to add new data to the end of an existing sequential data file:

(1) Open the input file.
(2) Open the temporary file as an output file.
(3) Test the input file for EOF. If found, go to step (7).
(4) Input the next dataset.
(5) Print the dataset to the new (temporary) file.
(6) Repeat steps (3) to (5) until the EOF for the input file is encountered.
(7) Enter and test the new data to be added to the end of the temporary file. Include a test for the user option to end data entry.
(8) Print the new dataset to the temporary file.
(9) Repeat steps (7) and (8) until all new data are entered.
(10) Close both files.
(11) Open the temporary file as an input file.
(12) Open the old file as an output file (destroying its previous contents).
(13) Repeat steps (3) to (5) until all old and new data have been copied back into the old file and the EOF is encountered.
(14) Close both files.

First look at the introductory module and the program routine to enter the first datasets.

```
100 REM      GROCERY LIST FILE APPLICATION
110 REM     INTRODUCTORY MODULE
120 :
130 REM     VARIABLES USED
140 REM        D$ = ITEM DESCRIPTION
150 REM        Q = QUANTITY TO ORDER
160 :
170 :
180 :
190 REM     FILES USED
200 REM        F$ = USER ENTERED INPUT FILE
210 REM        TEMPFIL = TEMPORARY FILE
220 :
```

(a) To write the next segment, fill in the blank statement lines according to the instructions given in the on-line REMARKS (lines 280 and 290).

```
250 REM     FILE INITIALIZATION
260 :
270 LINE INPUT "ENTER NAME OF INPUT FILE:"; F$
280                              :REM    OPEN INPUT FILE
290                              : REM   OPEN OUTPUT FILE
300 :
```

(a)

```
250 REM     FILE INITIALIZATION
260 :
270 LINE INPUT "ENTER NAME OF INPUT FILE:"; F$
280 OPEN "I", 1, F$
290 OPEN "O", 2, "TEMPFIL"
300 :
```

Notice that you open the input file, then the output file, using buffer 1, then buffer 2. This order is programming style rather than a requirement, but it makes the program easier to read.

The next program segment makes the copy into the temporary file (TEMPFIL).

```
310 REM     FILE COPY ROUTINE
320 :
330 GOSUB 830
340 :
350 :
800 REM     FILE COPY SUBROUTINE
810 REM    COPIES FILE 1 TO FILE 2
820 :
830 IF EOF(1) THEN RETURN
840 INPUT #1, D$, Q
850 PRINT #2, D$; ","; Q
860 GOTO 830
870 :
```

This segment completes the copy to the temporary file. A subroutine was used (at line 800), since the same statements can be used by another segment of this program. Check your understanding of the program so far by answering the following questions:

(a) If there are no data in the input data file, will the copy routine work?

(b) Assuming that data are read from the input file and copied to the output file, where will the file pointer in the output file be located when the program RETURNs from the subroutine to line 340?

(a) Yes, as long as the file exists on the disk. The data file may be empty or full of data. Note: If you get an error message such as FILE NOT FOUND IN 280, merely open the file in direct mode and RUN the program again.

(b) The pointer will be located just past the last data item in TEMPFIL, ready for more data to be added to the file.

Having determined that the program you are assembling would place the data pointer correctly, add another segment allowing the entry of new data and write it to the temporary file. Fill in the statements with on-line REMARKS (lines 410, 430, 520, and 560).

(a)
```
360 REM     DATA ENTRY ROUTINE
370 :
380 PRINT "ENTER 'STOP' WHEN FINISHED"
390 PRINT
400 LINE INPUT "ENTER ITEM DESCRIPTION:"; D$
410                                          REM     TEST FOR 'STOP'
420 IF LEN(D$) = 0 THEN PRINT "PLEASE ENTER A DESCRIPTION OR 'STOP'":
    GOTO 400
430                                          :REM    TEST FOR LENGTH
440 INPUT "ENTER QUANTITY:"; Q
450 IF Q => 1 AND Q < 10 THEN 520
460 PRINT "YOU ENTERED A QUANTITY OF"; Q
470 LINE INPUT "IS THAT WHAT YOU WANTED?"; R$
480 IF LEFT$(R$,1) = "N" THEN 440
490 :
500 REM     WRITE TO FILE ROUTINE
510 :
520                                          REM     WRITE TO OUTPUT FILE
530 GOTO 400
540 :
550 REM     FILE CLOSE
560                                          REM     CLOSE FILES
570 :
```

(a)
```
360 REM     DATA ENTRY ROUTINE
370 :
380 PRINT "ENTER 'STOP' WHEN FINISHED"
390 PRINT
400 LINE INPUT "ENTER ITEM DESCRIPTION:"; D$
```

```
410 IF D$ = "STOP" THEN 560
420 IF LEN(D$) = 0 THEN PRINT "PLEASE ENTER A DESCRIPTION OR 'STOP'":
    GOTO 400
430 IF LEN(D$) > 20 THEN PRINT "PLEASE LIMIT DESCRIPTION TO 20 CHARS.
    AND REENTER": GOTO 400
440 INPUT "ENTER QUANTITY:"; Q
450 IF Q >= 1 AND Q < 10 THEN 520
460 PRINT "YOU ENTERED A QUANTITY OF"; Q
470 LINE INPUT "IS THAT WHAT YOU WANTED?"; R$
480 IF LEFT$(R$,1) = "N" THEN 440
490 :
500 REM     WRITE TO FILE ROUTINE
510 :
520 PRINT #2, D$; ","; Q
530 GOTO 400
540 :
550 REM     FILE CLOSE
560 CLOSE 1,2
570 :
```

With the previous segment added to the program, the major work of the program is done. The old data and the new data are now in TEMPFIL. Next copy TEMPFIL back to the original file. Here the subroutine is used again. Complete the program segment (lines 610, 620, 650, and 690).

(a)
```
600 REM     INITIALIZE FILES
610                                 REM     OPEN INPUT FILE
620                                 REM     OPEN OUTPUT FILE
630 :
640 REM     FILE COPY ROUTINE
650                                 REM     EXIT TO SUBROUTINE
660 :
670 REM     CLOSE FILES
680 CLOSE 1,2
690                                 REM     JOB DONE MESSAGE
700 STOP
710 :
```

(a)
```
600 REM     INITIALIZE FILES
610 OPEN "I", 1, "TEMPFIL"
620 OPEN "O", 2, F$
630 :
640 REM     FILE COPY ROUTINE
650 GOSUB 830
660 :
670 REM     CLOSE FILES
680 CLOSE 1,2
690 PRINT "FILE COPY COMPLETED"
700 STOP
710 :
```

If your completion of the program segment was correct, you noticed that TEMPFIL becomes the input file.

(a) What happens to the old contents of file F$ when line 620 is executed?

____

____

(a) The previous contents are destroyed when the file is opened as an output file (and then replaced with the contents of TEMPFIL).

You may want to make a backup copy of the file F$ before using the program to add to the file in case something unforeseen happens to the data.

Following is a complete listing of the program you have developed. In this case a KILL statement could be included for the temporary file since it unnecessarily uses disk file space. It could be inserted as

```
695 KILL "TEMPFIL".
```

```
100 REM      GROCERY LIST FILE APPLICATION
110 REM     INTRODUCTORY MODULE
120 :
130 REM     VARIABLES USED
140 REM         D$ = ITEM DESCRIPTION
150 REM         Q = QUANTITY TO ORDER
160 :
170 :
180 :
190 REM     FILES USED
200 REM         F$ = USER ENTERED INPUT FILE
210 REM         TEMPFIL = TEMPORARY FILE
220 :
250 REM     FILE INITIALIZATION
260 :
270 LINE INPUT "ENTER NAME OF INPUT FILE"; F$
280 OPEN "I", 1, F$
290 OPEN "O", 2, "TEMPFIL"
300 :
310 REM     FILE COPY ROUTINE
320 :
330 GOSUB 830
340 :
350 :
360 REM     DATA ENTRY ROUTINE
370 :
380 PRINT "ENTER 'STOP' WHEN FINISHED"
390 PRINT
400 LINE INPUT "ENTER ITEM DESCRIPTION:"; D$
410 IF D$ = "STOP" THEN 560
```

continued on next page

```
420 IF LEN(D$) = 0 THEN PRINT "PLEASE ENTER A DESCRIPTION OR 'STOP'":
    GOTO 400
430 IF LEN(D$) > 20 THEN PRINT "PLEASE LIMIT DESCRIPTION TO 20 CHARS.
    AND REENTER": GOTO 400
440 INPUT "ENTER QUANTITY:"; Q
450 IF Q >= 1 AND Q < 10 THEN 520
460 PRINT "YOU ENTERED A QUANTITY OF"; Q
470 LINE INPUT "IS THAT WHAT YOU WANTED?"; R$
480 IF LEFT$(R$,1) = "N" THEN 440
490 :
500 REM     WRITE TO FILE ROUTINE
510 :
520 PRINT #2, D$; ","; Q
530 GOTO 400
540 :
550 REM     FILE CLOSE
560 CLOSE 1,2
570 :
600 REM     INITIALIZE FILES
610 OPEN "I", 1, "TEMPFIL"
620 OPEN "O", 2, F$
630 :
640 REM     FILE COPY ROUTINE
650 GOSUB 830
660 :
670 REM     CLOSE FILES
680 CLOSE 1,2
690 PRINT "FILE COPY COMPLETED"
700 STOP
710 :
800 REM      FILE COPY SUBROUTINE
810 REM     COPIES FILE 1 TO FILE 2
820 :
830 IF EOF(1) THEN RETURN
840 INPUT #1, D$, Q
850 PRINT #2, D$; ","; Q
860 GOTO 830
870 :
```

(a) Write the corresponding program line number(s) for each step in the outline.

(1) Open the input file. ______

(2) Open the temporary file as an output file. ______

(3) Test the input file for EOF. If found, go to step (7). ______

(4) Input the next dataset. ______

(5) Print the dataset to the new (temporary) file. ______

(6) Repeat steps (3) to (5) until the EOF for the input file is encountered.

______

(7) Enter and test the new data to be added to the end of the temporary file.

Include a test for the user option to end data entry. ______

______

(8) Print the new dataset to the temporary file. ______

(9) Repeat steps (7) and (8) until all new data are entered. ____________

____

(10) Close both files. ____________________

(11) Open the temporary file as an input file. ____________

(12) Open the old file as an output file (destroying its previous contents).

____

(13) Repeat steps (3) to (5) until all old and new data have been copied back into the old file and the EOF is encountered. ____________

(14) Close both files. ____________________

- - - - - - - - - - - - - - -

(a)

(1)	280	(8)	520
(2)	290	(9)	lines 400 to 530
(3)	830	(10)	560
(4)	840	(11)	610
(5)	850	(12)	620
(6)	830, 840, 850	(13)	830, 840, 850
(7)	lines 400 to 480	(14)	680

You can use another procedure to add data to the end of a sequential data file in BASIC. The success of this procedure depends on how much data the file contains and the amount of available memory in the computer itself. Follow these steps:

1. Open the file as an input file.
2. Load the contents of the data file into one or more arrays.
3. Close the input file.
4. Reopen the same file in output mode.
5. Write or "dump" the contents of the array into the file.
6. Add new data to the end of the output file.
7. Close the file.

Use this procedure only if the file is rather small and the datasets contain all data items packed into one string variable. If these two circumstances are present, you are not likely to encounter errors. However, when files are large or data are placed into more than one array or into a two-dimensional array, then the probability increases that data will get lost or "forgotten," resulting in errors.

We recommend the two-file procedure as illustrated by the grocery list program. It is clean and neat!

Changing Data in a File

Remember, you cannot write data into an input file, and you cannot read from an output file. This means that data already placed in a file cannot be changed easily, but can be changed. The procedure should look familiar: Copy all the unchanged data into a temporary file, make the changes in the temporary file, and then copy the temporary file back into the original file. A few tricks will be explained, as you are guided in writing this program.

The example uses a customer credit file for a small business. Each dataset consists of three items:

1. five-digit customer number (must have exactly five digits)
2. customer name (twenty characters maximum)
3. customer credit rating (a single digit number 1, 2, 3, 4, or 5)

The program task is to change the credit rating of selected customers, with the user entering the customer number and new credit rating. Below is a typical RUN sequence. Underlined items are user entries.

```
RUN

ENTER FILE NAME: CREDIT1
ENTER "STOP" TO FINISH
ENTER CUSTOMER NUMBER: 13762
ERROR, CUST. NOT FOUND. CHECK CUST. # & REENTER

ENTER CUSTOMER NUMBER: 13763

PALEO MECHANICS - RATING 3
NEW CREDIT RATING: 2
MORE ENTRIES (YES OR NO)? YES

ENTER CUSTOMER NUMBER: 11123

ABC SERVICE LTD - RATING 1
NEW CREDIT RATING: 2
MORE ENTRIES (YES OR NO)? NO
JOB COMPLETED

READY
```

While the procedure outlined below is tailored to the particular data structure of the example program, the basic idea is adaptable to data files with different data structures (more or less data items in a dataset, or data in fielded strings).

(1) Open the input file.
(2) Open the temporary output file.
(3) Enter the data item to search for, with data entry checks. Include user option for "no more searches."
(4) Check for EOF in input file. If found:
  (a) Display a message that the data search was unsuccessful.
  (b) Close both files (to reset data pointers to beginning of files).
  (c) Repeat steps (1) to (4) until the user specifies "no more searches."

(5) Read a complete dataset from the input file.
(6) Test customer number entered by user against customer number in the dataset read from the input file in step (5). Write rejected datasets to the temporary file.
(7) Display the data item found for user; also ask user to enter changes. Include data entry checks.
(8) Print dataset with new data to temporary (output) file.
(9) Print remainder of input file to temporary (output) file.
(10) Close both files.
(11) Open both files, but this time the original file is the output file and the temporary file is the input file. Note that the original contents of the original file are destroyed.
(12) Print the contents of the temporary file (now revised) into the original file with an EOF check.
(13) Close both files.
(14) Give the user the option to repeat the procedure starting at step (1).

The program will be developed a segment at a time, with blanks for you to fill in according to the on-line REMARKS. Below is the introductory module, which you understand by now, followed by the data entry routine with entry checks. Fill in the blanks in lines 350, 360, and 370.

(a)
```
100 REM     CREDIT FILE CHANGER
110 :
120 REM     VARIABLES USED
130 REM       F$ = FILE NAME
140 REM       C$ = CUST. #
150 REM       C1$ = CUST. #
160 REM       N$ = CUST. NAME
170 REM       R$ = ENTRY STRING
180 REM       R,R1 = CREDIT RATING VALUE
190 :
200 REM     FILES USED
210 REM       INPUT FILE = USED DEFINED
220 REM       OUTPUT FILE = "TEMPFIL"
230 :
240 REM     INITIALIZE FILES
250 CLS
260 LINE INPUT "ENTER FILE NAME:"; F$
270 OPEN "I", 1, F$
280 OPEN "O", 2, "TEMPFIL"
290 :
300 REM     DATA ENTRY ROUTINE
310 PRINT "ENTER 'STOP' TO FINISH"
320 PRINT
330 LINE INPUT "ENTER CUST. #:"; C$
340 IF C$ =  STOP  THEN 790
350                                   : REM     NULL STRING
                                                TEST WITH MSG
360                                   : REM     TEST FOR
                                                5 DIGITS
```

```
370                                   : REM    TEST FOR
                                               ALPHANUMERIC
                                               ENTRY
380 :
```

(a)
```
350 IF LEN(C$) = 0 THEN PRINT "ENTER NUMBERS OR STOP": GOTO 320
360 IF LEN(C$) <> 5 THEN PRINT "ENTRY ERROR. REENTER WITH 5
    DIGITS":GOTO 320
370 IF VAL(C$) = 0 THEN PRINT "ENTRY ERROR. NUMBERS ONLY": GOTO 320
```

Now for the interesting part. The program searches through the data file for the customer the user requested.

(a) When searching the data file for the customer and encountering the EOF marker without finding the customer, what should the program do?

(b) Before another search is made for a customer in the file, what must be done to the file?

(c) Fill in lines 410 and 430 below.

```
380 :
390 REM     FILE SEARCH ROUTINE
400 IF EOF(1) THEN 450
410                            :REM   READ FROM THE FILE TO C1$, N$, R
420 IF C$ = C1$ THEN 500
430                            :REM   REJECTS ARE TO BE PRINTED TO THE
                                      TEMPFIL
440 GOTO 400
450 PRINT "ERROR MESSAGE. WE CANNOT FIND CUST. #:"; C$; "ON THE FILE.
    PLEASE CHECK YOUR NUMBER AND REENTER"
460 CLOSE 1,2 : REM   RESET FILE POINTERS TO BEGINNING
470 GOTO 270
480 :
```

(d) Why was variable C1$ used in line 410 instead of C$?

(e) If you delete line 460 and then RUN the program, what will happen if an incorrect customer number is entered and then a correct customer number?

\- - - - - - - - - - - - - - - -

(a) Print an error message indicating that the customer was not in the file (see the sample RUN presented earlier). (see line 410 and 450 above.)

(b) Close and reopen the files to reset the file pointers to the beginning of the data (very important!). (see line 460 above.)

(c)
```
410 INPUT #1, C1$, N$, R
430 PRINT #2, C1$; ","; N$; ","; R
```

(d) Two values would have been assigned to C$, creating a program error. Note the error message at line 450. Also notice the CLOSE and OPEN to reset the data file pointer to the beginning of the file (line 460).

(e) The EOF check in line 400 will detect the EOF marker in both cases, and the error message will be printed both times.

When the file has been searched and the correct customer found, the program prints the customer name on the screen (line 510) as a double check to the computer operator that the correction is being made for the right customer.

```
480 :
490 REM    CUST # FOUND. PROCEED WITH DATA ENTRY
500 PRINT
510 PRINT N$, "CREDIT RATING:"; R
520 LINE INPUT "NEW CREDIT RATING:"; R$
530 IF LEN(R$) <> 1 THEN PRINT "ONLY A ONE DIGIT NUMBER IS ACCEPTABLE":
    GOTO 520
540 IF VAL(R$) < 1 OR VAL(R$) > 5 THEN PRINT "NUMBERS 1-5 ONLY, PLEASE":
    GOTO 520
550 LET R1 = VAL(R$)
560 :
570 REM    PRINT NEW INFO TO TEMPFIL
580 PRINT #2, C$; ","; N$; ","; R1
590 :
```

In line 580, the new customer rating is written into the TEMPFIL, along with the accompanying customer number and name. You now have completed routines to search the original file, and to place old and new data into TEMPFIL.

(a) Considering the location of the file pointer in FILE1, what should the program do next?

(a) Write the remaining data in the input file (FILE1) to the output file (TEMPFIL).

Fill in the blanks in this segment (610, 620 and 630).

(a)
```
590 :
600 REM    PRINT REMAINDER OF FILE TO TEMPFIL
610                                    :REM   TEST FOR EOF(1). GOTO CLOSE
620                                    :REM   READ FROM #1
630                                        :REM   PRINT TO #2
640 GOTO 610
650 :
660 REM    CLOSE FILES
670 CLOSE 1,2
680 :
```

(a)
```
610 IF EOF(1) THEN 670
620 INPUT #1, C$, N$, R
630 PRINT #2, C$; ","; N$; ","; R
```

The final program segment should copy TEMPFIL back into the original file. Complete the file program lines indicated (700, 710, 740, 750, and 790).

(a)
```
680 :
690 REM     INITIALIZE AND COPY TEMPFIL TO FILE
700                                    :REM    OPEN INPUT FILE
710                                    :REM    OPEN OUTPUT FILE
720 :
730 IF EOF(1) THEN 790
740                                    :REM    READ INPUT FILE
750                                    :REM    PRINT TO OUTPUT FILE
760 GOTO 730
770 :
780 REM     CLOSE FILES
790                                    :REM    CLOSE
800 :
810 REM     CONTINUE REQUEST
820 CLS
830 LINE INPUT "DO YOU HAVE MORE?"; R$
840 IF LEFT$(R$,1) = "Y" THEN 270
850 PRINT "JOB COMPLETED"
860 :
```

(a)
```
700 OPEN "I", 1, TEMPFIL
710 OPEN "O", 2, F$
740 INPUT #1, C$, N$, R
750 PRINT #2, C$; " ,"; N$; " , "; R
790 CLOSE 1,2
```

If you RUN this program with large files, each change will take considerable computer time. If you enter the data in the original file in customer number order, and also enter the changes in customer number order, the need to repeatedly execute the file copy routine (lines 600 to 800) after each change is eliminated, reducing computer time.

Here is a complete listing of the credit file change program so that you can see it all at once:

```
100 REM     CREDIT FILE CHANGER
110 :
120 REM     VARIABLES USED
130 REM       F$ = FILE NAME
140 REM       C$ = CUST. #
150 REM       C1$ = CUST. #
160 REM       N$ = CUST. NAME
170 REM       R$ = ENTRY STRING
180 REM       R,R1 = CREDIT RATING VALUE
190 :
200 REM     FILES USED
210 REM       INPUT FILE = USER DEFINED
220 REM       OUTPUT FILE = "TEMPFIL"
230 :
240 REM     INITIALIZE FILES
250 CLS
260 LINE INPUT "ENTER FILE NAME:"; F$
270 OPEN "I", 1, F$
280 OPEN "O", 2, "TEMPFIL"
290 :
300 REM     DATA ENTRY ROUTINE
310 PRINT "ENTER 'STOP' TO FINISH"
320 PRINT
330 LINE INPUT "ENTER CUST. #:"; C$
340 IF C$ = "STOP" THEN 790
350 IF LEN(C$) = 0 THEN PRINT "ENTER NUMBERS OR STOP": GOTO 320
360 IF LEN(C$) <> 5 THEN PRINT "ENTRY ERROR. REENTER WITH 5 DIGITS":
    GOTO 320
370 IF VAL(C$) = 0 THEN PRINT "ENTRY ERROR. NUMBERS ONLY": GOTO 320
380 :
390 REM     FILE SEARCH ROUTINE
400 IF EOF(1) THEN 450
410 INPUT #1, C1$, N$, R
420 IF C$ = C1$ THEN 500
430 PRINT #2; C1$; ","; N$; ","; R
440 GOTO 400
450 PRINT "ERROR MESSAGE. WE CANNOT FIND CUST. #:"; C$; "ON THE FILE.
    PLEASE CHECK YOUR NUMBER AND REENTER"
```

continued on next page

```
460 CLOSE 1, 2 : REM     RESET FILE POINTERS TO BEGINNING
470 GOTO 270
480 :
490 REM     CUST # FOUND. PROCEED WITH DATA ENTRY
500 PRINT
510 PRINT N$, "CREDIT RATING:"; R
520 LINE INPUT "NEW CREDIT RATING:"; R$
530 IF LEN(R$) <> 1 THEN PRINT "ONLY A ONE DIGIT NUMBER IS ACCEPTABLE":
    GOTO 520
540 IF VAL(R$) < 1 OR VAL(R$) > 5 THEN PRINT "NUMBERS 1-5 ONLY, PLEASE":
    GOTO 520
550 LET R1 = VAL(R$)
560 :
570 REM     PRINT NEW INFO TO TEMPFIL
580 PRINT #2, C$; ","; N$; ","; R1
590 :
600 REM     PRINT REMAINDER OF FILE TO TEMPFIL
610 IF EOF(1) THEN 670
620 INPUT #1, C$, N$, R
630 PRINT #2, C$; ","; N$; ","; R
640 GOTO 610
650 :
660 REM     CLOSE FILES
670 CLOSE 1, 2
680 :
690 REM     INITIALIZE AND COPY TEMPFIL TO FILE
700 OPEN "I", 1, "TEMPFIL"
710 OPEN "O", 2, F$
720 :
730 IF EOF(1) THEN 790
740 INPUT #1, C$, N$, R
750 PRINT #2, C$; ","; N$; ","; R
760 GOTO 730
770 :
780 REM     CLOSE FILES
790 CLOSE 1, 2
800 :
810 REM     CONTINUE REQUEST
820 CLS
830 LINE INPUT "DO YOU HAVE MORE?"; R$
840 IF LEFT$(R$,1) = "Y" THEN 270
850 PRINT "JOB COMPLETED"
860 :
```

(a) Write the corresponding program line number(s) for each step in the outline.

(1) Open the input file. ______________________

(2) Open the temporary output file. ______________________

(3) Enter the data item to search for, with data entry checks. Include user option for "no more searches." ______________________

(4) Check for EOF in input file. If found: ______________________

(a) Display a message that the data search was unsuccessful. ____________

(b) Close both files (to reset data pointers to beginning of files).

____

(c) Repeat steps (1) to (4) until the user specifies "no more searches." __________

(5) Read a complete dataset from the input file. __________

(6) Test customer number entered by user against customer number in the dataset read from the input file in step (5). Write rejected datasets to the temporary file. __________

(7) Display the data item found for user; also ask user to enter changes. Include data entry checks. __________

(8) Print dataset with new data to temporary (output) file. __________

(9) Print remainder of input file to temporary (output) file. __________

(10) Close both files. __________

(11) Open both files, but this time the original file is the output file and the temporary file is the input file. Note that the original contents of the original file are destroyed. __________

(12) Print the contents of the temporary file (now revised) into the original file with an EOF check. __________

(13) Close both files. __________

(14) Give the user the option to repeat the procedure starting at step (1). __________

(b) Modify the Credit Rating program to change customer names instead of credit rating (companies do change names). Only five program lines are involved. Show them below.

- - - - - - - - - - - - - - - -

(a) (1) 270
(2) 280

(3) lines 310 to 370
(4) 400
    (a) 450
    (b) 460
    (c) lines 270 to 460
(5) 410
(6) 420, 430
(7) lines 510 to 550
(8) 580
(9) lines 610 to 640
(10) 670
(11) 700, 710
(12) lines 730 to 760
(13) 790
(14) 830, 840

(b)
```
520 LINE INPUT "ENTER NEW NAME:"; N$
530 IF LEN(N$) = 0 THEN PRINT "PLEASE ENTER THE CORRECT NAME":
    GOTO 520
540 IF LEN(N$) > 20 THEN PRINT "20 CHAR. MAX. PLEASE REENTER":
    GOTO 520
550 REM*** STATEMENT DELETED
580 PRINT #2, C$; ","; N$; ","; R
```

Only five changes were necessary in this modularly designed program. A factor that minimized changes was that the entire data set was dealt with all at once instead of reading one data item at a time. Remember this when writing future programs.

Editing, Deleting, and Inserting File Data

Whenever we work extensively with files, we write a small utility program that lets us read through the file, one item at a time, to verify that everything is as it should be. A properly written data file editing program also lets you make changes in the file data as it reads through the file. Our example will use the previous application, the Credit Rating File. Remember that the dataset consists of:

1. five-digit customer number stored as a string
2. a twenty character customer name
3. a credit rating, stored as a numeric value from 1 to 5

The first program below allows you to look at each dataset, one item at a time, with the prompt "PRESS ENTER TO CONTINUE." (The entry key on your terminal may say RETURN or something similar instead of ENTER.) The PRESS ENTER TO CONTINUE technique is very popular for CRT screen-oriented systems. The program allows the user to review the data displayed for the length of time needed and then move on to the next dataset. The program then *refreshes* or clears the screen to remove "screen clutter" before the next data are displayed. Examine the program to see how the user INPUT statement is used in the PRESS ENTER TO CONTINUE technique.

```
100 REM     CREDIT FILE EDITOR(1)
110 :
120 :
130 REM     PRESS ENTER TO CONTINUE
140 :
150 REM     VARIABLES USED
160 REM       C$ = CUST #(5)
170 REM       N$ = CUST NAME(20)
180 REM       R = CREDIT RATING
190 REM       R$ = STRING VARIABLE RESPONSE
200 REM       F$ = FILE NAME
210 :
220 REM     FILES USED
230 REM       INPUT FILE IS USER DEFINED
240 :
250 REM     FILE INITIALIZATION
260 LINE INPUT "ENTER FILE NAME:"; F$
270 OPEN "I", 1, F$
280 :
290 REM     READ FILE AND DISPLAY
300 CLS
310 IF EOF(1) THEN 440
320 PRINT "PRESS ENTER TO CONTINUE"
330 INPUT #1, C$, N$, R
340 PRINT C$
350 LINE INPUT R$
360 :
370 PRINT N$
380 LINE INPUT R$
390 :
400 PRINT R
410 LINE INPUT R$
420 GOTO 300
430 REM     CLOSE FILE
440 CLOSE
450 PRINT "JOB COMPLETED"
460 :
```

(a) What is assigned to R$ in lines 350, 380, and 410? ______________________

____

(b) Since R$ acts as a dummy variable in the program above, what is the purpose of lines 350, 380, and 410?

(c) How often was the screen "refreshed" in the program above?

(a) Nothing (a null string)
(b) Keeps the data items on the CRT display until the user presses ENTER to continue. (Program waits at input statement until ENTER key is pressed, with or without any other entry.)
(c) Before (or after) each complete dataset of three items was displayed.

The next version of this program allows the user to change any data item displayed on the screen or accept it "as is" by pressing ENTER to continue. The procedure includes copying the credit data file to a temporary file "TEMPFIL" as you read through the file making changes. Here is the first part of the program, with the capability of changing the customer number.

```
100 REM    CREDIT FILE EDITOR(2)
110 :
120 :
130 REM    TYPE CHANGE OR C TO CHANGE ITEM
140 REM    PRESS ENTER TO CONTINUE
150 :
160 REM    VARIABLES USED
170 REM       C$ = CUST #(5)
180 REM       N$ = CUST NAME(20)
190 REM       R = CREDIT RATING
200 REM       R$ = STRING VARIABLE RESPONSE
210 REM       F$ = FILE NAME
220 :
230 REM    FILES USED
240 REM       INPUT FILE IS USER DEFINED
250 REM       OUTPUT FILE = TEMPFIL
260 :
270 REM    FILE INITIALIZATION
280 LINE INPUT "ENTER FILE NAME:"; F$
290 OPEN "I", 1, F$
300 OPEN "O", 2, "TEMPFIL"
310 :
320 REM    READ FILE AND DISPLAY
330 CLS
340 IF EOF(1) THEN 750
350 PRINT "TYPE CHANGE OR 'C' TO CHANGE ITEM"
360 PRINT "PRESS ENTER TO CONTINUE"
370 INPUT #1, C$, N$, R
380 PRINT C$
390 LINE INPUT R$
400 IF LEFT$(R$,1) = "C" THEN GOSUB 550
530 :
540 REM    CHANGE CUST # SUBROUTINE
550 LINE INPUT "ENTER NEW CUST. #:"; C$
560 IF LEN(C$) = 0 THEN PRINT "ENTER NUMBERS PLEASE": GOTO 550
570 IF LEN(C$) <> 5 THEN PRINT "ENTRY ERROR. REENTER WITH 5 DIGITS":
    GOTO 550
580 IF VAL(C$) = 0 THEN PRINT "ENTRY ERROR. NUMBERS ONLY": GOTO 550
590 RETURN
600 :
```

Notice the few additions: the output file (lines 250, 300); the instructions changes (lines 130, 350); and the entry test (line 400). For reasons that will become apparent, a subroutine (lines 540 to 590) is used for entering the change to the customer number. The same data entry checks are used that were originally used in the credit file creating program. A caution: This program segment does not write the new customer number to TEMPFIL. In order to maintain identical files, use one statement to write the entire dataset into TEMPFIL as was originally done with the credit rating data file. If you are particularly sharp, you may have noted that the new customer number was assigned to C$, replacing the old customer number stored there. Can you look ahead and see why?

Now it's your turn. Using the customary clues, write a routine that will allow a change in customer name. Use the subroutine format like that above. Fill in lines 620, 630, and 640.

```
410 :
420 PRINT N$
430 LINE INPUT R$
440 IF LEFT$(R$,1) = "C" THEN GOSUB 620
600 :
610 REM    CHANGE CUST NAME SUBROUTINE
620                                              :REM   DATA ENTRY
630                                                :REM   NULL
                                                          STRING TEST

640                                             :REM   TEST FOR LENGTH


650 RETURN
660 :
```

```
410 :
420 PRINT N$
430 LINE INPUT R$
440 IF LEFT$(R$,1) = "C" THEN GOSUB 620
600 :
610 REM    CHANGE CUST NAME SUBROUTINE
620 LINE INPUT "ENTER NEW NAME:"; N$
630 IF LEN(N$) = 0 THEN PRINT "PLEASE, WE NEED A NEW NAME":
    GOTO 620
640 IF LEN(N$) > 20 THEN PRINT "PLEASE REENTER NAME WITH 20
    CHARS OR LESS": GOTO 620
650 RETURN
660 :
```

Nice work! Now, write a program segment that allows a change to be entered for the credit rating. Upon returning from the subroutine, have the program record the entire dataset, including changes if any, to TEMPFIL. Fill in lines 510, 680, 690, 700, and 710.

```
450 :
460 PRINT R
470 LINE INPUT R$
480 IF LEFT$(R$,1) = "C" THEN GOSUB 680
490 :
500 REM    PRINT TO TEMPFIL
510                                          :REM    PRINT TO TEMPFIL
520 GOTO 330
530 :
660 :
670 REM    CHANGE CREDIT RATING SUBROUTINE
680                                          :REM    DATA ENTRY(R$)
690                                          :REM    LENGTH TEST
700                                          :REM    VALUE 1-5 TEST
710                                          :REM    CONVERT $ TO #(R)
720 RETURN
730 :
```

```
450 :
460 PRINT R
470 LINE INPUT R$
480 IF LEFT$(R$,1) = "C" THEN GOSUB 680
490 :
500 REM    PRINT TO TEMPFIL
510 PRINT #2, C$; ","; N$; ","; R
520 GOTO 330
530 :
660 :
670 REM    CHANGE CREDIT RATING SUBROUTINE
680 LINE INPUT "ENTER NEW CREDIT RATING:"; R$
690 IF LEN(R$) <> 1 THEN PRINT "ONLY A ONE DIGIT NUMBER IS ACCEPTABLE":
    GOTO 680
700 IF VAL(R$) < 1 OR VAL(R$) > 5 THEN PRINT "NUMBERS 1-5 ONLY, PLEASE":
    GOTO 680
710 LET R = VAL(R$)
720 RETURN
730 :
```

Did you get line 510 correct? Carefully planned, the routine that prints or writes to the file uses the same variables C$, N$, and R, that can contain either new data or old, unchanged data items.

(a) Describe the last routine needed to complete this program.

(a) Copy TEMPFIL back into the original file, F$.

The end of file test in line 340 to branch to the next program segment is already set up:

```
340 IF EOF(1) THEN 750
```

While experiencing a bit of dejá vu, complete the final section to copy TEMPFIL to the original file by filling in lines 780, 790, 810, 820, 830, and 860.

(a)
```
730 :
740 REM     CLOSE FILES
750 CLOSE 1,2
760 :
770 REM     INITIALIZE FILE AND COPY BACK TO ORIGINAL
780                                           :REM     OPEN INPUT FILE
790                                           :REM     OPEN OUTPUT FILE
800 :
810                                           :REM     EOF TEST TO 860
820                                           :REM     READ FROM INPUT
830                                           :REM     PRINT TO OUTPUT
840 GOTO 810
850 REM     CLOSE FILES
860                             :REM     CLOSE FILES (DID YOU FORGET?)
870 PRINT "COPY COMPLETED WITH CHANGES"
880 :
```

(a)
```
730 :
740 REM     CLOSE FILES
750 CLOSE 1,2
760 :
770 REM     INITIALIZE FILE AND COPY BACK TO ORIGINAL
780 OPEN "I", 1, "TEMPFIL"
790 OPEN "O", 2, F$
800 :
810 IF EOF(1) THEN 860
820 INPUT #1, C$, N$, R
830 PRINT #2, C$; ","; N$; ","; R
840 GOTO 810
850 REM     CLOSE FILES
860 CLOSE 1,2
870 PRINT "COPY COMPLETED WITH CHANGES"
880 :
```

Yet another desirable editing feature is the ability to delete a complete dataset from a data file. This is in addition to the program's ability to make changes in an existing dataset. To delete a dataset, have the program read the dataset from the input file, but *not* copy it into TEMPFIL. Thus, the dataset "disappears." This editing option can be integrated into the existing program you have been developing. First, enter a statement to inform the user of the option to delete a dataset.

```
355 PRINT "TYPE DELETE OR 'D' TO DELETE THIS DATASET"
```

Complete the other change (line 403) in a multiple statement line that tests for the user input "D" and, if present, branch to line 330 never writing this dataset to the file. Check the context (statements around 403) before writing line 403.

(a) 403 ______________________________

(a)
```
403 IF LEFT$(R$,1) = "D" THEN GOTO 330
```

You now have a model for a file editor that allows changes and deletions of data in a file. Another useful editing feature allows you to insert a new dataset *part way through* an existing data file to keep data in numerical or alphabetical order. After locating a certain dataset, the new dataset is then inserted. To insert a new dataset into a file, you can enter the new data using the subroutines used previously to make changes in the file. How's that for program efficiency! Following are some of the new statements needed, with blanks for you to complete (lines 404, 535, and 537).

(a)
```
357 PRINT "TYPE INSERT OR "I" TO INSERT A NEW DATASET AFTER THIS
      ONE."
404                          :REM TEST FOR "I". IF PRESENT GOTO 532
                                      (a routine developed next)
531 REM    FILE INSERT ROUTINE

533 GOSUB 550                          :REM ENTER NEW CUST. #

535                                    :REM ENTER NEW CUST. NAME

537                                    :REM ENTER NEW CREDIT RATING

539 GOTO 510
```

(a)
```
404 IF LEFT$(R$,1) = "I" THEN 532

535 GOSUB 620
537 GOSUB 680
```

Our "policy" is to insert the new dataset *after* the one just displayed. This means you cannot insert data before the first dataset! This also means that you must add a line 532.

(a) What will it do? ______________________________

____

(b) Write line 532.

532 ______________________________

\- - - - - - - - - - - - - - - -

(a) Line 532 will copy the current dataset to the TEMPFIL.

(b) `PRINT #2, C$; ","; N$; ","; R`

Now gather together this data file editing utility program for the credit file. It allows you to change, delete, insert, or add to the credit data file.

```
100 REM    CREDIT FILE EDITOR(3)
110 :
120 :
130 REM    TYPE CHANGE OR C TO CHANGE ITEM
140 REM    PRESS ENTER TO CONTINUE
150 :
160 REM    VARIABLES USED
170 REM        C$ = CUST #(5)
180 REM        N$ = CUST NAME(20)
190 REM        R = CREDIT RATING
200 REM        R$ = STRING VARIABLE RESPONSE
210 REM        F$ = FILE NAME
220 :
230 REM    FILES USED
240 REM        INPUT FILE IS USER DEFINED
250 REM        OUTPUT FILE = TEMPFIL
260 :
270 REM     FILE INITIALIZATION
280 LINE INPUT "ENTER FILE NAME:"; F$
290 OPEN "I", 1, F$
300 OPEN "O", 2, "TEMPFIL"
310 :
320 REM    READ FILE AND DISPLAY
330 CLS
340 IF EOF(1) THEN 750
350 PRINT "TYPE CHANGE OR 'C' TO CHANGE ITEM"
355 PRINT "TYPE DELETE OR 'D' TO DELETE THIS DATASET."
357 PRINT "TYPE INSERT OR 'I' TO INSERT A NEW DATASET AFTER THIS ONE"
360 PRINT "PRESS ENTER TO CONTINUE WITH NO CHANGE"
370 INPUT #1, C$, N$, R
380 PRINT C$
390 LINE INPUT R$
400 IF LEFT$(R$,1) = "C" THEN GOSUB 550: GOTO 420
```

continued on next page

```
403 IF LEFT$(R$,1) = "D" THEN GOTO 330
404 IF LEFT$(R$,1) = "I" THEN 532
410 :
420 PRINT N$
430 LINE INPUT R$
440 IF LEFT$(R$,1) = "C" THEN GOSUB 620
450 :
460 PRINT R
470 LINE INPUT R$
480 IF LEFT$(R$,1) = "C" THEN GOSUB 680
490 :
500 REM   PRINT TO TEMPFIL
510 PRINT #2, C$; ","; N$; ","; R
520 GOTO 330
530 :
531 REM   FILE INSERT ROUTINE
532 PRINT #2, C$; ","; N$; ","; R
533 GOSUB 550
535 GOSUB 620
537 GOSUB 680
539 GOTO 510
540 REM   CHANGE CUST # SUBROUTINE
550 LINE INPUT "ENTER NEW CUST. #:"; C$
560 IF LEN(C$) = 0 THEN PRINT "ENTER NUMBERS PLEASE": GOTO 550
570 IF LEN(C$) <> 5 THEN PRINT "ENTRY ERROR. REENTER WITH 5 DIGITS":
    GOTO 550
580 IF VAL(C$) = 0 THEN PRINT "ENTRY ERROR. NUMBERS ONLY": GOTO 550
590 RETURN
600 :
610 REM   CHANGE CUST NAME SUBROUTINE
620 LINE INPUT "ENTER NEW NAME:"; N$
630 IF LEN(N$) = 0 THEN PRINT "PLEASE, WE NEED A NEW NAME": GOTO 620
640 IF LEN(N$) > 20 THEN PRINT "PLEASE REENTER NAME WITH 20 CHARS OR
    LESS": GOTO 620
650 RETURN
660 :
670 REM   CHANGE CREDIT RATING SUBROUTINE
680 LINE INPUT "ENTER NEW CREDIT RATING:"; R$
690 IF LEN(R$) <> 1 THEN PRINT "ONLY A ONE DIGIT NUMBER IS ACCEPTABLE":
    GOTO 680
700 IF VAL(R$) < 1 OR VAL(R$) > 5 THEN PRINT "NUMBERS 1-5 ONLY, PLEASE":
    GOTO 680
710 LET R = VAL(R$)
720 RETURN
730 :
740 REM   CLOSE FILES
750 CLOSE 1,2
760 :
770 REM   INITIALIZE FILE AND COPY BACK TO ORIGINAL
780 OPEN "I", 1, "TEMPFIL"
790 OPEN "O", 2, F$
800 :
810 IF EOF(1) THEN 860
820 INPUT #1, C$, N$, R
830 PRINT #2, C$; ","; N$; ","; R
840 GOTO 810
850 REM   CLOSE FILES
860 CLOSE 1,2
870 PRINT "COPY COMPLETED WITH CHANGES"
880 :
```

The following outline for the final version of the program allows for insertion, deletion, or changes of data in the file.

(1) Open the input file.
(2) Open the temporary file as an output file.
(3) Check for EOF in the input file; if encountered, go to step (11).
(4) Display a "menu" for the user to select changes to be made, including a "no changes" option.
(5) Read the entire dataset from the file and display the first data *item* (not dataset) in the current dataset.
(6) Allow the user to enter a selection from the "menu" and test for the selection possibilities.
(7) If user entered "C" for change:
    (a) Allow user to enter change with data entry checks.
    (b) Display next data item from data file for current dataset (if any items remain in this dataset) and display it.
    (c) User entered option for another change and test selection.
    (d) User entered change with data entry checks.
    (e) Repeat (7) (b), (c), and (d) until all items in a dataset have been through the change option.
    (f) Print the dataset (with any changes) to the temporary file.
    (g) Go to step (3).
(8) If user entered "I" for insert:
    (a) Print the dataset to the temporary file.
    (b) User enters new dataset with data entry checks.
    (c) Print the newly entered data to the temporary file.
    (d) Go to step (3).
(9) If user entered "D" for delete, go to step (3).
(10) If the user entered no response (just pressed the ENTER key), go to steps (7) (b) to (g).
(11) Close both files.
(12) Open the original file as an output file and the temporary file as an input file.
(13) Test for EOF for the temporary file (output) and, if found, close both files.
(14) Input a complete dataset from the temporary file and print it to the original file.
(15) Repeat steps (13) and (14) until EOF is found and files are closed.

Write the corresponding program line number(s) for each step in the outline below, except for items (10) and (15), where you are to fill in the blanks in the parentheses.

(1) Open the input file. ____________________

(2) Open the temporary file as an output file. ____________________

(3) Check for EOF in the input file; if encountered, go to step (11). __________

____

(4) Display a "menu" for the user to select changes to be made, including a "no changes" option. ______________________________

(5) Read the entire dataset from the file and display the first data *item* (not dataset) in the current dataset. ______________________________

(6) Allow the user to enter a selection from the "menu" and test for the selection possibilities. ______________________________

(7) If user entered "C" for change:

(a) Allow user to enter change with data entry checks. ______________________________

(b) Display next data item from data file for current dataset (if any items remain in this dataset) and display it. ______________________________

(c) User entered option for another change and test selection. ______________________________

(d) User entered change with data entry checks. ______________________________

(e) Repeat (7) (b), (c), and (d) until all items in a dataset have been through the change option. ______________________________

(f) Print the dataset (with any changes) to the temporary file. ______________________________

(g) Go to step (3). ______________________________

(8) If user entered "I" for insert:

(a) Print the dataset to the temporary file. ______________________________

(b) User enters new dataset with data entry checks. ______________________________

(c) Print the newly entered data to the temporary file. ______________________________

(d) Go to step (3). ______________________________

(9) If user entered "D" for delete, go to step (3). ______________________________

(10) Same as steps (__) (__) to (__) (__). (Fill in the blanks.)

(11) Close both files. ______________________________

(12) Open the original file as an output file and the temporary file as an input file. ______________________________

(13) Test for EOF for the temporary file (output) and, if found, close both files.

____

(14) Input a complete dataset from the temporary file and print it to the original file. ____

(15) Repeat steps (__) and (__). (Fill in the blanks.)

- - - - - - - - - - - - - - -

(1) 290
(2) 300
(3) 340
(4) lines 350 and 360
(5) lines 370 and 380
(6) lines 390 to 404
(7) (a) lines 550 to 590
 (b) lines 410 and 420
 (c) lines 470 and 480
 (d) lines 620 to 650
 (e) lines 450, 460, and 680 to 720
 (f) 510
 (g) 520
(8) (a) 532
 (b) lines 550 to 590, 620 to 650, and 680 to 720
 (c) 510
 (d) (if program rewritten or) 520
(9) 403
(10) steps (7) (b) to (7) (g)
(11) 750
(12) lines 780 and 790
(13) lines 810 and 860
(14) lines 820 and 830
(15) steps (13) and (14)

MERGING THE CONTENTS OF FILES

In many business applications of computers, information in data files is maintained in alphabetic or numeric order. This can be done by customer number, customer name, product number, or some other key to filing. It is often necessary or desirable to merge the contents of two data files, both already in some order, to a make a third data file with the same order or sequence. A utility program to merge files also allows you to learn some new file programming techniques with wider applications.

Follow these steps to merge two data files into one.

(1) Open the two files to be merged (#1 and #2) as input files and check for EOF in both files to be certain there is data to merge. If not, go to step (11).
(2) Open the file (#3) that will contain the merged data as an output file.
(3) Test file #1 for EOF and, if found, go to step (10).
(4) Read the first dataset from file #1.
(5) Test file #2 for EOF and, if found, go to step (10).
(6) Read the first dataset from file #2.
(7) Test datasets to see which file dataset (#1 or #2) is to be copied or printed to the merge file (#3).
(8) Print the selected dataset to file #3; this requires two separate routines:
    (a) One if file #1 dataset is selected, or
    (b) Another if file #2 dataset is selected.
(9) Test for EOF and read another dataset from whichever file's dataset was printed to file # 3 in step (8). Again, two separate routines are needed:
    (a) Test for EOF and read another dataset from file #1, or
    (b) Test for EOF and read another dataset from file #2.
(10) Again, separate routines are needed to "dump" or transfer the remaining data in file #1 or #2 to file #3:
    (a) If file #1 comes to EOF first, copy the remaining datasets in file #2 to file #3, or
    (b) If file #2 comes to EOF first, copy the remaining datasets in file #1 to file #3.
(11) Close all files.
(12) Optional routine to display merged data files for confirmation of a successful merge.

The model program merges two transaction files into a third larger file that combines the other two. In the example, each transaction produces a dataset stored as one fourteen-character string with three fields, as shown below.

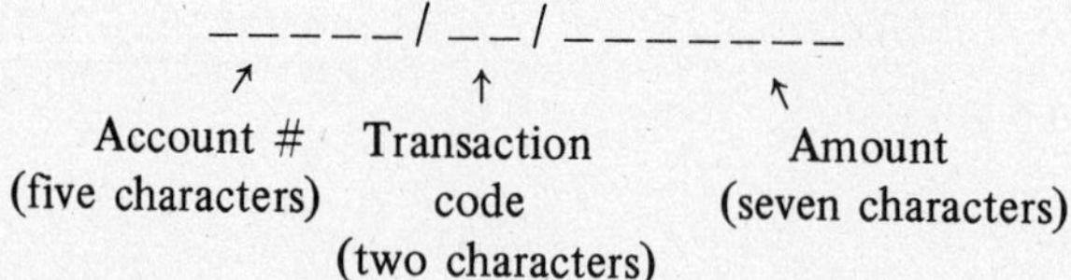

Account number = five character field
Transaction code = two character field (for a bank, 1 = check, 2 = deposit, etc.)
Amount = seven character field

Assume that the datasets are stored in two data files each in ascending numerical order by account number (problem 3 in the Chapter 4 Self-Test). The goal is to produce a third file that combines the data in the first two files, but maintains the numerical order when the file merging is complete. Also assume that more than one dataset can have the same account number in either or both data files.

This last assumption requires a decision. When merging, if two datasets have the same account number, the program will copy the dataset from file #1 first, then the dataset with the same number from file #2.

```
FILE #1          FILE #2
10762            10761
18102            18203
43611            43611
43611            80111
43611            80772
80223            80772
98702            89012
```

File #3 (files #1 and #2 merged into one)

```
10761
10762
18102
18203
43611
43611
43611
43611
80111
80223
80772
80772
89102
98702
```

(Note: Only the account numbers are shown here; the complete datasets also include transaction codes and amounts.)

This program is called MERGE. It gets tricky, so read the text and program segments carefully. The initializing process is familiar.

```
100 REM     FILE MERGE APPLICATION
110 :
120 REM     VARIABLES USED
130 REM       F1$, F2$, F3$ = FILE NAMES
140 REM       D1$, D2$ = DATASETS FROM FILE 1,2
150 REM       D1, D2 = ACCOUNT NUMBERS
160 REM       R$ = STRING VARIABLE ENTRY
170 REM     FILES USED
180 REM      TWO INPUT FILES = USER ENTERED
190 REM       OUTPUT FILE = USER ENTERED
200 :
210 REM     FILE INITIALIZATION
220 LINE INPUT "ENTER INPUT FILE #1:"; F1$
230 LINE INPUT "ENTER INPUT FILE #2:"; F2$
240 LINE INPUT "ENTER OUTPUT FILE:"; F3$
250 :
260 OPEN "I", 1, F1$
270 OPEN "I", 2, F2$
280 OPEN "O", 3, F3$
290 :
```

For program readability, file F1$ uses buffer #1, file F2$ uses buffer #2, etc.

Next, the first dataset is read from file #1. Notice that an EOF test is made before the first dataset is read, just in case the file has no data. (We added line 315 just in case both files are empty. At 900 an error message appears.)

```
300 :
310 REM      READ #1
315 IF EOF(1) AND EOF(2) THEN 900
320 IF EOF(1) THEN INPUT #2,D2$: GOTO 610
330 INPUT #1, D1$
```

If file #1 is empty to begin with, we read one item from file #2 and GOTO 610.

Line 340 converts the part of the dataset field string that contains the account number into a numeric value.

```
340 LET D1 = VAL(LEFT$(D1$,5))
```

You write the next segment. The program should check for EOF (and branch to line 670 if the test is true), read the first data item from file #2, and convert the account number part of the dataset string into a numeric value.

(a)
```
360 REM      READ #2
370
380
390
400 REM
```

(a)
```
350 :
360 REM      READ #2
370 IF EOF(2) THEN 670
380 INPUT #2, D2$
390 LET D2 = VAL(LEFT$(D2$,5))
400 :
```

The next decision is which dataset, that from file #1 or from file #2, will be copied into file #3 first?

```
400 :
410 REM      MERGE TESTING
420 IF D1 = D2 THEN 470
430 IF D1 < D2 THEN 470
440 GOTO 540
450 :
```

The program so far:

```
100 REM     FILE MERGE APPLICATION
110 :
120 REM     VARIABLES USED
130 REM       F1$, F2$, F3$ = FILE NAMES
140 REM       D1$, D2$ = DATASETS FROM FILE 1,2
150 REM       D1, D2 = ACCOUNT NUMBERS
160 REM       R$ = STRING VARIABLE ENTRY
170 REM     FILES USED
180 REM      TWO INPUT FILES = USER ENTERED
190 REM       OUTPUT FILE = USER ENTERED
200 :
210 REM     FILE INITIALIZATION
220 LINE INPUT "ENTER INPUT FILE #1:"; F1$
230 LINE INPUT "ENTER INPUT FILE #2:"; F2$
240 LINE INPUT "ENTER OUTPUT FILE:"; F3$
250 :
260 OPEN "I", 1, F1$
270 OPEN "I", 2, F2$
280 OPEN "O", 3, F3$
290 :
300 :
310 REM     READ #1
320 IF EOF(1) THEN 610
330 INPUT #1, D1$
340 LET D1 = VAL(LEFT$(D1$,5))
350 :
360 REM     READ #2
370 IF EOF(2) THEN 670
380 INPUT #2, D2$
390 LET D2 = VAL(LEFT$(D2$,5))
400 :
410 REM     MERGE TESTING
420 IF D1 = D2 THEN 470
430 IF D1 < D2 THEN 470
440 GOTO 540
450 :
```

(a) What should happen in the program routine that starts at line 470?

(b) The program tests for equality in line 420. In line 430, the test was for D1 less than D2. If both tests are false, then what is the relationship of D1 to D2?

(c) What should happen in the program routine at line 540 that line 440 branches to?

_ _ _ _ _ _ _ _ _ _ _ _ _ _ _

(a) Copy the contents of D1$ to file #3.
(b) D1 is greater than D2.
(c) Print the contents of D2$ into file #3.

Continue with the file copying segment for copying a dataset from file #1 to file #3.

```
450 REM
460 REM      COPY FROM #1 TO #3
470 PRINT #3, D1$
```

(a) After executing the above segment, the program should now read another dataset from file #1. You might want to have the program branch back to the routine at line 310 and continue executing from there. Why would this result in a program error?

(a) The routine at 310 reads from file #1, but then goes right on to read another dataset from file #2, replacing the dataset already assigned to D2$ without it having been copied to file #3.

Another program segment is used for reading the next data item from file #1.

```
480 IF EOF(1) THEN 610
490 INPUT #1, D1$
500 LET D1 = VAL(LEFT$(D1$,5))
510 GOTO 420
```

(a) When the program finds the end of file #1, it branches to line 610. Think ahead. What should happen in the routine at line 610?

(a) Since all datasets have been read from file #1 and copied to file #3, all the remaining data in file #2 should be copied into file #3. You'll see this routine soon.

Here is the routine we need to copy a dataset from file #2 to file #3.

```
520 :
530 REM      PRINT #2 TO #3
540 PRINT #3, D2$
550 IF EOF(2) THEN 670
560 INPUT #2, D2$
570 LET D2 = VAL(LEFT$(D2$,5))
580 GOTO 420
590 :
```

Notice how carefully you must think through these file utility programs. You are nearing the end with a few more "clean-up" routines needed. Two similar routines are needed to copy or dump the remainders of file #2 to #3, and #1 to #3.

```
600 REM      DUMP #2 TO #3
610 ___________
```

(a) The routine begun just above is branched to from line 480, where the program had just finished copying a file #1 dataset into #3. The EOF for file #1 is detected, showing that all data in that file has now been copied to file #3 and the program has branched to line 610. Since a dataset has been assigned to D2$, what must happen at line 610?

____

(a) Copy the contents of D2$ to file #3.

The rest is easy. Check file #2 for the EOF marker and dump any remaining datasets into file #3.

```
590 :
600 REM      DUMP #2 TO #3
610 PRINT #3, D2$
620 IF EOF(2) THEN 730
630 INPUT #2, D2$
640 GOTO 610
650 :
```

Write the corresponding routine to dump file #1 to file #3. The EOF check statement should branch to line 730.

(a)
```
650 REM
660 REM      DUMP #1 TO #3
670
680
690
700
710 REM
```

(b) The EOF test statements in lines 620 and 680 branch to line 730. What final routine should appear there?

(a)
```
650 :
660 REM      DUMP #1 TO #3
670 PRINT #3, D1$
680 IF EOF(1) THEN 730
690 INPUT #1, D1$
700 GOTO 670
710 :
```

(b) Close all files, since all data has been copied and merged.

Once the files are closed, the program gives the user the option to display the contents of the merged files to verify that it did happen and to judge whether the program works properly. In MERGE all the activity takes place between the computer memory and the disk with no evidence of the action appearing on the CRT screen. You see only RUN and READY, so did it really happen? The routine included at the end of the complete listing of MERGE lets you be sure (see 760 through 870).

```
100 REM     FILE MERGE APPLICATION
110 :
120 REM     VARIABLES USED
130 REM        F1$, F2$, F3$ = FILE NAMES
140 REM        D1$, D2$ = DATASETS FROM FILE 1,2
150 REM        D1, D2 = ACCOUNT NUMBERS
160 REM        R$ = STRING VARIABLE ENTRY
170 REM     FILES USED
180 REM        TWO INPUT FILES = USER ENTERED
190 REM        OUTPUT FILE = USER ENTERED
200 :
210 REM     FILE INITIALIZATION
220 LINE INPUT "ENTER INPUT FILE #1:"; F1$
230 LINE INPUT "ENTER INPUT FILE #2:"; F2$
240 LINE INPUT "ENTER OUTPUT FILE:"; F3$
250 :
260 OPEN "I", 1, F1$
270 OPEN "I", 2, F2$
280 OPEN "O", 3, F3$
```

```
290 :
300 :
310 REM     READ #1
315 IF EOF(1) AND EOF(2) THEN 900
320 IF EOF(1) THEN INPUT #2; D2$: GOTO 610
330 INPUT #1, D1$
340 LET D1 = VAL(LEFT$(D1$,5))
350 :
360 REM     READ #2
370 IF EOF(2) THEN 670
380 INPUT #2, D2$
390 LET D2 = VAL(LEFT$(D2$,5))
400 :
410 REM     MERGE TESTING
420 IF D1 = D2 THEN 470
430 IF D1 < D2 THEN 470
440 GOTO 540
450 :
460 REM     PRINT #1 TO #3
470 PRINT #3, D1$
480 IF EOF(1) THEN 610
490 INPUT #1, D1$
500 LET D1 = VAL(LEFT$(D1$,5))
510 GOTO 420
520 :
530 REM     PRINT #2 TO #3
540 PRINT #3, D2$
550 IF EOF(2) THEN 670
560 INPUT #2, D2$
570 LET D2 = VAL(LEFT$(D2$,5))
580 GOTO 420
590 :
600 REM     DUMP #2 TO #3
610 PRINT #3, D2$
620 IF EOF(2) THEN 730
630 INPUT #2, D2$
640 GOTO 610
650 :
660 REM     DUMP #1 TO #3
670 PRINT #3, D1$
680 IF EOF(1) THEN 730
690 INPUT #1, D1$
700 GOTO 670
710 :
720 REM     CLOSE FILES
730 CLOSE 1, 2, 3
740 PRINT "MERGE COMPLETED"
750 PRINT:PRINT
760 LINE INPUT "WOULD YOU LIKE TO SEE THE MERGED FILE?"; R$
770 IF LEFT$(R$,1) = "N" THEN 870
780 :
790 REM     PRINT CONTENTS OF MERGED FILE
800 OPEN "I", 1, F3$
810 IF EOF(1) THEN 860
820 INPUT #1, D1$
830 PRINT D1$
840 GOTO 810
850 REM     CLOSE FILE
860 CLOSE 1
870 STOP
880 :
```

continued on next page

```
890 REM    EOF ERROR MESSAGES
900 PRINT "BOTH FILES ARE EMPTY AT THE BEGINNING OF THE MERGE"
910 :
920 END
```

Write the corresponding program line number(s) for each step of the following outline:

(1) Open the two files to be merged (#1 and #2) as input files and check for EOF in both files to be certain there is data to merge. If not, go to step (11).

____

(2) Open the file (#3) that will contain the merged data as an output file.

____

(3) Test file #1 for EOF and, if found, go to step (10). _______________

(4) Read the first dataset from file #1. _______________

(5) Test file #2 for EOF and, if found, go to step (10). _______________

(6) Read the first dataset from file #2. _______________

(7) Test datasets to see which file dataset (#1 or #2) is to be copied or printed to the merge file (#3). _______________

(8) Print the selected dataset to file #3; this requires two separate routines:

(a) One if file #1 dataset is selected, _______________ or

(b) Another if file #2 dataset is selected. _______________

(9) Test for EOF and read another dataset from whichever file's dataset was printed in file #3 in step (8). Again, two separate routines are needed:

(a) Test for EOF and read another dataset from file #1, _______________

_______________ or

(b) Test for EOF and read another dataset from file #2. _______________

____

(10) Again, separate routines are needed to "dump" or transfer the remaining data in file #1 or #2 to file #3:

(a) If file #1 comes to EOF first, copy the remaining datasets in file #2 to file #3, _______________ or

(b) If file #2 comes to EOF first, copy the remaining datasets in file #1 to file #3. _______________

(11) Close all files. _______________

____

(12) Optional routine to display merged data files for confirmation of a successful merge. ______________________________

---

(1) lines 260 and 270
(2) 280
(3) 320
(4) 330
(5) 370
(6) 380
(7) lines 420 and 430
(8) (a) 470
    (b) 670
(9) (a) lines 480 and 490
    (b) lines 680 and 690
(10) (a) lines 610 to 640
     (b) lines 670 to 700
(11) 730
(12) lines 760 to 860

PROBLEMS WITH SEQUENTIAL DATA FILES

You should be aware of some frequent errors made in using sequential files and some programming techniques used for successful programs accessing data files.

The most frequent programming error is failing to keep track of the file pointers. In TRS-80 BASIC and BASIC-80, where the computer distinguishes between input and output files at the time the file is opened, the problem is usually greater with input files. Each time you use an INPUT # statement in a program, ask yourself how the file pointer is affected and where it is located before and after executing the statement.

(a) How can you reset the datafile pointer to the beginning of a file? ______________________________

(a) Close the file. Pointer is at beginning of file when file is reopened.

Another frequent error occurs when a program sequentially searches through a data file for a particular dataset or data item. Let's say you have a data file of names arranged alphabetically by last names. After you enter the name to be searched, the program searches through the file until it finds the name and then prints the information on your printer for that person. Then you enter a second name. When writing the program, ask yourself where the file pointer will be located after the first search.

Assume the first name searched and located is DORIAN SCHMIDT and the second name is HAMILTON ANDERSON. The data file search for the second name takes up where the search for the first name left off. The second name obviously will not be found before you reach the end-of-file. If the data file pointer was not reset to the beginning of the file after the first search, ANDERSON will never be found because the file was in alphabetical order and the search for the second name started at SCHMIDT. The solution, of course, is to make sure the program resets the pointer to the beginning of the file after every search, by using a CLOSE followed by an OPEN statement.

(a) When a file has been partially read through during a data search, why must the file pointer be reset to the beginning of the file before a new search of the file commences?

\- - - - - - - - - - - - - - - -

(a) Because if the pointer is midway in the file and the new datum searched for is near the beginning of the file, the search would not find the datum.

Another program situation to watch out for is a file application program containing routines that sequence through a data file using one INPUT # statement in a program loop. Think through this situation carefully when writing a program. Go through the loop in your mind or on paper two or three times before running the program to make certain the program will perform as expected. You may find (as we did in the MERGE program) that the first INPUT # statement cannot be part of a file reading loop without data being lost. Your program may need two different INPUT # statements, in separate routines. One may read only the first dataset or data item, while the other reads the rest of the file, or as far as necessary, in a program loop routine. This is common.

(a) How could data be lost when all data file inputs are included in data file reading loops? ______________________________

\- - - - - - - - - - - - - - - -

(a) In cases where one file or the other is empty to begin with.

Errors also occur when the contents of arrays are copied into a data file, a topic not covered earlier. The contents of a one- or two-dimensional array can be copied into a file or read from a file back into an array, provided you use the correct programming techniques. Such data manipulation has many uses. There is a tendency to think of array data as something that is used up or consumed, but storing array data in a file gives it permanence.

To load array data into a data file from a one-dimensional array:

P	
(1)	1761
(2)	18
(3)	1942
(4)	24
(5)	8209
(6)	2

The wrong way:

```
PRINT #1, P
```

The correct procedure:

```
FOR X = 1 TO 6
PRINT #1, P(X)
NEXT X
```

The correct procedure could also be done as one multiple statement line. Using this format PRINT #1, P(X); (note the semicolon) could possibly save a little file space.

Similarly, to load array data into a data file from a two-dimensional array:

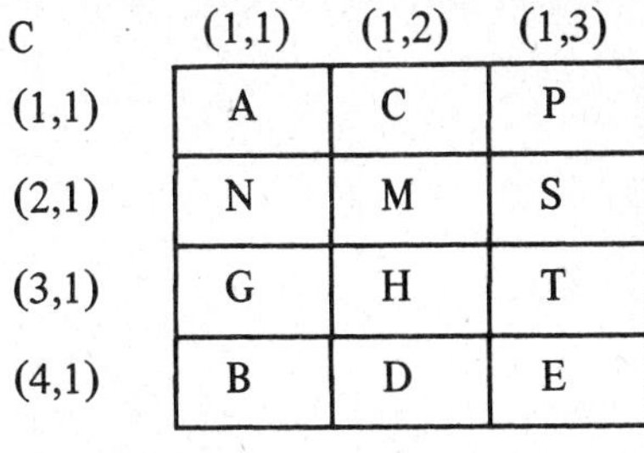

C	(1,1)	(1,2)	(1,3)
(1,1)	A	C	P
(2,1)	N	M	S
(3,1)	G	H	T
(4,1)	B	D	E

The wrong way:

```
PRINT #1, C
```

The correct procedure:

```
FOR X = 1 TO 4
FOR Y = 1 TO 3
PRINT #1, C(X,Y)
NEXT Y
NEXT X
```

(a) To read data into (or out of) an array from (or to) a data file, what programming technique is used? ____________________

- - - - - - - - - - - - - - - - -

(a) FOR NEXT loop

Another useful technique deals with applications where data are to be added to a file. Let's say a client number needs to be assigned to a new client or customer as part of a new dataset. In a business environment, the new client number might be assigned by data preparation personnel or the data entry person, relying on a list or on their knowledge of what number was last used. However, if you let the computer do it you can avoid "human error" commonly mislabeled "computer error." In the data file and after any copy made for modification of the file, reserve the very first file data position for the next available client number. Then when new clients are added to the file, follow these steps.

1. Read the first data item (next available client number) = N.
2. Assign N to the next client.
3. Increment N by 1 (or perhaps by +2 or +5 or +10 to leave room for future client data to be squeezed in) = N1.
4. Then have the program place N1 as the first item in the temporary file.
5. Copy the rest of the old file to the temporary file.
6. Place the new client data in the temporary file.
7. Copy the temporary file (including N1) back to the old file.
8. Repeat from step 1 for each new client.

Using the first part of a data file to hold information needed by the program, followed by the regular data, is a broadly useful technique. For example, the contents of an array could be placed at the head or beginning of a file, followed by the main datasets that make up the file. This procedure prevents using a separate data file for array data that are a part of the file. Just don't forget how the data file is set up, or some rather horrific file input errors could ensue. Such information should be included in the documentation prepared for each program and its corresponding data files.

A LETTER-WRITING PROGRAM

The next sequential file application example is a letter-writing program you may find useful in your home or business. This application presents some new techniques and reviews others.

Assume that you did the Chapter 4 Self-Test and have three form letters stored in data files called LETTER1, LETTER2, and LETTER3. When these letters are printed, you want the program to put the inside address and salutation in the letter from data located in yet another sequential data file called ADDRESS. The file ADDRESS contains the names and addresses in the mailing list. The data have the format shown below, with each dataset containing five items in fields within one string.

```
                                                        55
/1                  20/21                40/41      50/12/53      57/
______________________ ______________________ ___________ __ ___________
        name                 address            city     state  zip code
```

The salutation for each letter will be:

Dear resident of <u>(name of city)</u>

To print the letters on your line printer, use the LPRINT statement.

The program uses the CRT screen to enter which form letter (1, 2, or 3) you want to send to each name on the mailing list. This program, then, uses four data files (only two data files at a time), a line printer, and a CRT screen. If you don't have a line printer, the program is easily adapted to have all the program output displayed on a CRT screen. Some interesting techniques can be learned from this example.

Follow these steps for this particular program.

(1) Open the address data file as an input file.
(2) Check for EOF of address file and, if found, close all files and end the program.
(3) Input the address dataset and display the name.
(4) User entry option to select the form letter to this address with data entry checks.
(5) Open selected form letter file as an input file.
(6) Print inside heading address.
(7) Print salutation with addressee's last name.
(8) Test letter file for EOF and, if found,
    (a) close that form letter file, and
    (b) repeat from step (2).
(9) Input a dataset (one line of text from the letter file) and print it.
(10) Repeat steps (8) and (9).

Look at the introductory module of the program. The ADDRESS file is opened and, as indicated in the line 240 remark, the LETTER files are user selected and opened when selected.

```
100 REM    LETTER WRITING PROGRAM
110 :
120 REM    VARIABLES USED
130 REM       N$ = NAME, ADDRESS, ETC
140 REM       R$ = RESPONSE STRING
150 REM       R$ = LETTER READ STRING
160 REM       F$ = LETTER FILE NAME
170 REM    FILES USED
180 REM       INPUT FILE = ADDRESS
190 REM       INPUT FILES = LETTER1, LETTER2, LETTER3
200 CLEAR 1000
210 REM    FILE INITIALIZATION
220 OPEN "I", 1, "ADDRESS"
230 :
240 REM    OTHER INPUT FILE IS USER SELECTED AND OPENED AT THAT TIME
250 :
```

```
260 REM    READ NAME, ADDRESS
270 IF EOF(1) THEN 620
280 INPUT #1, N$
290 :
```

The program assigns the first name and address dataset string to variable N$ in line 280. Notice that the program tests for the EOF marker *before* the first datum is read from the file. Always include this test before a file input statement.

Now it's your turn. Have the program display the party's name on the CRT, and then ask the user to select the letter to be printed to this party. Fill in lines 320, 330, and 340.

(a)
```
290 :
300 REM    DISPLAY NAME/ LETTER REQUEST
310 CLS
320                                          :REM   PRINT NAME,
                                                    LINE FEED
330                                          :REM   ASK FOR LETTER
                                                    #(R$)
340                                          :REM   TEST IF R$ IS
                                                    1,2, OR 3
350 :
```

(a)
```
290:
300 REM    DISPLAY NAME/ LETTER REQUEST
310 CLS
320 PRINT LEFT$(N$,20): PRINT
330 LINE INPUT "WHICH LETTER?"; R$
340 IF VAL(R$) < 1 OR VAL(R$) > 3 THEN PRINT "ERROR. LETTERS 1-3
    ONLY": GOTO 330
350 :
```

Examine the following routine for creating the name of an existing data file.

```
350 :
360 REM    INITIALIZE LETTER FILE
370 LET F$ = "LETTER"+ R$
380 OPEN "I", 2, F$
390 :
```

(a) If the user enters 2, in response to "WHICH LETTER?", what file name is created and assigned to F$?

(a) LETTER2 (note the string concatenation in line 370).

Write the inside address printing statements (to be printed by the line printer). Fill in lines 410, 420, 430, and 440.

(a)
```
390 :
400 REM    PRINT INSIDE ADDRESS
410                                       :REM    LINE FEED 3 TIMES
                                                  USING CHR$(138)
420
430                                       :REM    PRINT NAME
440                                       :REM    ADDRESS
450 :                                     :REM    CITY, STATE, ZIP
```

(a)
```
390:
400 REM    PRINT INSIDE ADDRESS
410 PRINT CHR$(138): LPRINT CHR$(138): LPRINT CHR$(138)
420 LPRINT LEFT$(N$,20)
430 LPRINT MID$(N$,21,20)
440 LPRINT MID$(N$,41,10), MID$(N$,51,2), RIGHT$(N$,5)
450 :
```

This next routine prints the salutation. Notice how the city name is extracted from N$ in line 480.

```
450 :
460 REM    PRINT SALUTATION
470 LPRINT CHR$(138): LPRINT CHR$(138)
480 LPRINT "DEAR RESIDENT OF"; MID$(N$,41,10)
490 :
```

(a) For practice, write a BASIC statement that would print this alternate salutation: HELLO THERE ALL YOU FOLKS AT (street address)

(a) LPRINT "HELLO THERE ALL YOU FOLKS AT"; MID$(N$,21,20)

The next routine to print the text of the letter is fairly straightforward. The data input loop continues until that file data are exhausted. Assume that all line feeds and carriage returns are included with the text in the data file.

```
490 :
500 REM    PRINT LETTER TEXT
510 REM      WHICH INCLUDES TOP OF FORM CODES
520 IF EOF(2) THEN 580
530 LINE INPUT #2, R$
540 LPRINT R$
550 GOTO 520
```

continued on next page

```
560 :
570 REM     CLOSE LETTER FILE AND RETURN FOR NEXT ADDRESS
580 CLOSE 2
590 GOTO 270
600 :
```

(a) Give two reasons for closing the letter file in line 580.

(b) Why use LINE INPUT #2 in line 530 instead of just INPUT?

(c) Without checking back, what happens in line 270, which is branched to from line 590 GOTO 270?

— — — — — — — — — — — — — — —

(a) Resets the pointer so that the letter can be used again, and only one OPEN statement is needed for all letter files.
(b) LINE INPUT permits entering data that includes commas and quotation marks, as might be included in the text of a letter. (MICROSOFT BASIC)
(c) EOF tests and next name and address data set is read.

And now, you write the last routine necessary to properly complete this program by completing line 620.

(a) 610 REM
620
630 PRINT "JOB COMPLETED"

— — — — — — — — — — — — — — —

(a)
```
600 :
610 REM CLOSE ADDRESS FILE
620 CLOSE 1
630 PRINT "JOB COMPLETED"
640 :
```

Following is a complete listing of the letter-writing program.

```
100 REM     LETTER WRITING PROGRAM
110 :
120 REM     VARIABLES USED
130 REM       N$ = NAME, ADDRESS, ETC
140 REM       R$ = RESPONSE STRING
150 REM       R$ = LETTER READ STRING
160 REM       F$ = LETTER FILE NAME
170 REM     FILES USED
180 REM       INPUT FILE = ADDRESS
190 REM       INPUT FILES = LETTER1, LETTER2, LETTER3
200 CLEAR 1000
210 REM     FILE INITIALIZATION
220 OPEN "I", 1, "ADDRESS"
230 :
240 REM     OTHER INPUT FILE IS USER SELECTED AND OPENED AT THAT TIME
250 :
260 REM     READ NAME, ADDRESS
270 IF EOF(1) THEN 620
280 INPUT #1, N$
290 :
300 REM     DISPLAY NAME/LETTER REQUEST
310 CLS
320 PRINT LEFT$(N$,20): PRINT
330 LINE INPUT "WHICH LETTER?"; R$
340 IF VAL(R$) < 1 OR VAL(R$) > 3 THEN PRINT "ERROR. LETTERS 1-3 ONLY":
    GOTO 330
350 :
360 REM     INITIALIZE LETTER FILE
370 LET F$ = "LETTER" + R$
380 OPEN "I", 2, F$
390 :
400 REM     PRINT INSIDE ADDRESS
410 LPRINT CHR$(138): LPRINT CHR$(138): LPRINT CHR$(138)
420 LPRINT LEFT$(N$,20)
430 LPRINT MID$(N$,21,20)
440 LPRINT MID$(N$,41,10), MID$(N$,51,2), RIGHT$(N$,5)
450 :
460 REM     PRINT SALUTATION
470 LPRINT CHR$(138): LPRINT CHR$(138)
480 LPRINT "DEAR RESIDENT OF"; MID$(N$,41,10)
490 :
500 REM     PRINT LETTER NEXT
510 REM      WHICH INCLUDES TOP OF FORM CODES
520 IF EOF(2) THEN 580
530 LINE INPUT #2, R$
540 LPRINT R$
550 GOTO 520
560 :
570 REM      CLOSE LETTER FILE AND RETURN FOR NEXT ADDRESS
580 CLOSE 2
590 GOTO 270
```

continued on next page

```
600 :
610 REM CLOSE ADDRESS FILE
620 CLOSE 1
630 PRINT "JOB COMPLETED"
640 :
```

CHAPTER 5 SELF-TEST

1. Write a program to make a copy of the ADDRESS file that you created in the Chapter 4 Self-Test problem (5).

2a. Write a program to create a sequential data file whose data items are the titles of computer magazines. Use the files shown below, and enter the items in each file in alphabetical order.

File One:	File Two:
BYTE Magazine	Creative Computing
Compute	DATAMATION
Dr. Dobbs Journal	Interface Age
Kilobaud Microcomputing	ON Computing
Recreational computing	Personal Computing

2b. Write a program to merge into one alphabetically organized sequential data file, two data files whose data items are the titles of computer magazines. The data in the two files are already in alphabetical order and contain the following two sets of data:

3. Write a program that allows you to enter into a data file a list of household maintenance tasks to be done and allows you to add to or delete from the data file.

Answer Key

1.
```
100 REM     PROB 5-1
110 :
120 REM     VARIABLES USED
130 REM     N$(20) = NAME
140 REM     A$(20) = ADDRESS
150 REM     C$(10) = CITY
160 REM     S$(2) = STATE
170 REM     Z$(5) = ZIP CODE
180 REM     D$(57) = ENTIRE DATASET
190 REM     F$ = COPY FILE
200 :
210 REM     FILES USED = ADDRESS
220 REM     COPY FILE = USER DEFINED
230 :
240 REM     INITIALIZE
250 LINE INPUT "ENTER NAME OF COPY FILE"; F$
260 OPEN "I", 1, "ADDRESS"
270 OPEN "O", 2, F$
280 :
290 REM     READ/COPY FILE
300 IF EOF(1) THEN 360
310 INPUT #1, D$
320 PRINT #2, D$
330 GOTO 300
340 :
350 REM     CLOSE FILE
360 CLOSE
370 :
```

2a.
```
100 REM     PROB5-2A SOLUTION
110 :
120 REM     VARIABLES USED
130 REM       F$ = FILE NAME
140 REM       M$ = DATA (MAGAZINE)
150 REM       R$ = USER RESPONSE
160 :
170 REM     FILES USED
180 REM      USER DEFINED SEQ. OUTPUT FILE
190 :
200 REM     INITIALIZATION
210 CLEAR 500
220 LINE INPUT "ENTER FILE NAME:"; F$
230 OPEN "O", 1, F$
240 :
250 REM     DATA ENTRY
260 PRINT "IF NO MORE MAGAZINES TO ENTER, TYPE 'STOP'."
270 LINE INPUT "MAGAZINE NAME?"; M$
280 IF M$ = "STOP" THEN 360
290 IF ASC(M$) = 0 THEN PRINT "PLEASE ENTER MAGAZINE NAME.": GOTO 260
300 IF LEN(M$) < 40 THEN LET M$ = M$ + " " : GOTO 300
310 REM     OTHER DATA ENTRY TESTS WOULD GO HERE
320 PRINT #1, M$
330 CLS
340 GOTO 260
350 REM     CLOSE FILE
360 CLOSE
370 PRINT "FILE CLOSED"
380 :
```

2b.

```
100 REM     PROB5-2B
110 :
120 REM     VARIABLES USED
130 REM       F1$,F2$,F3$ = FILE NAMES
140 REM       D1$,D2$ = DATA FROM FILES 1,2
150 REM       R$ = USER RESPONSE
160 :
170 REM     FILES USED
180 REM       TWO SEQ. INPUT FILES, USER DEFINED
190 REM       SEQ OUTPUT FILE, USER DEFINED
200 :
210 REM     INITIALIZATION
220 CLEAR 500
230 LINE INPUT "ENTER NAME OF INPUT FILE #1:"; F1$
240 LINE INPUT "ENTER NAME OF INPUT FILE #2:"; F2$
250 LINE INPUT "ENTER NAME OF OUTPUT FILE:"; F3$
260 :
270 OPEN "I", 1, F1$
280 OPEN "I", 2, F2$
290 OPEN "O", 3, F3$
300 PRINT "WORKING - - - MERGE IN PROGRESS"
310 :
320 REM     READ FILE 1
330 IF EOF(1) THEN 590
340 INPUT #1, D1$
350 :
360 REM     READ FILE 2
370 IF EOF(2) THEN 640
380 INPUT #2, D2$
390 :
400 REM     MERGE TESTING
410 LET K = 1
420 IF ASC(MID$(D1$,K,1)) < ASC(MID$(D2$,K,1)) THEN 470
430 IF ASC(MID$(D1$,K,1)) = ASC(MID$(D2$,K,1)) THEN K = K + 1: GOTO 420
440 GOTO 530
450 :
460 REM     PRINT FILE 1 TO 3
470 PRINT #3, D1$
480 IF EOF(1) THEN 590
490 INPUT #1, D1$
500 GOTO 410
510:
520 REM     PRINT FILE 2 TO 3
530 PRINT #3, D2$
540 IF EOF(2) THEN 640
550 INPUT #2, D2$
560 GOTO 410
570 :
580 REM    DUMP FILE 2 TO 3
590 PRINT #3, D2$
600 IF EOF(2) THEN 700
605 INPUT #2, D2$
610 GOTO 590
620 :
630 REM     DUMP FILE 1 TO 3
640 PRINT #3, D1$
650 IF EOF(1) THEN 700
660 INPUT #1, D1$
670 GOTO 640
680 :
```

continued on next page

```
690 REM    CLOSE FILES
700 CLOSE 1,2,3
710 CLS
720 PRINT "MERGE COMPLETED"
730 PRINT: PRINT
740 LINE INPUT "WOULD YOU LIKE TO SEE THE MERGED FILE?"; R$
750 IF LEFT$(R$,1) = "N" THEN 850
760 :
770 REM    DISPLAY CONTENTS OF MERGED FILE
780 OPEN "I", 1, F3$
790 IF EOF(1) THEN 840
800 INPUT #1, D1$
810 PRINT D1$
820 GOTO 790
830 REM    CLOSE FILE
840 CLOSE
850 END
```

3.

```
100 REM    PROB 5-3 SOLUTION
110 :
120 REM    VARIABLES USED
130 REM      F$ = FILE NAME
140 REM      R$,C$ = RESPONSE STRING
150 REM      M$ = TASK
160 REM    INITIALIZE
170 LINE INPUT "ENTER FILE NAME:"; F$
180 OPEN "I", 1, F$
190 OPEN "O", 2, "TEMPFIL"
200 :
210 LINE INPUT "DO YOU WISH TO ADD OR DELETE FROM THE FILE (A/D):"; R$
220 IF R$ <> "A" AND R$ <> "D" THEN PRINT "ENTRY ERROR. REENTER":GOTO 210
230 IF R$ = "A" THEN 390
240 :
250 REM    DELETE ROUTINE
260 PRINT "AS THE FILE DATA APPEARS ON THE SCREEN"
270 PRINT "PRESS ENTER TO ACCEPT, TYPE D TO DELETE"
280 :
290 IF EOF(1) THEN 500
300 INPUT #1, M$
310 PRINT M$
320 LINE INPUT "PRESS ENTER OR D:"; C$
330 IF LEN(C$) = 0 THEN 290
340 :
350 PRINT #2, M$
360 GOTO 290
370 :
380 REM    ADD TO FILE ROUTINE
390 IF EOF(1) THEN 440
400 INPUT #1, M$
410 PRINT #2, M$
420 GOTO 390
430 :
440 LINE INPUT "ENTER NEW TASK OR STOP:"; M$
450 IF M$ = "STOP" THEN 500
460 PRINT #2, M$
470 GOTO 440
480 :
490 REM    COPY TEMPFIL TO FILE
500 CLOSE 1,2
510 :
```

```
520 OPEN "I", 1, "TEMPFIL"
530 OPEN "O", 2, F$
540 :
550 IF EOF(1) THEN 600
560 INPUT #1, M$
570 PRINT #2, M$
580 GOTO 550
590 :
600 CLOSE 1,2
610 END
```

CHAPTER SIX

Cassette Tape Data Files

Objectives: In this chapter, you will learn to use those sequential disk data file techniques and statements that apply to sequential *cassette* data files and to write programs for creating and using cassette data files.

INTRODUCTION

Now that you can use sequential data files, let's extend this understanding to saving data files on *cassette* tapes rather than magnetic disks. Radio Shack TRS-80 users will find this chapter tailored especially for them.

If you want to apply your knowledge of data files to cassette files and have the computer system to do so, this chapter teaches you to manipulate data files on cassettes. This is a different operation than saving BASIC programs onto a cassette (using CSAVE) or loading programs from cassettes (using CLOAD). This discussion is on sequential data files; the same kind you learned to use in Chapters 4 and 5.

Before getting into the subject, however, we offer our editorial opinion on cassette data files. If you are planning to do a lot of serious programming using data files, then buy a disk drive at your earliest convenience. Cassette data files are not only difficult to work with, but are also limited in the scope of things you can do with them. They are sensitive to sound, interference, tape quality, dirt, recorder operation errors, and a host of other factors difficult to control. Cassette tape files are neither fun nor easy to work with, especially after using a computer system with disks. In contrast to disks, cassettes are notoriously slow. At the very least, we recommend using a dual recorder system to increase the capabilities available to you as a user of cassette data files.

In spite of the horror stories of erased tapes, tape reading errors, writing and recording errors, and the like, if you are calm, methodical, and cautious, you can successfully use cassette data files. And practice, of course, helps.

A good way to eliminate some potential problems is to always use high quality cassette tapes made specifically for computer use, rather than trying to get by with inexpensive audio recording tapes. Cassettes made for computer use come without a blank leader at either end. The leader material found in audio recording tapes is not magnetically coated like the rest of the tape and, therefore, will not record data. When the cassette is read, the first part of the data simply will not be there. Using cassettes made for computer applications will eliminate aggrevation and errors caused by your system trying to record data on the leader. So leaderless tape is highly recommended.

In your programs to read from or write to cassettes, include messages giving instructions on the recorder's physical operation. While software and recorders that give more program control over cassette operation are becoming available, you may find that a certain amount of button pushing is inevitable. Avoid errors by having reminder messages at appropriate places, such as in the following excerpt from a program RUN.

```
LOAD EMPTY CASSETTE TAPE
PRESS RECORD/PLAY BUTTONS
PRESS ENTER KEY TO CONTINUE
.
.
.
STOP CASSETTE
REWIND TO BEGINNING OF TAPE
PRESS PLAY BUTTON
PRESS ENTER KEY TO CONTINUE
```

PRINTING TO AND READING FROM A CASSETTE TAPE DATA FILE

The set of BASIC instructions used with cassette tape files is much like that of disk files, only easier! The file number (after #) for a cassette recording device is a negative number (-1); for a second recorder the number is -2. Therefore, the file input statement has the following format:

```
180 INPUT #-1, A, B$, C$
```

Similarly, the format for the file print statement includes that same negative number to indicate "cassette" to the computer.

```
200 PRINT #-1, A, B$, C$
```

Easy! Note that in the PRINT #-1 statement, you do *not* have to force commas between the string variables with quotation marks, as was necessary in the version of MICROSOFT BASIC for disks used in the previous chapters. Also cassette files do *not* need OPEN or CLOSE statements since no directory of data files exists on a cassette for the computer to refer to, and the rest is taken care of by turning the recorder on and off. Furthermore, there is no buffer to worry about. The cassette INPUT # and PRINT # statements operate directly with the cassette recorder with no buffer as intermediary.

It sounds easy, doesn't it? So why the concern expressed earlier? Wait – you have only begun. There are other rules of syntax and usage that must be followed.

(1) On the TRS-80 with Level II, you must disable the timing mechanism before any cassette operations. Use the DOS command CMD"T" to disable the timer or you will get nothing but "garbage" data on the tape. The DOS command CMD"R" reenables the timer.

(2) Data items in a cassette tape file are separated by a gap of blank tape (no data recorded). If you use three separate PRINT # statements with one variable each, instead of a single PRINT # statement with three variables, you use three times as much tape. For example, these three statements:

```
PRINT #-1, A
PRINT #-1, B
PRINT #-1, C
```

use three times as much tape as:

```
PRINT #-1, A, B, C
```

This circumstance further reinforces the desireability of using one INPUT # or PRINT # statement for an entire dataset, rather than one data item at a time.

(3) If you use a statement such as PRINT #-1, A, B, C (with three variables) to copy datasets onto the file, then you must use an INPUT # statement with an identical number of variables to read back the datasets. The statement INPUT #-1, X, Y, Z would work since it also has three numeric variables. If the INPUT # statement has only one or two variables, the result will be input errors. The real problem arises if you forget or lose track of how the data were printed to the file. Therefore, always immediately and accurately label the cassette with information on how to read back the contents of the data file, by specifying the format of the PRINT # statement.

(4) If the data was printed to the file with a numeric variable to start with, our reference manual says that you must then read that numeric value from the tape into a numeric variable. That means to read data that were recorded with a statement such as PRINT #-1, A use a statement such as INPUT #-1, A. In practice, we found this untrue. We tried this:

```
PRINT #-1, A, B, C
```

followed by:

```
INPUT #-1, A$, B$, C$
```

And it worked. The numeric values in the data file were correctly assigned to string variables, but as strings, of course. However, the reverse was not true. Data placed in the file as strings, whether numbers or other alphanumeric characters, could not be assigned to numeric variables. The following sequence resulted in an error message and the program stopped execution:

```
PRINT #-1, A$, B$, C$
```

followed by:

```
100 INPUT #-1, A, B, C
```

gave us this error message:

```
WRONG DATA TYPE IN LINE 100
```

(5) We found that the computer would sometimes "hang up" and not respond to the BREAK key or anything else if it was looking for data on a part of the cassette tape past the place where data actually existed. We had to reset the system, thereby losing the program in the computer's memory. Resolve this problem by using a program-generated end-of-file marker or flag, essentially a piece of "dummy data," that the program can test for. The technique will be presented as a substitute for the EOF test used for disk files. It is always good practice to rewind cassettes so you don't accidentally try to read from an unrecorded section of tape.

With this background, you are ready to proceed with some practice examples. First, go back to the program developed in Chapter 4 to be used for a property inventory file. The datasets for the disk file included a property description, number of items, and a dollar value. Here is the sequential *disk* file program for you to adapt for cassette files.

```
100 REM    INVENTORY FILE LOAD PROGRAM
110 :
120 REM    VARIABLES USED
130 REM       D$ = DESCRIPTION (20)
140 REM       N = NUMBER OF ITEMS
150 REM       V = DOLLAR VALUE
160 :
170 REM    FILES USED
180 REM       PROPERTY = SEQUENTIAL FILE
190 :
200 REM    INITIALIZE
210 OPEN "O", 1, "PROPERTY"
220 :
230 REM    DATA ENTRY ROUTINES
240 LINE INPUT "ENTER ITEM DESCRIPTION:"; D$
250 IF LEN(D$) > 20 THEN PRINT "PLEASE ABBREVIATE TO 20 CHAR. AND
    REENTER": GOTO 240
260 IF LEN(D$) = 0 THEN PRINT "PLEASE ENTER A DESCRIPTION OR WE CANNOT
    CONTINUE": GOTO 240
270 INPUT "HOW MANY ITEMS"; N
280 IF N <> INT(N) THEN PRINT "ENTER INTEGER NUMBERS ONLY.": GOTO 270
290 IF N = <0 THEN PRINT "THERE MUST BE SOME UNITS. PLEASE ENTER A
    QUANTITY": GOTO 270
300 INPUT "WHAT IS THE DOLLAR VALUE OF EACH"; V
310 IF V =< 0 THEN 350
```

```
320 PRINT #1, D$; ","; N; V
325 LINE INPUT "MORE DATA (YES OR NO):"; R$
326 IF LEFT$(R$,1) = "N" THEN 410
330 GOTO 240
340 :
350 LINE INPUT "DID YOU REALLY MEAN ZERO VALUE, YES OR NO:"; R$
360 IF LEFT$(R$,1) = "N" THEN PRINT "THEN REENTER THE CORRECT VALUE":
    GOTO 300
370 GOTO 320
380 :
400 REM    FILE CLOSE ROUTINE
410 CLOSE 1
420 :
499 END
```

(a) List the changes, including deletions, to make in the program above to adapt it to cassette tape data files.

(a)

```
180 REM*** PROPERTY *CASSETTE TAPE FILE
200 DELETE
210 DELETE
320 PRINT #-1, D$, N, V
400 DELETE
410 DELETE
```

In addition to the above changes, a well-designed program would include these instructions:

```
200 REM*** INITIALIZE
210 PRINT "PLACE CASSETTE TAPE INTO RECORDER"
220 PRINT "PRESS RECORD/PLAY BUTTONS"
400 REM
410 PRINT "STOP RECORDER AND REWIND TAPE"
```

If you have a cassette recorder handy, run this program and load a cassette file with some property data. You can also write the companion program to read from the file and prepare a screen display or printed report on the data. Complete lines 210 and 220.

(a)
```
100 REM     PROPERTY CASSETTE FILE READER
110 :
120 REM     VARIABLES USED
130 REM       D$ = DESCRIPTION(20)
140 REM       N = NUMBER OF ITEMS
150 REM       V = DOLLAR VALUE OF EACH ITEM
160 :
170 REM     FILES USED
180 REM       PROPERTY - CASSETTE FILE
190 :
200 REM     INITIALIZE
210 REM                                   :REM    GIVE THE OPERATOR
                                                  INSTRUCTIONS FOR
                                                  RECORDER
220 REM                                   :REM    PRESS ENTER TO
                                                  CONTINUE MESSAGE
230 :
240 REM     PRINT REPORT HEADINGS
250 PRINT "ITEMS", "QUANTITY", "VALUE EACH"
260 :
```

(a)
```
210 PRINT "LOAD CASSETTE TAPE. IS IT REWOUND?"
220 INPUT "PRESS ENTER TO CONTINUE": X$
```

Now, complete the program by following the on-line remarks.

(a)
```
260 :
270 REM   READ THE FILE/PRINT REPORT
280                                  :REM    READ FILE DATA
290                                  :REM    PRINT REPORT
300                                  :REM    RETURN TO FILE READ
310 :
```

(a)
```
280 INPUT #-1, D$, N, V
290 PRINT D$, N, V
300 GOTO 280
```

(Note: you can use different variable names, but they should be a string variable followed by two numeric variables.)

Here is a complete listing of the program:

```
100 REM     PROPERTY CASSETTE FILE READER
110 :
120 REM     VARIABLES USED
130 REM       D$ = DESCRIPTION(20)
140 REM       N = NUMBER OF ITEMS
150 REM       V = DOLLAR VALUE OF EACH ITEM
160 :
170 REM     FILES USED
180 REM       PROPERTY - CASSETTE FILE
190 :
200 REM     INITIALIZE
210 PRINT "LOAD CASSETTE TAPE. IS IT REWOUND?"
220 INPUT "PRESS ENTER TO CONTINUE"; X$
230 :
240 REM     PRINT REPORT HEADINGS
250 PRINT "ITEMS", "QUANTITY", "VALUE EACH"
260 :
270 REM     READ THE FILE/PRINT REPORT
280 INPUT #-1, D$, N, V
290 PRINT D$, N, V
300 GOTO 280
310 :
```

(a) When the program above is RUN, how will it terminate?

(a) With an "out of data" message. (There is no end-of-file test.)

Cassette tape file operations do not include an end-of-file test. Under normal conditions the program aborts with an error message when the last data item is read. To avoid this problem, go back to the file loading program and make an addition. The easy way to create an end of file marker is to place false or dummy data at the end of the file – something that can be checked by an IF. . .THEN statement. You can use STOP, or *, or 999, or -1, or whatever false data item you choose. However, choose something that is easy to remember and that will definitely not be part of the file's legitimate data. Also remember to note on the cassette label the end of the file marker you have used, as well as the format for the variable list or dataset.

(a) Refer to the program for placing the property inventory data into a cassette file. Using an asterisk (*) as a dummy string item, write a statement to place an end-of-file marker in the proper program location to be written as the last data in the cassette file.

(b) Why are three items needed for the dummy data?

(c) Refer to the previous program. Write a statement in the correct program location to test for the end-of-file marker and, if present, branch to the following segment:

```
400 PRINT "JOB COMPLETED"
410 END
```

(a) `410 PRINT #-1, "*", 0, 0` (Change the other 410 "message" to 415)
(Note: statement must be placed before END and before the recorder has been turned off.)

(b) The dataset is loaded into and is read back from the file in this format. If only one data item is available for the last INPUT # statement, a file reading error will occur.

(c) `285 IF D$ = "*" THEN 400`

To remove old data from a cassette tape, whether data files or programs, always use a magnetic tape bulk eraser. If you count on the erase head built into your recorder to adequately erase old data before new data are recorded on the same area of tape, you are likely to end up with problems. The built-in erase head doesn't always adequately clear the tape for computer applications. An unerased "bit" or two would be inaudible if you were reusing a tape for audio recordings, but an unerased "bit" from a previous data file could cause errors in a second data file recorded over the same stretch of tape. This is also a reason for putting only one data file on a cassette tape. Besides the convenience of not having to search a tape for a particular data file, you can bulk erase an entire tape for reuse when the contents are no longer of value.

Your greatest problems probably will not be in programming, but rather in actually operating the cassette recorder and dealing with the tapes. Programming complexity is further reduced if you have two cassette recorders. The programs developed in Chapter 5 work with dual cassettes with only minor modifications. You can adapt those programs to copy, make changes in data, edit, etc., as you did for disk data files and as discussed later in this chapter.

If you have only one cassette recorder, you can still write file utility programs as you did before, but it takes more programming. Most of the previous utility applications used a temporary disk file, a technique not available to cassette users. Instead of a temporary disk file, cassette users must use an array or multiple arrays in the computer's electronic memory as the temporary file. Otherwise, procedures are similar to those used for disk files. The limitation of the array storage method for the temporary file is the amount of computer memory available. For cassette files with large amounts of data to be transferred to arrays, you may find your computer's memory filled beyond its capacity, meaning the program will not be able to do its job.

Now let's develop a model utility program to copy an existing cassette data file onto a new cassette tape. But first, write a program to enter the data for the original cassette data file, the one that will later be copied. Here are the specifications for that program and data file:

1. The data items are numeric values in the range from 1 to 100, representing statistical information (such as age, driving speed, or the like). Include a data entry check for these parameters.
2. The values are copied onto the file with a PRINT # statement using one variable (one value at a time).
3. You may enter as few values as you wish. We suggest a minimum of a couple of dozen values and as many as 350 to 400 values. Using a large number of values in the file gives you a feel for the amount of time it takes to manipulate cassette data files.
4. Place -999 as the ending data flag at the end of the file data.

(a) Now write the program and create the data file on your computer.

(a)

```
100 REM    STAT1 DATA ENTRY
120 REM    FILES-  STAT1 CASSETTE TAPE
130 :
240 REM    DATA ENTRY WITH TESTS
210 INPUT "ENTER VALUE OR -999"; V
220 IF V = -999 THEN 299
230 IF V < 1 OR V > 100 THEN PRINT "DATA ERROR. PLS. REENTER":
    GOTO 210
240 PRINT #-1, V
250 GOTO 210
299 PRINT #-1, -999
300 END
```

Now write a simple cassette file copy routine, assuming you have only one recorder. The key to the technique involved is to think of the array(s) as the temporary file. You have a cassette file filled with numeric values originally recorded onto the file with a program that had a PRINT # statement that looked like this:

```
PRINT #-1, V
```

Remember, you need to know that information in order to read the file correctly. Assume that the values in the file represent statistical data you want to send to a friend in another state, so you need a cassette copy. The file has between 350 and 400 values. You need to know how many data items are in the file so you can correctly dimension the array. Here is the introductory module.

```
100 REM    NUMERIC FILE COPY
110 :
120 REM    VARIABLES USED
130 REM      V = VALUE FROM FILE
140 REM      K = COUNTER
150 REM      T = ARRAY
160 REM      X = ARRAY DIMENSION(VARIABLE)
170 :
180 REM    FILES USED
190 REM      STAT1 = CASSETTE TAPE FILE
200 REM      STAT1A = OUTPUT FILE COPY
210 REM    END-OF-FILE FLAG IS # -999
220 :
230 REM    INITIALIZE
240 CLS
250 PRINT "PLACE STAT1 CASSETTE ON RECORDER."
```

```
260 INPUT "REWIND AND THEN PRESS PLAY BUTTON"
270 INPUT "PRESS ENTER TO CONTINUE"; R$
280 :
290 INPUT "ABOUT HOW MANY ITEMS ON THE FILE"; X
300 DIM T(X)
310 LET K = 0
320 :
```

Look at line 290. At the moment you can't know exactly how many data items are in the file, so you have the program ask "ABOUT HOW MANY?" The program uses this value to dimension the array. If you overestimate this value by too much, you could be reserving more computer memory space for the array than is available on your system, so be realistic. Line 310 initializes a variable, K, used to count the data items as they are read from the cassette data file into the array. Now, fill in the blanks in the next program segment (lines 340, 350, 360, and 370).

(a)
```
320 :
330 REM     READ FILE INTO ARRAY
340                                         :REM    READ VALUE
                                                    FROM FILE
350                                         :REM    FLAG TEST/
                                                    GOTO 410
360                                         :REM    INCREMENT
                                                    COUNTER K BY 1
370                                         :REM    PLACE VALUE
                                                    INTO T ARRAY
380 GOTO 340
390 :
```

(a)
```
320 :
330 REM     READ FILE INTO ARRAY
340 INPUT #-1, V
350 IF V = -999 THEN 410
360 LET K = K + 1
370 LET T(K) = V
380 GOTO 340
390 :
```

In line 340 you may have done this: INPUT #-1, T(K) which is acceptable, but for later applications it is better not to assign the data item to an array element directly. Rather, temporarily assign each data item to the variable V until the end of file check and counter incrementing is accomplished.

(a) If the statement at line 350 detects the end of data marker, what routines will start at line 410?

- - - - - - - - - - - - - - - -

(a) Instructions to change cassette tapes, followed by the array copy routine.

Now, complete the crucial statement in the next program segment (line 490).

(a)
```
390 :
400 REM     INITIALIZE FILE COPY
410 CLS
420 PRINT "REWIND STAT1 TAPE"
430 PRINT "PLACE STAT1A TAPE ON RECORDER"
440 PRINT "PRESS RECORD/PLAY BUTTONS"
450 INPUT "PRESS ENTER TO CONTINUE"; R$
460 :
470 REM     COPY ARRAY TO CASSETTE
480 FOR Y = 1 TO K
490                              :REM    PRINT VALUE TO CASSETTE
500 NEXT Y
510 :
```

(b) Why is it necessary to use counter K to count the data items?

- - - - - - - - - - - - - - - -

(a)
```
490 PRINT #-1, T(Y)
```
(b) When the array is copied to the new cassette, the program must know how much of the array contains valid data.

For this application the program concludes by writing an end of file marker (-999) in the data file just copied.

```
510 :
520 REM     PRINT EOF MARKER
530 PRINT #-1, -999
540 PRINT "JOB COMPLETE"
550 :
```

Use part of the copy program to prepare an add-to-file program. Can you see what changes have to be made?

```
100 REM     NUMERIC FILE COPY
110 :
120 REM     VARIABLES USED
130 REM       V = VALUE FROM FILE
140 REM     K = COUNTER
150 REM       T = ARRAY
160 REM     X = ARRAY DIMENSION(VARIABLE)
170 :
180 REM     FILES USED
190 REM       STAT1 = CASSETTE TAPE FILE
200 REM       STAT1A = OUTPUT FILE COPY
210 REM     END-OF-FILE FLAG IS # -999
220 :
230 REM     INITIALIZE
240 CLS
250 PRINT "PLACE STAT1 CASSETTE ON RECORDER."
260 INPUT "REWIND AND THEN PRESS PLAY BUTTON"
270 INPUT "PRESS ENTER TO CONTINUE"; R$
280 :
290 INPUT "ABOUT HOW MANY ITEMS ON THE FILE"; X
300 DIM T(X)
310 LET K = 0
320 :
330 REM     READ FILE INTO ARRAY
340 INPUT #-1, V
350 IF V = -999 THEN 410
360 LET K = K + 1
370 LET T(K) = V
380 GOTO 340
390 :
400 REM     INITIALIZE FILE COPY
410 CLS
420 PRINT "REWIND STAT1 TAPE"
430 PRINT "PLACE STAT1A TAPE ON RECORDER"
440 PRINT "PRESS RECORD/PLAY BUTTONS"
450 INPUT "PRESS ENTER TO CONTINUE"; R$
460 :
470 REM     COPY ARRAY TO CASSETTE
480 FOR Y = 1 TO K
490 PRINT #-1, T(Y)
500 NEXT Y
510 :
```

Surprise! You can use all of the copy program up to line 510.

Up to now the program can copy the original file into an array and then onto a new cassette file. You can just reuse the original tape if you're confident that you don't need a back-up copy.

(a) Describe what the program to add-to-file should do in the routine beginning at line 520.

(b) Fill in the blanks for the routine you described in (a) (540, 550, and 560).

```
510 :
520 REM     ENTER NEW DATA ITEMS(-999 TO STOP)
530 REM     PRINT TO FILE
540                                        :REM    DATA ENTRY
                                                   TO V
550                                        :REM    PRINT TO
                                                   FILE
560                                        :REM    END TEST/
                                                   GOTO 540
570 END
580 :
```

(c) How does the program know to stop asking for more new data?

(a) Provide for entry of new data and add it to the new file.

(b)

```
510 :
520 REM     ENTER NEW DATA ITEMS(-999 TO STOP)
530 REM     PRINT TO FILE
540 INPUT "ENTER DATA ITEM"; V
550 PRINT #-1, V
560 IF V <> -999 THEN 540
570 END
580 :
```

(c) By checking to see whether the user has entered the end of file marker (-999).

In summary, merely follow the same procedures you would use for disk files, except use an array instead of a temporary disk file.

With the use of arrays as temporary files, it is important to know how many data items are stored in a file so you can properly dimension the arrays. Before you estimated, but here is a variation you might want to consider. You could, as a policy, always keep track of the number of data items in a file and place this figure as the first data item in the cassette tape file. Then use this value to dimension the array. Some changes in procedure are required.

The new procedures are:

1. Read first data item (number of datasets or data items) = X.
2. Ask how many new datasets are to be added = Y.
3. Dimension the array(s) with X + Y.
4. Read the file into the array.

5. Add the new data for the file into the array rather than the new file.
6. When a user signal indicates all new data have been entered, then print the new total number of data items into the new file.
7. Copy the array data items into the new file.

As an example of this procedure, consider the grocery list program from Chapter 5. Here the data entered are item descriptions and quantity (how much of that grocery item to buy). The first data item in the data file tells how many datasets are already contained in the file. The program follows the seven steps outlined above.

```
100 REM     ADD TO CASSETTE GROCERY FILE
110 :
120 REM     VARIABLES USED
130 REM       K = DATASET COUNT
140 REM       A = HOW MANY ADDED DATASETS
150 REM       D$ = ITEM DESCRIPTION
160 REM       N$ = NUMBER NEEDED
170 REM       G$ = ARRAY
180 REM       R$ = RESPONSE STRING
190 :
200 REM     FILES USED
210 REM       GROCERY = CASSETTE FILE
220 :
230 REM     INITIALIZE
240 PRINT "PLACE GROCERY CASSETTE INTO RECORDER"
250 PRINT "PRESS PLAY BUTTON AND IMMEDIATELY"
260 INPUT "PRESS ENTER TO CONTINUE"; R$
270 INPUT #-1, K
280 INPUT "HOW MANY DATASETS WILL BE ADDED"; A
290 DIM G$(K+A,2)
300 :
```

(a) What does line 270 do?

(b) Explain what line 290 does.

(c) Complete line 330.

```
300 :
310 REM     LOAD FILE INTO ARRAY
320 FOR X = 1 TO K
330                                         :REM    INPUT DATASET FROM FILE
340 NEXT X
350 :
```

(d) Examine the FOR NEXT loop in the next program segment and complete lines 430 and 440. Line 370 controls how many new datasets are entered. Line 380 gives the number of the next empty element in the G$ array

```
350 :
360 REM    DATA ENTRY ROUTINE
370 FOR X = 1 TO A
380 LET K = K + 1
390 LINE INPUT "ENTER ITEM DESCRIPTION"; D$
400 LINE INPUT "ENTER QUANTITY NEEDED:"; N$
410 :
420 REM    PLACE DATA INTO ARRAY
430                                              :REM    LOAD D$ INTO ARRAY
440                                              :REM    LOAD N$ INTO ARRAY
450 NEXT X
460 :
```

- - - - - - - - - - - - - - - -

(a) Reads the first data item in the file (number of datasets in the file).

(b) Dimensions array G$ to size K (number of datasets in the file) plus A (number of datasets to be added) by 2 (two items in each dataset).

(c) `330 INPUT #-1, G$(X,1), G$(X,2)`

(d)
```
430 LET G$(K,1) = D$
440 LET G$(K,2) = N$
```

And now to copy the data-filled array onto the new cassette data file or over the old one complete lines 540 and 580.

(a)
```
460 :
470 REM    RECORDER INSTRUCTIONS
480 CLS
490 PRINT "PLACE REWOUND TAPE INTO RECORDER"
500 PRINT "PRESS RECORD/PLAY BUTTONS"
510 INPUT "PRESS ENTER TO CONTINUE"; R$
520 :
530 REM    PRINT NUMBER OF DATASETS INTO FILE
540                                                        :REM
550 :
560 REM    PRINT ARRAY CONTENTS INTO FILE
570 FOR X = 1 TO K
580                                                        :REM
590 NEXT X
600 :
610 PRINT "JOB COMPLETE"
620 :
```

- - - - - - - - - - - - - - - -

(a) Here is the complete program.

```
100 REM     ADD TO CASSETTE GROCERY FILE
110 :
120 REM     VARIABLES USED
130 REM       K = DATASET COUNT
140 REM       A = HOW MANY ADDED DATASETS
150 REM       D$ = ITEM DESCRIPTION
160 REM       N$ = NUMBER NEEDED
170 REM       G$ = ARRAY
180 REM       R$ = RESPONSE STRING
190 :
200 REM     FILES USED
210 REM       GROCERY = CASSETTE FILE
220 :
230 REM     INITIALIZE
240 PRINT "PLACE GROCERY CASSETTE INTO RECORDER"
250 PRINT "PRESS PLAY BUTTON"
260 INPUT "PRESS ENTER TO CONTINUE"; R$
270 INPUT #-1, K
280 INPUT "HOW MANY DATASETS WILL BE ADDED"; A
290 DIM G$(K+A,2)
300 :
310 REM     LOAD FILE INTO ARRAY
320 FOR X = 1 TO K
330 INPUT #-1, G$(X,1), G$(X,2)
340 NEXT X
350 :
360 REM     DATA ENTRY ROUTINE
370 FOR X = 1 TO A
380 LET K = K + 1
390 LINE INPUT "ENTER ITEM DESCRIPTION"; D$
400 LINE INPUT "ENTER QUANTITY NEEDED:"; N$
410 :
420 REM     PLACE DATA INTO ARRAY
430 LET G$(K,1) = D$
440 LET G$(K,2) = N$
450 NEXT X
460 :
470 REM     RECORDER INSTRUCTIONS
480 CLS
490 PRINT "PLACE REWOUND TAPE INTO RECORDER"
500 PRINT "PRESS RECORD/PLAY BUTTONS"
510 INPUT "PRESS ENTER TO CONTINUE"; R$
520 :
530 REM     PRINT NUMBER OF DATASETS INTO FILE
540 PRINT #-1, K
550 :
560 REM     PRINT ARRAY CONTENTS INTO FILE
570 FOR X = 1 TO K
580 PRINT #-1, G$(X,1), G$(X,2)
590 NEXT X
600 :
610 PRINT "JOB COMPLETE"
620 :
```

You now have a background for working with cassette files and can take the disk file programs in the previous chapters and adapt them for cassette data files. Remember, the basic technique is to use arrays as temporary files. Also be aware of the limitations of these procedures, especially the size of the files in relation to the size of your computer's memory. With patience and great care, you can have the advantages of using data files and the inexpensiveness of cassette data storage.

CHAPTER 6 SELF-TEST

1. (a) Write a program to enter datasets into a cassette file. Each dataset contains two string data items, followed by two numeric data items. Include a user response for "MORE DATA?" after each dataset entry and place an end of file dummy data item as the last item of data in the file.

```
110 :
120 REM     VARIABLE LIST
130 REM       A$,B$ = ALPHA DATA
140 REM       C$(C), D$(D) = NUMERIC DATA
150 :
```

1. (b) Write a companion program to Problem 1a to display the contents of the cassette file. Include the end of file test.

```
110 :
120 REM     VARIABLE LIST
130 REM       A$,B$ = ALPHA DATA
140 REM       C,D = NUMERIC DATA
150 :
```

2. (a) Write a grocery list program that allows you to enter the following into a cassette file:

   Item description – twenty characters maximum
   Quantity to buy

   The data entry tests should include a section that displays the entry if the quantity is less than one or more than ten and allows the user to reenter that quantity if needed.

```
120 :
130 REM     VARIABLES USED
140 REM       D$ = ITEM DESCRIPTION
150 REM       Q = QUANTITY TO BUY
160 REM       R$ = USER RESPONSE
170 :
```

2. (b) Write a companion program to the one written in 2a, that displays the grocery file contents.

```
110 :
120 REM    INTRODUCTORY MODULE
130 REM     VARIABLES USED
140 REM       D$ = ITEM DESCRIPTION
150 REM       Q = QUANTITY TO ORDER
160 :
```

3. (a) Write a program to create a cassette file mailing list, as indicated in the variable list below. Concatenate the data items into one dataset per person.

```
110 :
120 REM     VARIABLES USED
130 REM     N$(20) = NAME
140 REM     A$(20) = ADDRESS
150 REM     C$(10) = CITY
160 REM     S$(2) = STATE
170 REM     Z$(5) = ZIP CODE
180 REM     D$(57) = ENTIRE DATASET
190 REM     R$ = USER RESPONSE VARIABLE
200 :
```

3. (b) Write a companion program to count each data item as it is displayed and display the number of the total datasets in the file (1,2,3. . . . Total is 14).

```
110 :
120 REM      VARIABLES USED
130 REM      D$ = ONE ENTIRE DATASET (57 CHAR.)
140 REM      K = DATASET COUNTING VARIABLE
150 :
```

3. (c) Write a program, including recorder user instructions, to make a copy of the mailing list on a separate tape.

```
110 :
120 REM VARIABLES USED
130 REM     D$ = ONE COMPLETE DATASET (57 CHARS.)
140 REM     K = NO. OF DATASETS IN FILE
141 REM     X = FOR-NEXT LOOP CONTROL VARIABLE
142 REM     R$ = 'PRESS ENTER TO CONTINUE' RESPONSE VARIABLE
150 :
```

Answer Key

1 a.

```
100 REM   PROB 6-1A SOLUTION
110 :
120 REM    VARIABLE LIST
130 REM       A$,B$ = ALPHA DATA
140 REM       C$(C), D$(D) = NUMERIC DATA
150 :
160 REM    DATA ENTRY ROUTINE
170 LINE INPUT "ENTER DATA ITEM:"; A$
180 IF LEN(A$) = 0 THEN PRINT "PLEASE ENTER SOMETHING": GOTO 170
190 LINE INPUT "ENTER DATA ITEM 2:"; B$
200 IF LEN(B$) = 0 THEN PRINT "PLEASE ENTER SOME DATA": GOTO 190
210 LINE INPUT "ENTER NUMERIC DATA:"; C$
220 IF LEN(C$) = 0 THEN PRINT "PLEASE ENTER SOMETHING": GOTO 210
230 IF VAL(C$) = 0 THEN PRINT "PLEASE ENTER NUMBERS ONLY": GOTO 210
240 LET C = VAL(C$)
250 LINE INPUT "ENTER NUMERIC ITEM 2:"; D$
260 IF LEN(D$) = 0 THEN PRINT "PLEASE ENTER SOMETHING": GOTO 250
270 IF VAL(D$) = 0 THEN PRINT "PLEASE ENTER NUMBERS ONLY": GOTO 210
280 LET D = VAL(D$)
290 :
300 PRINT #-1, A$, B$, C, D
310 :
320 LINE INPUT "MORE DATA?"; R$
330 IF LEFT$(R$,1) = "Y" THEN 170
340 :
350 REM END-OF-DATA FLAG AND 'DUMMY' DATA FOR OTHER DATA ITEMS
360 PRINT #-1, -999, 0, 0, 0
370 END
```

1 b.

```
100 REM   PROB 6-1B SOLUTION
110 :
120 REM    VARIABLE LIST
130           A$,B$ = ALPHA DATA
140 REM       C,D = NUMERIC DATA
150 :
160 REM    DATA ENTRY FROM FILE
170 :
180 INPUT #-1, A$, B$, C, D
190 IF A$ = -999 THEN 240
200 PRINT A$, B$, C, D
210 GOTO 180
220 :
230 :
240 END
```

2 a.

```
100 REM   PROB 6-2A
110 REM    INTRODUCTORY MODULE
120 :
130 REM    VARIABLES USED
140 REM       D$ = ITEM DESCRIPTION (20 CHAR. MAX.)
150 REM       Q = QUANTITY TO BUY
160 REM       R$ = USER RESPONSE
170 :
180 REM   DATA ENTRY ROUTINE
190 PRINT "ENTER '-999' WHEN FINISHED ENTERING DATA"
```

```
200 PRINT
210 LINE INPUT "ENTER ITEM DESCRIPTION:"; D$
220 IF D$ = "-999" THEN 350
230 IF LEN(D$) = 0 THEN PRINT "PLEASE ENTER A DESCRIPTION OR '-999'":
    GOTO 210
240 IF LEN(D$) > 20 THEN PRINT "PLEASE LIMIT DESCRIPTION TO 20 CHARS.
    AND REENTER": GOTO 210
250 INPUT "ENTER QUANTITY:"; Q
260 IF Q >= 1 AND Q < 10 THEN 320
270 PRINT "YOU ENTERED A QUANTITY OF"; Q
280 LINE INPUT "IS THAT WHAT YOU WANTED?"; R$
290 IF LEFT$(R$,1) = "N" THEN 250
300 :
310 REM    WRITE TO FILE ROUTINE
320 PRINT #-1, D$, Q
330 GOTO 210
340 :
345 REM    END-OF-DATA FLAG AND 'DUMMY' DATA FOR Q
350 PRINT #-1, -999, 0
360 END
```

2 b.

```
100 REM     PROBLEM 6-2B SOLUTION
110 :
120 REM    INTRODUCTORY MODULE
130 REM     VARIABLES USED
140 REM       D$ = ITEM DESCRIPTION
150 REM       Q = QUANTITY TO ORDER
160 :
170 :
180 REM    READ AND PRINT FILE
190 :
200 PRINT "ITEM"; TAB(24); "QUANTITY"
210 INPUT #-1, D$, Q
220 IF D$ = "-999" THEN 250
230 PRINT D$; TAB(24); Q
240 GOTO 210
250 END
```

3 a.

```
100 REM     PROB 6-3A SOLUTION
110 :
120 REM     VARIABLES USED
130 REM     N$(20) = NAME
140 REM     A$(20) = ADDRESS
150 REM     C$(10) = CITY
160 REM     S$(2) = STATE
170 REM     Z$(5) = ZIP CODE
180 REM     D$(57) = ENTIRE DATASET
190 REM     R$ = USER RESPONSE VARIABLE
200 :
210 REM     INITIALIZE
220 CLEAR 1000
230 :
240 REM     DATA ENTRY/TESTS
250 LINE INPUT "ENTER NAME:"; N$
260 REM     DATA TESTS
270 IF LEN(N$) < 20 THEN LET N$ = N$ + " ": GOTO 270
280 LINE INPUT "ENTER ADDRESS:"; A$
```

```
290 REM    DATA TEST
300 IF LEN(A$) < 20 THEN LET A$ = A$ + " ": GOTO 300
310 LINE INPUT "ENTER CITY NAME:"; C$
320 REM    DATA TESTS
330 IF LEN(C$) < 10 THEN LET C$ = C$ + " ": GOTO 330
340 LINE INPUT "ENTER STATE CODE:"; S$
350 REM    DATA TEST
360 IF LEN(S$) <> 2 THEN PRINT "PLEASE ENTER 2 CHARACTER CODE": GOTO 340
370 LINE INPUT  ENTER ZIP CODE: ; Z$
380 IF LEN(Z$) <> 5 THEN PRINT "PLEASE ENTER 5-DIGIT CODE": GOTO 370
390 :
400 LET D$ = N$+A$+C$+S$+Z$
410 :
420 PRINT #-1, D$
430 :
440 LINE INPUT "MORE ENTRIES?"; R$
450 IF LEFT$(R$,1) = "Y" THEN 250
460 :
470 PRINT #-1, "-999"
480 END
```

3 b.

```
100 REM    PROB 6-3B SOLUTION
110 :
120 REM    VARIABLES USED
130 REM    D$ = ONE ENTIRE DATASET (57 CHAR.)
140 REM    K = DATASET COUNTING VARIABLE
150 :
160 REM    INITIALIZE
170 CLEAR 500
180 LET K = 0
190 :
200 REM    READ, COUNT, AND DISPLAY DATASETS
210 READ #-1, D$
220 LET K = K + 1
230 IF D$ = "-999" THEN 270
240 PRINT K; "  "; D$
250 GOTO 210
260 PRINT
270 PRINT "TOTAL DATASETS INCLUDING END OF FILE FLAG;"; K
280 END
```

3 c.

```
100 REM    PROB 6-3C SOLUTION
110 :
120 REM    VARIABLES USED
130 REM    D$ = ONE COMPLETE DATASET (57 CHARS.)
140 REM    K = NO. OF DATASETS IN FILE
141 REM    X = FOR-NEXT LOOP CONTROL VARIABLE
142 REM    R$ = 'PRESS ENTER TO CONTINUE' RESPONSE VARIABLE
150 :
160 REM    INITIALIZE
170 CLEAR 500
180 INPUT "HOW MANY ITEMS IN THIS DATAFILE"; K
190 DIM A$(K)
200 :
210 REM    READ DATASETS INTO ARRAY
220 FOR X = 1 TO K
230 READ #-1, D$
```

```
240 LET A$(X) = D$
250 NEXT X
260 :
270 PRINT "STOP RECORDER. REWIND TAPE. REMOVE FROM RECORDER."
280 PRINT "PLACE NEW TAPE IN RECORDER, REWIND TO BEGINNING."
290 PRINT "PUT RECORDER IN RECORD MODE."
300 LINE INPUT "PRESS 'ENTER' WHEN READY TO CONTINUE."; R$
310 :
320 REM    FIRST DATA ITEM IN NEW FILE IS NO. OF DATASETS
330 PRINT #-1, K
340 :
350 REM    COPY ARRAY TO CASSETTE DATA FILE
360 FOR X = 1 TO K
370 LET D$ = A$(X)
380 PRINT #-1, D$
390 NEXT X
400 :
410 PRINT "COPY COMPLETE"
420 END
```

CHAPTER SEVEN

Random Access Data Files

Objectives: When you complete this chapter, you will be able to use the following statements and functions in programs to create, verify, copy, and change random access disk data files: FIELD, LSET, RSET, PUT, GET, LOF( ), MKS$( ), MKI$( ), MKD$( ), CVS( ), CVI( ), and CVD( ). You will also be able to convert sequential files to random access files.

INTRODUCTION

The next two chapters illustrate the use of random access data files.

Programs using random access data files present more variations in the BASIC instructions among different versions of MICROSOFT BASIC than any other BASIC language procedure. Therefore, while most of what you have learned so far has worked on nearly any microcomputer that uses a version of MICROSOFT BASIC, that will not be the case with this chapter and the next. However, continue working through this material, even if you do not have a Radio Shack TRS-80 computer with DOS BASIC, the system used to write these chapters and to which the programming procedures specifically apply. BASIC-80 uses the same language syntax as TRS-80. Every effort has been made to show you how to use random access files with good, general, fundamental procedures that will apply to any BASIC language syntax. Only the exact statements and syntax may be different. After you have read these chapters, you can refer to the reference manual for your system and make sense of it. You can then apply the specific programming syntax for your system to the general concepts presented here.

WHAT IS A RANDOM ACCESS FILE?

A random access data file is a disk file divided into sections called records that permit you to easily change data. The structure also allows very fast access of data, whether located in the first or last record in the file. These two strengths of random access files are the greatest weaknesses of sequential data files.

Random access files use a different set of instructions than sequential files, except for the OPEN and CLOSE procedure. Random access files use a complete record of 256 bytes for each dataset (255 bytes on some computers, and user selected length files on still others). The file is read as one complete record (and dataset) at a time. When a dataset is printed or recorded to the file, a complete record is used each time. The technique stressed earlier, that you set up your program to read or write a complete dataset at a time, will help you understand the workings of random access files.

The only disadvantage of using random access files is that the fixed record length file wastes disk space if you place only a small amount of information in each record; that is, if the dataset size is considerably less than the length of a record in bytes. For example, if each record is 256 bytes and you place only 100 bytes of data in each record, then 60 percent of the space in each record becomes blanks, leaving a lot of unused disk space. The selected length record available on some computers eliminates the wasted disk space. Dividing full records into "sub-records" is another way to reduce wasted disk space but is a complex technique you should delay using until you are confident in your use of random access files.

Using random access files requires more preplanning and more carefully designed systems for organizing and using data. Once planned, random access files require much less programming to accomplish the same activities as sequential files. Random access files are put to best use when the data in the files change frequently. This might be the case with a customer charge account file or when you have a large data base, such as a customer credit information file that you will be accessing in no particular order (randomly). For large scale applications, you may find yourself designing systems that use some sequential files and some random access files in concert.

(a) On a system that uses a complete 256 byte record for each dataset in a random access file, what size datasets use disk space most efficiently?

(b) What are two advantages of random access disk files compared to sequential files?

- - - - - - - - - - - - - - - -

(a) A dataset that uses most or all of the 256 bytes in a record.
(b) (1) Fast access to all datasets (records), regardless of position within the file.
(2) Easy to change data within a particular dataset or record.

Initializing Random Access Files

For random access files, the OPEN statement serves the same purpose of assigning a buffer to the file(s) as in sequential files. The difference is that the buffer assigned can be used for both input and output. The format of the OPEN statement for random access files is as follows:

```
120 OPEN "R", 3, "RNDTEST"
```

The "R" indicates random access files, followed by the buffer number (3 in this case), followed by the file name.

The CLOSE statement operates exactly the same for both sequential and random access files. A CLOSE statement by itself, such as:

```
860 CLOSE
```

will close all open files. The statement to close only the file opened in example line 120 above uses this notation:

```
860 CLOSE 3
```

Explain what each of the following statements does.

(a) `310 OPEN "I", 1, "ADDRESS"` ______________________________

____

(b) `310 OPEN "O", 2, "TEMPFIL"` ______________________________

____

(c) `310 OPEN "R", 1, "MASTER"` ______________________________

____

- - - - - - - - - - - - - - - -

(a) opens a sequential disk data file as an input file named ADDRESS, assigned to buffer #1.
(b) opens a sequential disk data file as an output file named TEMPFIL, assigned to buffer #2.

(c) opens a random access disk data file named MASTER as an input or output file, assigned to buffer #1.

BUFFER FIELDS

The second step after opening a file is to "field" the buffer(s) that the program will use; that is, to define the fields for data within the 256 byte record. The *FIELD statement* organizes the assigned buffer into discrete data fields into which data are placed and from which data are read. Those of you with experience during the punch card era will recognize this concept of fields, which assigns the same specific data to the same location in the buffer for each dataset. The concept is very similar to the data fields within a string used in some sequential data files.

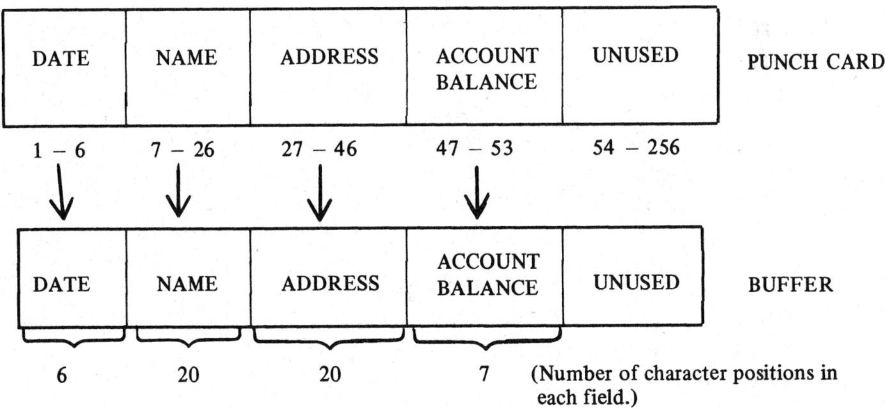

The fields in the illustration are defined by the following field statement, where the buffer number assigned in the OPEN statement is 3.

```
130 FIELD 3, 6 AS DATE$, 20 AS NAME$, 20 AS ADD$, 7 AS BAL$
```

In some versions of BASIC it is not necessary to "field the buffer" or define the data fields within the 256 byte-length record. However, it is always necessary to think in terms of data fields, so you know where in the record each part of the dataset is located. Therefore, it is nice to have a FIELD statement as a required part of a program. Those computer systems that do not use a FIELD statement require the programmer to annotate the program with REMARK statements providing the same information.

A series of five datasets occupying the first five records in a random access file with the format defined by the FIELD statement previously can be visualized like this (only part of the second and third fields are actually shown):

	1	2	3	4	5	6	7	8	9	10	11	12	13	14
Record 1	0	4	0	1	8	0	S	M	I	T	H		L	
Record 2	1	2	2	5	8	0	J	O	N	E	S		B	
Record 3	0	7	0	4	8	0	C	A	R	R		S		
Record 4	1	0	2	1	7	9	H	U	N	T	E	R		T
Record 5	1	1	1	7	8	2	T	R	I	C	E		J	

	27	28	29	30		
Record 1	3	0	1	7		B
Record 2	1		A		S	T
Record 3	2	4	3	#	1	
Record 4	4	0		A	R	C
Record 5	1	1	5		S	O

	47	48	49	50	51	52	53	54	55
Record 1					5	0	0		
Record 2				1	6	0	0		
Record 3		3	2	5	1	2	1		
Record 4						4	8		
Record 5			3	4	7	1	5		

Refer to record 2 in the illustration and answer these questions.

(a) What is the name of the person in record 2? ____________________

(b) What is the street address? ____________________

(c) What is the balance recorded in this record? ____________________

(d) On what date was this transaction? ____________________

- - - - - - - - - - - - - - -

(a) B. Jones
(b) 1 A Street
(c) 1600
(d) 12-25-80

Let's plan the buffer fields for a customer data file named MASTER that includes the data listed below for each customer. The maximum length of each data item in bytes or characters is indicated in parentheses. All data items are entered as strings.

Customer number (6)
Customer name (20)
Street address (20)
City, state, and zip code (20)
Phone number (10)
Total: 76 bytes (out of 256 bytes available)

The FIELD statement for this data could look like this:

```
130 FIELD 3, 6 AS CF$, 20 AS NF$, 20 AS AF$, 20 AS SF$, 10 AS PF$
```

Line 130 tells the computer to divide buffer number 5 into sections, reserving six bytes for CF$, twenty for NF$, twenty for AF$, etc. The remaining unused 180 bytes in each record do not have to be FIELDed.

Notice that each field is identified by length and a variable. The variable name follows the normal rules for string variable names. Throughout this text simple variable names have been used and have been defined in an introductory module. Simple variables consist of one alphabetic character, sometimes followed by one numeric character, such as A, A$, P, P1, P1$. The letter F is convenient for Field as the last character in the buffer variable names. This convention is a constant reminder that the variables in question are fielded buffer variables – *not* the usual string variables. No rule says you must use a "reminder" character in the buffer variable names; these variable names follow the same rules as string variables. However, it is easier to follow a program's logic by using the F. If N$ (for Name) is the variable to which a customer name is assigned, and NF$ is the buffer variable for the customer name field; consistency in the BASIC program code makes the program easier to read and follow. Using the same "reminder" character (F) also eliminates the need to list buffer variables separately in the introductory module.

Many versions of BASIC allow you to use long variable names; that is, variables with more than one or two characters. However, many versions of BASIC check and use only the first two characters of a long variable name as the actual label for the value or string assigned to them (TRS-80 BASIC). These versions of BASIC allow use of both NAME$ and NAMEF$ as variables, but actually only use NA$ as the variable label internally, making the two apparently different variables actually the same. In order to use the F reminder for long variable names in these versions of BASIC, use the F as the leading rather than the last character in the variable name, i.e., use FNAME$ instead of NAMEF$. Remember that only the first two characters may actually count; the rest of the long variable name is strictly for the program reader's convenience in recalling what the value or string assigned to that variable represents.

The buffer field variable names used in the earlier examples are all string variable names, but not in the ordinary sense. They do not reserve or consume string variable space in the computer's memory. They do assign field space in the buffer, which is different. You can perform some, but not all, string variable operations with buffer variables. It is important to remember that you canNOT use the same variable name for both a regular string variable and a buffer field variable. If a program contained the following sequence of statements, an error would result because the second statement essentially nullifies the assignment action of the first.

```
120 FIELD 1, 25 AS B$, 25 AS CF$
130 LET B$ = X$
```

In this case, after line 130 is executed, B$ is no longer available as a buffer field variable; it has been reassigned as an ordinary string variable.

(a) Write a FIELD statement for a random access file assigned to buffer number 2 for the following dataset:

A catalog number with seven characters entered as a string. (C$)

A catalog description with up to sixty characters maximum. (D$)

A price for the item with up to six characters entered as a string. (P$)

540 FIELD ____________________

(b) Which of the following FIELD statements is not acceptable and why?

(1) `240 FIELD 2, 5 AS NF$, 10 AS PF$, 4 AS CF$, 4 AS BF$`

(2) `540 FIELD 1, 85 AS AF$, 85 AS BF$, 85 AS CF$, 85 AS DF$`

(3) `320 FIELD 2, 25 AS GF$, 4 AS PF, 16 AS NF$, 10 AS CF`

- - - - - - - - - - - - - - - -

(a) 540 FIELD 1, 7 AS CF$, 60 AS DF$, 6 AS PF$

(b) 2, because more characters are reserved in the field than are available in one record. 3, because two field variables are not in string variable format.

SIMPLE READ AND WRITE OPERATIONS TO RANDOM ACCESS FILES WITH STRING DATA

Now consider the sequence of procedures to use random access files with string variables (not numeric data assigned to numeric variables).

1. OPEN the file(s).
2. FIELD the buffer(s).
3. Enter the data, assigning it to ordinary string variables.
4. Assign the position of string variables data to the buffer fields, using LSET and/or RSET.
5. PUT the buffer to the disk file, *or* GET data from the disk file into the buffer.
6. Display, move, copy, or otherwise manipulate the buffer contents.
7. CLOSE the files.

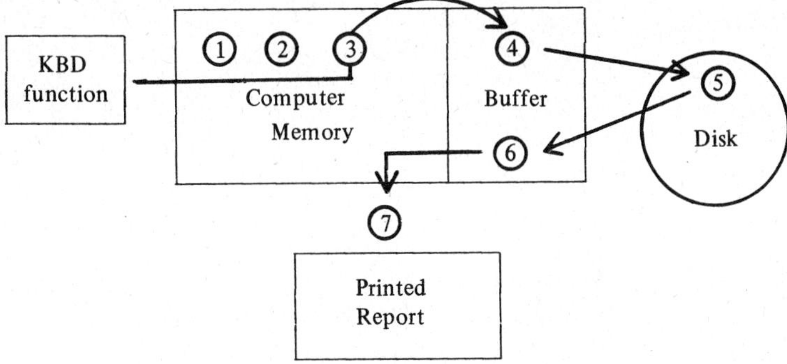

FIGURE 7-1. Seven steps for using random access files with string variables.

Now try a simple application program using random access files, following the steps outlined. The program will enter data into a random access file. The datum is an inventory of repair parts, including a six-digit product number entered as a string and a product description of up to twenty characters, with one of these datasets per record. "How many" or quantity in stock will be added later. The introductory module looks like this. Fill in the OPEN and FIELD statements at lines 210 and 220 below.

(a)
```
100 REM    PARTS INVENTORY (R-A FILE DEMO)
110 :
120 REM    VARIABLES USED
130 REM      N$ = PART NUMBER(6)
140 REM      D$ = DESCRIPTION(20)
150 :
160 :
170 REM    FILES USED
180 REM      INVEN = R-A FILE
190 :
200 REM    FILE INITIALIZATION
210                                            :REM    OPEN FILE
220                                            :REM    FIELD THE BUFFER
230 :
```

\- - - - - - - - - - - - - - - -

(a)
```
210 OPEN "R", 1, "INVEN"
220 FIELD 1, 6 AS NF$, 20 AS DF$
```

A data entry module should include data entry checks or validity tests which are merely noted here since you already know how to do them.

```
240 REM     DATA ENTRY MODULE
250 LINE INPUT "ENTER PRODUCT NUMBER(6)"; N$
260 REM     DATA ENTRY TESTS HERE
270 LINE INPUT "ENTER DESCRIPTION(20)"; D$
280 REM     DATA ENTRY TESTS HERE
290 :
```

The preceding segment assigns the data to regular string variables. To assign the data to buffer variables, use the LSET or RSET statements. These statements place string variable data into previously defined buffer fields. The statement LSET left-justifies the information in the field; that is, the datum starts at the first character position in the field to the "left end" of the field space. If there are fewer characters in the data than the space reserved for them, the remaining unused character positions in the field are automatically filled with blank spaces. On the other hand, if the data to be fit into the field have more characters than are reserved, the excess characters are truncated (left out), and no error message alerts you to this occurrence. Consider the case of a twenty-character (maximum) data string and a defined twenty-character buffer field. Instead of using a string assigned to a variable, use a direct assignment of the string to the buffer variable for clarity.

```
LSET DF$ = "MOTHERBOARD"
```

This statement fills the buffer field like this:

/M/O/T/H/E/R/B/O/A/R/D/ / / / / / / / / /

The remaining character positions in the field are filled with blanks. Notice that LSET places the data into the field starting at the left-most character position in the field. *RSET* does the exact opposite. *Data are right-justified in the field;* that is, the last character in the data is located at the end or right-most character position in the buffer field. In this case, if the data have fewer than twenty characters, the extra leading spaces in the field are filled with blank spaces.

```
RSET DF$ = "MOTHERBOARD"
```

This statement fills the buffer field like this:

/ / / / / / / / / /M/O/T/H/E/R/B/O/A/R/D/

The leading character positions are filled with blanks. Note that if the data contain more than twenty characters, some leading characters in the data are lost by truncation.

```
310 LET D$ = "COMPUTER MEMORY BOARDS"
320 LSET DF$ = D$
```

If DF$ was fielded for twenty characters, this is all that would be included in the data field:

/C/O/M/P/U/T/E/R/ /M/E/M/O/R/Y/ /B/O/A/R/

If you used RSET instead of LSET:

```
320 RSET DF$ = D$
```

then the data would be truncated to fit the twenty character field like this:

/M/P/U/T/E/R/ /M/E/M/O/R/Y/ /B/O/A/R/D/S/

To assign data to a buffer variable and place it into the field, use either RSET or LSET. However, RSET is seldom used except, perhaps, to right-justify numeric data. Be consistent in your procedures by using only one or the other.

Consider again this representation of a series of records in a random access file and the FIELD statement that structured the dataset.

```
130 FIELD 3, 6 AS DATE$, 20 AS NAME$, 20 AS ADD$, 7 AS BAL$
```

	1	2	3	4	5	6	7	8	9	10	11	12	13	14	
Record 1	0	4	0	1	8	0	S	M	I	T	H		L		
Record 2	1	2	2	5	8	0	J	O	N	E	S		B		
Record 3	0	7	0	4	8	0	C	A	R	R		S			
Record 4	1	0	2	1	7	9	H	U	N	T	E	R		T	
Record 5	1	1	1	7	8	2	T	R	I	C	E		J		

	27	28	29	30		
Record 1	3	0	1	7		B
Record 2	1		A		S	T
Record 3	2	4	3	#	1	
Record 4	4	0		A	R	C
Record 5	1	1	5		S	O

	47	48	49	50	51	52	53	54	55
Record 1					5	0	0		
Record 2				1	6	0	0		
Record 3		3	2	5	1	2	1		
Record 4						4	8		
Record 5			3	4	7	1	5		

(a) Which buffer variable(s) were definitely assigned with LSET? ______________

____

(b) Which buffer variable(s) were definitely assigned with RSET? ______________

(c) Which buffer variable(s) could have been assigned with either LSET or RSET?

____

- - - - - - - - - - - - - - -

(a) NAME$, ADD$
(b) BAL$
(c) DATE$

Notice that if the datasets in a series of records like the preceding were to be displayed on the CRT or printed one after the other in their fielded format, the alphanumeric data would be left-justified and the dollar (or dollar and cents) entries would be right-justified (as expected for a column of figures), so the decimal points in the column are aligned.

Now that you understand the use of LSET and RSET, let's return to the example program under consideration which looks like this so far:

```
100 REM    PARTS INVENTORY (R-A FILE DEMO)
110 :
120 REM    VARIABLES USED
130 REM      N$ = PART NUMBER (6)
140 REM      D$ = DESCRIPTION(20)
150 :
160 :
170 REM    FILES USED
180 REM      INVEN = R-A FILE
190 :
200 REM    FILE INITIALIZATION
210 OPEN "R", 1, "INVEN"
220 FIELD 1, 6 AS NF$, 20 AS DF$
230 :
240 REM    DATA ENTRY MODULE
250 LINE INPUT "ENTER PRODUCT NUMBER(6)"; N$
260 REM    DATA ENTRY TESTS HERE
270 LINE INPUT "ENTER DESCRIPTION(20)"; D$
280 REM    DATA ENTRY TESTS HERE
290 :
```

Complete lines 310 and 320 to assign entered data to the buffer fields.

(a)
```
290 :
300 REM    PLACE DATA INTO BUFFER
310                                         :REM   PLACE N$
320                                         :REM   PLACE D$
330 :
```

(a)
```
310 LSET NF$ = N$
320 LSET DF$ = D$
```

Note that data are not entered directly into the buffer. Instead, the data entered are assigned to a regular string variable and then placed into the buffer with LSET.

At this point, all the data are in place. The buffer contains the data to be recorded into the random access file. How? *Use the PUT statement to tell the computer to copy or print the entire contents of the buffer into a record in the file.* Which record? You can either specify exactly which record is to be filled, or you can let the computer fill what is called the "current record." When you OPEN a file, the current record is record number 1. After each execution of the PUT statement, the current record number is increased by one. Then that record is filled (number 2, then number 3, etc.). If the PUT statement looks like this:

```
PUT 1
```

where the "1" is the buffer number, then each execution of the PUT statement fills the current record and automatically increases the record number by one.

If the PUT statement looks like this:

```
PUT 1, R
```

where the R is the specified record number, then record number R is filled with the buffer contents and the current record number becomes R + 1. You can think of the record number as the position of the *record pointer,* similar to the data pointer in sequential files.

Continuing with the program, fill in line 350.

(a)
```
330:
340 REM    PRINT TO FILE
350                                  :REM    WITHOUT A RECORD #
360 :
```

(a)
```
350 PUT 1
```

The program is nearly complete. Execution of the program so far allows you to enter data, and to print one dataset to the first record in the file. Complete the program with the segment below, and it will accept data and place it in a random access data file until you tell it to stop.

```
360 :
370 REM    MORE DATA?
380 LINE INPUT "DO YOU HAVE MORE ENTRIES?"; R$
390 IF LEFT$(R$,1) = "Y" THEN 250
400 :
410 REM    CLOSE FILE
420 CLOSE 1
430 :
```

Here are the program segments gathered into a complete listing:

```
100 REM    PARTS INVENTORY (R-A FILE DEMO)
110 :
120 REM    VARIABLES USED
130 REM      N$ = PART NUMBER (6)
```

continued on next page

```
140 REM      D$ = DESCRIPTION(20)
150 :
160 :
170 REM   FILES USED
180 REM      INVEN = R-A FILE
1N[ :
200 REM   FILE INITIALIZATION
210 OPEN "R", 1, "INVEN"
220 FIELD 1, 6 AS NF$, 20 AS DF$
230 :
240 REM   DATA ENTRY MODULE
250 LINE INPUT "ENTER PRODUCT NUMBER(6)"; N$
260 REM   DATA ENTRY TESTS HERE
2N[ LINE INPUT "ENTER DESCRIPTION(20)"; D$
280 REM   DATA ENTRY TESTS HERE
290 :
300 REM   PLACE DATA INTO BUFFER
310 LSET NF$ = N$
320 LSET DF$ = D$
330 :
340 REM   PRINT TO FILE
350 PUT 1
360 :
370 REM   MORE DATA?
380 LINE INPUT "DO YOU HAVE MORE ENTRIES?"; R$
390 IF LEFT$(R$,1) = "Y" THEN 250
400 :
410 REM   CLOSE FILE
420 CLOSE 1
430 :
```

Before proceding, consider the following information. 1) You can refield a buffer (that is, change the data structure for the same R-A file) using another FIELD statement in a program, but usually you should avoid doing so. If "refielding" is necessary, always provide ample explanation of your program's procedures in REMARK statements or the program's actions will be totally unclear to a reader/user. 2) If a program PUTs to a record whose record number is beyond the end of the file, the statement will be executed. However, the records between the last used record and the one indicated by the current PUT statement are allocated to the file and left unfilled. For example, if the highest used record number is 25 and the program encounters the statement:

```
PUT 1, 226
```

then 200 new, empty records are created between record number 25 and record number 226, using a lot of disk space. 3) The maximum number of records in a random access file on the Radio Shack computer with a 5¼″ disk is 335.

Using the program just developed, assume that you have filled the random access file called INVEN with the following data:

ITEM #	DESCRIPTION
112131	MOTHERBOARD
341232	5 IN. DISKETTES
341233	8 IN DISKETTES
871256	RS232 INTERFACE
983476	5 IN DISK DRIVE

Now let's write another program to display the contents of this random access file. You could incorporate this program into the previous one later. Again, fill in the OPEN and FIELD statements in the introductory module of the program at lines 200 and 210 below.

(a)
```
100 REM    INVEN RANDOM FILE READ/PRINT
110 :
120 REM    VARIABLES USED
130 REM      NF$ = PRODUCT NUMBER(6)
140 REM      DF$ = DESCRIPTION(20)
150 :
160 REM    FILES USED
170 REM      INVEN = RANDOM ACCESS FILE
180 :
190 REM    INITIALIZATION
200                                              :REM    OPEN FILE
210                                              :REM    FIELD BUFFER
220 :
230 PRINT "ITEM #", "DESCRIPTION"
240 :
```

(a)
```
200 OPEN "R", 1, "INVEN"
210 FIELD 1, 6 AS NF$, 20 AS DF$
```

Note the use of the buffer variable names in lines 130 and 140 since the data will be read from the disk record directly to the buffer. The OPEN and FIELD statements are identical to those used in the previous program that created the file.

To input or copy data from the disk to the buffer, use the GET statement. GET works like the PUT statement in reverse. Data are input or copied from the disk file to the buffer with the GET statement. The formats for the GET and PUT statements are the same.

```
270 GET 2
```

means copy the contents of the "current record" to buffer number 2 and then increment the current record number by one (advance the record pointer by one record).

```
270 GET 1, R
```

means copy the contents of record number R to buffer number 1 and increment the current record counter by one (advance the record pointer by one record).

The program module to read the file and print the report looks like this:

```
240 :
250 REM    READ THE FILE/PRINT REPORT
260 IF EOF(1) THEN 320
270 GET 1
```

continued on next page

```
280 PRINT NF$, DF$
290 GOTO 260
300 :
310 REM    CLOSE FILE
320 CLOSE 1
330 :
```

Notice the end-of-file test in line 260. Without this test, the program would hang-up in a loop and keep trying to GET data forever. You would have to use the BREAK key to terminate the program. The CRT screen would print the data in the file and then continue displaying "blank" records until the other data were pushed off the screen. For unknown reasons, no end-of-file error message is associated with random access GET statements in our version of TRS-80 BASIC.

The GET statement in line 270 above copies the entire contents of the current record into the buffer. Line 280 prints the fielded buffer contents on the screen. It is not necessary to reassign the buffer data to regular string variables before printing or displaying it on the screen. However, it is necessary to first place data in a regular string variable before you place it into the buffer with a field variable, for copying to the data file. Watch out for that distinction.

An alternative to detect the end of file uses the LOF function. *LOF stands for length of file and tells the number of the last record presently used in the file.* The format is LOF(1) where the number in the parentheses is the buffer number of the file in question. The program module below is a substitute for the read and print module in the previous program. The use of LOF( ) as the upper parameter in a FOR NEXT loop will GET and PRINT exactly the number of records that are used in the file.

```
240 :
250 REM    READ THE FILE/PRINT REPORT
260 FOR X = 1 TO LOF(1)
270 GET 1
280 PRINT NF$, DF$
290 NEXT X
300 :
310 REM    CLOSE FILE
320 CLOSE 1
330 :
```

The LOF( ) function can also tell the computer into which record to start placing new data when you want to add data to an existing random access file. Examine the following program segment to see the technique for adding a record to the end of an existing random access data file.

```
240 LET R = LOF(3) + 1
250 PUT 3, R
```

Using the introductory and data entry modules that follow as a guide, complete the program to add new datasets into an existing random access file of customer phone numbers. Complete lines 370, 380, 390, 420, and 490.

(a)
```
100 REM   RANDOM FILE COMPLETION
110 :
120 REM   VARIABLES USED
130 REM     N$ = CUSTOMER NUMBER (5)
140 REM     C$ = CUST. NAME (20)
150 REM     P$ = PHONE NUMBER (10)
160 REM     R = CURRENT RECORD COUNTER
170 :
180 REM   FILES USED
190 REM     PHONE = RANDOM ACCESS FILE
200 :
210 REM   FILE INITIALIZATION
220 OPEN "R", 1, "PHONE"
230 FIELD 1, 5 AS NF$, 20 AS CF$, 10 AS PF$
240 :
250 REM   LOCATE LAST USED RECORD
260 LET R = LOF(1) + 1
270 :
280 REM   DATA ENTRY MODULE
290 LINE INPUT "ENTER CUST. #:"; N$
300 REM   DATA ENTRY TEST
310 LINE INPUT "ENTER CUST. NAME:"; C$
320 REM   DATA ENTRY TESTS
330 LINE INPUT "ENTER PHONE #:"; P$
340 REM   DATA ENTRY TESTS
350 :
360 REM   MOVE DATA TO BUFFER
370
380
390
400 :
410 REM   COPY BUFFER TO FILE
420
430 :
440 REM   MORE DATA TO ENTER?
450 LINE INPUT "DO YOU HAVE MORE:"; R$
460 IF LEFT$(R$,1) = "Y" THEN 290
470 :
480 REM   CLOSE FILE
490
500 :
```

(a)
```
360 REM   MOVE DATA TO BUFFER
370 LSET NF$ = N$
380 LSET CF$ = C$
390 LSET PF$ = P$
400 :
410 REM   COPY BUFFER TO FILE
420 PUT 1,R
430 :
440 REM   MORE DATA TO ENTER?
450 LINE INPUT "DO YOU HAVE ANY MORE?"; R$
460 IF LEFT$(R$,1) = "Y" THEN 290
470 :
480 REM   CLOSE FILE
490 CLOSE 1
500 :
```

Now add to the previous program a module to read and print the entire contents of the file, including the new entries. This segment will begin at line 510.

(a)
```
510 REM    READ/PRINT ENTIRE FILE
```

- - - - - - - - - - - - - - -

(a)
```
510 REM    READ/PRINT ENTIRE FILE
520 OPEN "R", 1, "PHONE"
530 FIELD 1, 5 AS NF$, 20 AS CF$, 10 AS PF$
540 :
550 FOR X = 1 TO LOF(1)
560 GET 1
570 PRINT NF$, CF$, PF$
580 NEXT X
590 :
600 CLOSE 1
610 :
```

USING RANDOM ACCESS FILES WITH NUMERIC DATA

So far only alphabetic or string data have been used in the random access files. Now that you have a basic knowledge of random access files, you are ready for the extra steps necessary to use numeric data with random access files.

To avoid problems, always remember: Only string information can be placed into a buffer for random access files. Therefore, all numeric data must be converted to strings before the data are placed in the buffer. Likewise, all numeric data read from a file must be converted from a string to numeric form before the values are manipulated mathematically or otherwise used in expressions or functions. This process requires extra steps, but fortunately, BASIC provides the functions needed to make these conversions easy. To convert numeric data to string form before placing in the buffer and hence to the file, use the three functions explained below. The parentheses after each function can contain a value or a numeric variable to which a value has been assigned.

MKS$( ) – make (MK) a single (S) precision value into a string that is four bytes in length. Examples:

```
340 LSET DF$ = MKS$(476.23)
```

or the equivalent with the value assigned to a numeric variable:

```
330 LET X = 476.23
340 LSET DF$ = MKS$(X)
```

The similar functions for making integer values and double precision values into strings for random access file storage look like this:

MKI$( ) – make an integer (I) value into a two-byte string.
MKD$( ) – make a double (D) precision value into an eight-byte string.

The length of the strings (in bytes) that result from using these functions is important, because you have to FIELD the buffer differently according to whether the values are integers, or single or double precision values (two, four, or eight bytes). The examples use single precision numbers. Note in the example statements above that LSET places the converted numeric data into the buffer. If you use RSET, do some thorough testing for possible errors when these strings are read from the file and converted back to numeric values.

From line 340 in the preceding example, DF$ was assigned the string representation of a numeric value. If you attempt to PRINT DF$ on your display, you will get some interesting but undecipherable hieroglyphics. This is because the string variable conversion performed by MKS$( ) makes a "representation" of the numeric value that is not necessarily usable in its converted form. To restore these converted numbers to usable numeric values, use the three conversion functions that reverse the action of the ones discussed earlier. (The buffer variable to be converted back to numeric value form is enclosed in parentheses.)

CVS( ) – convert (CV) or restore to single (S) precision numeric form the string indicated in the parentheses.

Typically, this string variable in the parentheses is a fielded buffer variable that was made into a string with the MKS$( ) function. If the length of the string to be converted is fewer than four characters, you will get an error message. If the length of the string is greater than four characters, only the first four characters are used in the conversion. Here are examples of CVS( ) in the context of statements:

```
460 PRINT CVS(DF$)

310 LET D = CVS(DF$)
```

CVI( ) – convert or restore to integer (I) numeric form the string indicated in the parentheses. If the string length is less than two an error message results. If the string has more than two characters, only the first two are used.

CVD( ) – convert or restore to a double (D) precision numeric value the string indicated in the parentheses. If the string length is fewer than eight characters, you'll get an error message. If the string length is greater than eight characters, only the first eight characters are used.

Remember: *Use matching functions to make numeric values into strings and to convert them back to numeric form when dealing with random access file data.* If you mismatch functions, you may get an error message or erroneous data.

If you use MKS$( ) to make a value into a string, use CVS( ) to convert it back.
If you use MKD$( ) to make a value into a string, use CVD( ) to convert it back.
If you use MKI$( ) to make a value into a string, use CVI( ) to convert it back.

The INVEN file created earlier contains product numbers and product descriptions. Assume you now want to add to that program the statements to place the quantity available of each item into the same file. Following is the original program:

```
100 REM     PARTS INVENTORY (R-A FILE DEMO)
110 :
120 REM     VARIABLES USED
130 REM        N$ = PART NUMBER (6)
140 REM        D$ = DESCRIPTION(20)
150 :
160 :
170 REM     FILES USED
180 REM        INVEN = R-A FILE
190 :
200 REM     FILE INITIALIZATION
210 OPEN "R", 1, "INVEN"
220 FIELD 1, 6 AS NF$, 20 AS DF$
230 :
240 REM     DATA ENTRY MODULE
250 LINE INPUT "ENTER PRODUCT NUMBER(6)"; N$
260 REM     DATA ENTRY TESTS HERE
2N[ LINE INPUT "ENTER DESCRIPTION(20)"; D$
280 REM     DATA ENTRY TESTS HERE
290 :
300 REM     PLACE DATA INTO BUFFER
310 LSET NF$ = N$
320 LSET DF$ = D$
330 :
340 REM     PRINT TO FILE
350 PUT 1
360 :
370 REM     MORE DATA?
380 LINE INPUT "DO YOU HAVE MORE ENTRIES?"; R$
390 IF LEFT$(R$,1) = "Y" THEN 250
400 :
410 REM     CLOSE FILE
420 CLOSE 1
430 :
```

To modify the program, add this statement:

```
150 REM            Q = QUANTITY (SINGLE PRECISION)
```

You modify the FIELD statement in line 220 to include the quantity variable.

(a)
```
210 OPEN "R", 1, "INVEN2"
220 ______________________________
```

(a)
```
220 FIELD 1, 6 AS NF$, 20 AS DF$, 4 AS QF$
```

Also add to the program:

```
290 INPUT "QUANTITY AVAILABLE"; Q
295 REM          DATA ENTRY TESTS
```

Write the buffer placement statement for quantity.

(a)
```
330 ______________
```

(b) What change is needed for the print to file statement?

(a)
```
330 LSET QF$ = MKS$(Q)
```

(b) No change. The entire dataset in the buffer will be PUT, so line 350 is unchanged.

Following is the program used to print the contents of the earlier version of the INVEN file, with lines 150, 170, 200 and 230 changed. Make the changes to lines 210 and 280 to print the quantity:

(a)
```
100 REM     INVEN2 RANDOM FILE PRINT
110 :
120 REM     VARIABLES USED
130 REM       NF$ = PRODUCT NUMBER(6)
140 REM       DF$ = DESCRIPTION(20)
150 REM       QF$ = QUANTITY (SINGLE PREC)
160 REM     FILES USED
170 REM      INVEN2 = R-A FILE
```

continued on next page

```
180 :
190 REM     INITIALIZATION
200 OPEN "R", 1, "INVEN2"
210                                                  :REM    FIELD
                                                             THE BUFFER
220 :
230 PRINT "ITEM #", "DESCRIPTION", "QUANTITY"
240 :
250 REM     READ THE FILE/PRINT REPORT
260 IF EOF(1) THEN 320
270 GET 1
280                                                   REM    PRINT
                                                             BUFFER DATA
290 GOTO 260
300 :
310 REM     CLOSE FILE
320 CLOSE 1
330 :
```

(a)
```
210 FIELD 1, 6 AS NF$, 20 AS DF$, 4 AS QF$
280 PRINT NF$, DF$, CVS(QF$)

OR LINE 280 CAN BE DONE IN TWO STATEMENTS:

280 LET Q = CVS(QF$)
285 PRINT NF$, DF$, Q
```

RANDOM ACCESS FILE UTILITY PROGRAMS

Having covered the essentials for using random access files, let's write two file utility programs to further your understanding and provide models for similar programs you can write.

The first program simply copies the data from one random access file into another random access file, record for record. The data are both alphabetic and numeric.

Follow these steps to create a random access file copying program:

(1) Open the original file (the one to be copied).
(2) Open the file to be copied into. Use a different buffer number from step (1).
(3) FIELD the buffer for the step (1) file.
(4) FIELD the buffer for the step (2) file. Use different variable names than in step (3), but use identical data structure or field format.
(5) In a FOR NEXT loop with LOF for the upper limit to the FOR control variable,
    (a) Input a dataset from the original file.
    (b) Reassign the strings assigned to variables of the original file to the fielded variables for the copy.
    (c) Print the reassigned dataset to the copy file.

(6) Close the files.

Here is the introductory module:

```
100 REM     R-A FILE COPY
110 :
120 REM     VARIABLES USED
130 REM        GF$ = FF$ = (20)
140 REM        SF$ = RF$ = (8)
145 REM        QF$ = PF$ = (4)
150 REM        MF$ = NF$ = (30)
160 :
170 REM     FILES USED
180 REM        MASTER = R-A FILE TO BE COPIED
190 REM        STORE1 = FILE COPY
200 :
```

Go back to page 228 and write the program to create the file named MASTER, of which our example program will make a copy. Also write the companion program to display MASTER.

Notice how line 130 indicates the variable and field size used in the program. This format indicates the equivalent variables in the two files involved in the program, the file copied from and the file copied to. Variable GF$ in file 1 is equivalent to FF$ in file 2, and both have the same maximum length (twenty characters).

Complete the following program module to initialize the two files. Fill in lines 220, 230, 240, and 250.

(a)
```
200 :
210 REM     FILE INITIALIZATION
220                                            :REM   OPEN
                                                      MASTER
230                                            :REM   OPEN
                                                      STORE1
240                                            :REM   FIELD
                                                      BUFFER 1
250                                            :REM   FIELD
                                                      BUFFER 2
260 :
```

(a)
```
200 :
210 REM     FILE INITIALIZATION
220 OPEN "R", 1, "MASTER"
230 OPEN "R", 2, "STORE1"
240 FIELD 1, 20 AS GF$, 8 AS SF$, 4 AS QF$, 30 AS MF$
250 FIELD 2, 20 AS FF$, 8 AS RF$, 4 AS PF$, 30 AS NF$
260 :
```

In the final part of the program, the data are read from file 1 and then assigned into buffer number 2 and PUT to file 2. You have six statements to complete; lines 290, 300, 310, 320, 330, and 340.

(a)
```
260 :
270 REM     COPY FILE
280 FOR R = 1 TO LOF(1)
290                                    :REM   READ FROM MASTER FILE
300                                    :REM   MOVE DATA TO BUFFER 2
310
320
330
340                                    :REM   PRINT TO FILE 2
350 NEXT R
360 CLOSE 1,2
370 PRINT "COPY COMPLETE"
```

(a)
```
260 :
270 REM    COPY FILE
280 FOR R = 1 TO LOF(1)
290 GET 1
300 LSET FF$ = GF$
310 LSET RF$ = SF$
320 LSET PF$ = QF$
330 LSET NF$ = MF$
340 PUT 2
350 NEXT R
360 CLOSE 1,2
370 PRINT "COPY COMPLETE"
```

You probably found completing that program easy. Random access files *are* easy to manipulate, once you get the hang of it.

Following is the complete program:

```
100 REM     R-A FILE COPY
110 :
120 REM     VARIABLES USED
130 REM       GF$ = FF$ = (20)
140 REM       SF$ = RF$ = (8)
145 REM       QF$ = PF$ = (4)
150 REM       MF$ = NF$ = (30)
160 :
170 REM     FILES USED
180 REM       MASTER = R-A FILE TO BE COPIED
190 REM       STORE1 = FILE COPY
200 :
210 REM     FILE INITIALIZATION
220 OPEN "R", 1, "MASTER"
230 OPEN "R", 2, "STORE1"
240 FIELD 1, 20 AS GF$, 8 AS SF$, 4 AS QF$, 30 AS MF$
250 FIELD 2, 20 AS FF$, 8 AS RF$, 4 AS PF$, 30 AS NF$
260 :
```

```
270 REM      COPY FILE
280 FOR R = 1 TO LOF(1)
290 GET 1
300 LSET FF$ = GF$
310 LSET RF$ = SF$
320 LSET PF$ = QF$
330 LSET NF$ = MF$
340 PUT 2
350 NEXT R
360 CLOSE 1,2
370 PRINT "COPY COMPLETE"
```

(a) Check your understanding of the file copying program by filling in the corresponding program line number(s) for each step in the following outline:

(1) Open the original file (the one to be copied). ______________________

(2) Open the file to be copied into. Use a different buffer number from step (1).

____

(3) FIELD the buffer for the step (1) file. ______________________

(4) FIELD the buffer for the step (2) file. Use different variable names than in step (3), but use identical data structure or field format. ______________________

(5) In a FOR NEXT loop with LOF for the upper limit to the FOR control variable,

____

- (a) Input a dataset from the original file. ______________________
- (b) Reassign the strings assigned to variables of the original file to the fielded variables for the copy. ______________________
- (c) Print the reassigned dataset to the copy file. ______________________

(6) Close the files. ______________________

- - - - - - - - - - - - - - -

(a) (1) 220
(2) 230
(3) 240
(4) 250
(5) 280 (FOR statement) and 350 (NEXT statement)
(a) 290
(b) lines 300 to 330
(c) 340
(6) 360

Now let's consider a versatile utility program that allows a number of options for changing the data in a random access file (in particular, the one created earlier in this chapter called INVEN). For simplicity, let's use the version that contains only two data items per record: the code number (six characters) and the description (twenty characters maximum). You want the program to display the datasets in the file, one record at a time, and allow the user the following options:

1 – Change both the code number and description.
2 – Change the code number only.
3 – Change the description only.
4 – Delete the information in this record.
5 – No change for this record.

Follow these steps:

(1) Open the file.
(2) Field the buffer.
(3) Assign R, the record pointer variable (record counter), an initial value of zero.
(4) Increase the current value of R by one.
(5) Check the value of R against the length of file value plus one to see whether the last record in the file has already been retrieved. The comparison is IF R = LOF (1) + 1 THEN step (19), where the file is closed. Note that if you used R = LOF(1) for the comparison, and the comparison is true, the last record (where the file pointer is located) is not processed through the rest of the program.
(6) Retrieve the dataset in record number R.
(7) Clear the display screen.
(8) Display the items in the dataset.
(9) Display the "menu" choices for the user.
(10) Ask the user to input a choice from the "menu."
(11) Check the entry for legal "menu" options.
(12) Design subroutine one:
    (a) Enter change for code number.
    (b) Data entry checks.
    (c) Assign entry to correct buffer variable.
    (d) Return.
(13) Design subroutine two:
    (a) Enter change for description.
    (b) Data entry checks.
    (c) Assign entry to correct buffer variable.
    (d) Return.
(14) For "menu" option 1:
    (a) Go to subroutine one.
    (b) Go to subroutine two.
    (c) Place the changed dataset into the same record from which the old dataset was retrieved.
    (d) Go back to step (4).
(15) For "menu" option 2, follow steps (14) (a), (c), and (d).

(16) For "menu" option 3, follow steps (14) (b), (c), and (d).
(17) For "menu" option 4:
  (a) Assign null strings to all buffer variables.
  (b) Follow steps (14) (c) and (d).
(18) For "menu" option 5, merely go back to step (4).
(19) Display the message END OF DATA IN THIS FILE and close the file.

Here is the complete program:

```
100 REM   INVEN FILE EDITOR
110 :
120 REM   VARIABLES USED
130 REM      C$, CF$ = PART NUMBER (6)
140 REM      D$, DF$ = DESCRIPTION (20)
150 REM      R$ = RESPONSE VARIABLE
160 REM      R = RECORD NUMBER
170 :
180 REM   FILES USED
190 REM      INVEN - RA FILE
200 :
210 REM   INITIALIZE
220 OPEN "R", 1, "INVEN"
230 FIELD 1, 6 AS CF$, 20 AS DF$
240 :
250 LET R = 0
260 LET R = R + 1
270 IF R = LOF(1) + 1 THEN 480
280 GET 1, R
290 :
300 CLS
310 PRINT CF$, DF$
320 PRINT "ENTER ONE OF THE FOLLOWING OPTIONS:"
330 PRINT "1  CHANGE ALL (BOTH CODE AND DESCRIPTION)"
340 PRINT "2  CHANGE CODE ONLY"
350 PRINT "3  CHANGE DESCRIPTION ONLY"
360 PRINT "4  DELETE ITEM FROM FILE"
370 PRINT "5  NO CHANGE FOR THIS DATA"
380 :
390 LINE INPUT "ENTER YOUR CHOICE FROM THE OPTIONS ABOVE:"; R$
400 IF VAL(R$) <1 OR VAL(R$) >5 THEN PRINT "ENTER NUMBER 1-5 ONLY
    PLEASE": GOTO 390
410 IF VAL(R$) = 1 THEN GOSUB 520 :GOSUB 570 :PUT 1,R : GOTO 260
420 IF VAL(R$) = 2 THEN GOSUB 520 :PUT 1,R: GOTO 260
430 IF VAL(R$) = 3 THEN GOSUB 570 :PUT 1,R: GOTO 260
440 IF VAL(R$) = 4 THEN LSET CF$ = "": LSET DF$ = "":PUT 1,R:
    GOTO 260
450 IF VAL(R$) = 5 THEN 260
460 PRINT "PLEASE ENTER 1-5 ONLY": GOTO 260
470 :
480 PRINT "END OF DATA IN THIS FILE"
490 CLOSE 1
500 GOTO 620
510 :
520 LINE INPUT "ENTER NEW CODE #:"; C$
530 REM   DATA ENTRY CHECKS
540 LSET CF$ = C$
550 RETURN
560 :
```

continued on next page

```
570 LINE INPUT "ENTER NEW DESCRIPTION:"; D$
580 REM    DATA ENTRY TESTS
590 LSET DF$ = D$
600 RETURN
610 :
620 END
```

(a) Write the corresponding program line number(s) for each step in the outline.

(1) Open the file. ____________________

(2) Field the buffer. ____________________

(3) Assign R, the record pointer variable (record counter), an initial value of zero.

____

(4) Increase the current value of R by one. ____________________

(5) Check the value of R against the length of file value plus one to see whether the last record in the file has already been retrieved. The comparison is IF R = LOF(1) + 1 THEN step (19), where the file is closed. Note that if you used R = LOF(1) for the comparison, and the comparison is true, the last record (where the file pointer is located) is not processed through the rest of the program.

____

(6) Retrieve the dataset in record number R. ____________________

(7) Clear the display screen. ____________________

(8) Display the items in the dataset. ____________________

(9) Display the "menu" choices for the user. ____________________

(10) Ask the user to input a choice from the "menu." ____________________

(11) Check the entry for legal "menu" options. ____________________

(12) Design subroutine one: ____________________

- (a) Enter change for code number. ____________________
- (b) Data entry checks. ____________________
- (c) Assign entry to correct buffer variable. ____________________
- (d) Return. ____________________

(13) Design subroutine two: ____________________

- (a) Enter change for description. ____________________
- (b) Data entry checks. ____________________
- (c) Assign entry to correct buffer variable. ____________________
- (d) Return. ____________________

(14) For "menu" option 1: ______

(a) Go to subroutine one. ______

(b) Go to subroutine two. ______

(c) Place the changed dataset into the same record from which the old dataset was retrived. ______

(d) Go back to step (4). ______

(15) For "menu" option 2, follow steps (14) (a), (c), and (d). ______

(16) For "menu" option 3, follow steps (14) (b), (c), and (d). ______

(17) For "menu" option 4: ______

(a) Assign null strings to all buffer variables. ______

(b) Follow steps (14) (c) and (d). ______

(18) For "menu" option 5, merely go back to step (4). ______

(19) Display the message END OF DATA IN THIS FILE and close the file.

______

- - - - - - - - - - - - - - -

(a) (1) 220
(2) 230
(3) 250
(4) 260
(5) 270
(6) 280
(7) 300
(8) 310
(9) 320–370
(10) 390
(11) 400
(12) (a) 520
(b) 530
(c) 540
(d) 550
(13) (a) 570
(b) 580
(c) 590
(d) 600
(14) (a) 410
(b) 410
(c) 410
(d) 410
(15) 420
(16) 430
(17) (a) 440
(b) 440
(18) 450
(19) 480

CONVERTING SEQUENTIAL FILES TO RANDOM ACCESS FILES

Another useful file utility program converts a sequential file to a random access file. The procedure involves making a copy of the sequential file and placing one dataset from the sequential file into one record in a random access file. If at some point you want to standardize your entire software collection or system into random access file format, a program modeled on the one you are about to write would do the job.

The example is a small business-type application where a sequential file contains data in this format:

> Customer number = five-character string
> Customer phone number = ten-character string
> Credit status code = number from 1 to 10 (single precision value)
> Current balance owed = numeric value (single precision value)

Create this sequential file by modifying the Chapter 4 Self-test problem 3. Name this file CUST. The task is to copy a sequential data file into a random access file, one dataset (as described above) per record. The outline of steps is as follows.

(1) Open the sequential data file as an input file.
(2) Open the random access file into which the copy is to be made.
(3) Field the random access file.
(4) Check the sequential file for EOF and, if found, go to step (9).
(5) Input a complete dataset from the sequential file.
(6) Reassign the data items to fielded variables. Remember to make any numeric data items in the dataset into the acceptable random access file format.
(7) Print the dataset to the random access file.
(8) Repeat steps (4) to (8) until all data have been copied.
(9) Close the files.

Here is the introductory and initializing module. You write lines 230, 240, and 250. Assume single precision values for credit status and current balance.

(a)
```
100 REM        SEQ TO R-A FILE COPY
110 :
120 REM      VARIABLES USED
130 REM        N$ = CUST. # (5)
140 REM        P$ = PHONE # (10)
150 REM        C = CREDIT STATUS
160 REM        B = BALANCE OWED
170 :
180 REM      FILES USED
190 REM        CUST = SEQ FILE
200 REM        CUST1 = R-A FILE
210 :
220 REM      FILE INITIALIZATION
230                                                     :REM    OPEN SEQ FILE
240                                                     :REM    OPEN R-A FILE
250                                                     :REM    FIELD BUFFER
260 :
```

— — — — — — — — — — — — — — —

(a)
```
230 OPEN "I", 1, "CUST"
240 OPEN "R", 2, "CUST1"
250 FIELD 2, 5 AS NF$, 10 AS PF$, 4 AS CF$, 4 AS BF$
```

Note that the two numeric values are fielded as four-byte strings, since single precision numbers were assumed. You could have used only two bytes for the credit status since it is expressed as an integer, and you could have used eight bytes for the current balance if you had assumed a double precision number (big business!).

In the next program section, fill in the blank at line 280 to test for end-of-file for the sequential file and branch to line 420 if the end of file is found. Then fill in line 290 to read one dataset from the sequential file.

(a)
```
260 :
270 REM    READ SEQ FILE
280                                          :REM    TEST EOF(1)
290                                          :REM    READ DATASET
300 :
```

(a)
```
260 :
270 REM    READ SEQ FILE
280 IF EOF(1) THEN 420
290 INPUT #1, N$, P$, C, B
300 :
```

A GOTO loop causes the repeated execution of the program segment above, reading one dataset at a time from the sequential file until the end of file marker is encountered. When that happens, the task is complete.

Meanwhile, the first execution of the preceding program segment places one dataset into buffer number 1. Next, the program must copy the data into buffer number 2 directly. The first such transfer statement has been completed. You complete the others.

(a)
```
300 :
310 REM    COPY DATA TO BUFFER
320 LSET NF$ = N$
330
340
350
360 :
```

(a)
```
300 :
310 REM    COPY DATA TO BUFFER
320 LSET NF$ = N$
330 LSET PF$ = P$
340 LSET CF$ = MKS$(C)
350 LSET BF$ = MKS$(B)
360 :
```

The final section of the program is all that remains to complete the utility example. The program reads the sequential file and copies the data to the random access file buffer. Next the random access file buffer is to be copied into the random access file itself (line 380, which is left for you to complete). Then the program goes back to line 280 for more data, as shown by line 390. The close file operation is completed in lines 410 to 430. You fill in line 380.

(a)
```
360 :
370 REM    WRITE TO R-A FILE
380                           :REM    PRINT TO R-A FILE
390 GOTO 280
400 :
410 REM    CLOSE FILES
420 CLOSE 1,2
430 PRINT "COPY COMPLETE"
```

(a)
```
380 PUT 2
```

You may have noticed that you do not have to use a record number in the GET and PUT statements. For these applications, the current record counter provided record numbers automatically. The next chapter contains programs where the automatic record counter is not necessarily used.

Here is the complete sequential to the random access file conversion program:

```
100 REM       SEQ TO R-A FILE COPY
110 :
120 REM      VARIABLES USED
130 REM        N$ = CUST. #(5)
140 REM        P$ = PHONE # (10)
150 REM        C = CREDIT STATUS
160 REM        B = BALANCE OWED
170 :
180 REM      FILES USED
190 REM        CUST = SEQ FILE
200 REM        CUST1 = R-A FILE
210 :
220 REM      FILE INITIALIZATION
230 OPEN "I", 1, "CUST"
240 OPEN "R", 2, "CUST1"
250 FIELD 2, 5 AS NF$, 10 AS PF$, 4 AS CF$, 4 AS BF$
260 :
270 REM      READ SEQ FILE
280 IF EOF(1) THEN 420
290 INPUT #1, N$, P$, C, B
300 :
310 REM      COPY DATA TO BUFFER
320 LSET NF$ = N$
330 LSET PF$ = P$
340 LSET CF$ = MKS$(C)
350 LSET BF$ = MKS$(B)
360 :
370 REM      WRITE TO R-A FILE
380 PUT 2
390 GOTO 280
```

```
400 :
410 REM      CLOSE FILES
420 CLOSE 1,2
430 PRINT "COPY COMPLETE"
```

(a) Check your understanding of the sequential file to random access file copying procedure by writing the corresponding program line numbers for each step in the outline:

(1) Open the sequential data file as an input file. ______

(2) Open the random access file into which the copy is to be made. ______

(3) Field the random access file. ______

(4) Check the sequential file for EOF and, if found, go to step (9). ______

(5) Input a complete dataset from the sequential file. ______

(6) Reassign the data items to fielded variables. ______

(7) Print the dataset to the random access file. ______

(8) Repeat steps (4) to (8) until all data have been copied. ______

(9) Close the files. ______

(a) (1) 230
(2) 240
(3) 250
(4) 280
(5) 290
(6) lines 320 to 350
(7) 380
(8) lines 280 to 390
(9) 420

A Technique for Changing the Order of Records Within a Random Access File

The use of the record pointer value (record counter) in GET and PUT statements provides a simple technique for moving datasets from one record position in the file to another in the same file. By fielding the buffer so that the entire record is considered one dataset or data item with 256 characters, you can GET an entire record from one place in the file (let's say the last record in the file), and then PUT it into another record (say a record whose dataset is no longer needed and is to be deleted from the file).

```
420 FIELD 1, 256 AS F$
430 GET 1, LOF(1)
440 PUT 1, 43
```

(a) What value is used in line 430 to retrieve the last record in a file? ____________

(a) The value of the length of file (which is the same as the last record number in a file).

A Universal Random Access File Display Program

In the little program below, the LOF function helps you go through a random access file and displays every record in the file, regardless of how the data were fielded when originally placed in the file.

```
10 LINE INPUT "NAME OF FILE YOU WANT DUMPED (DISPLAYED)"; A$
20 OPEN "R", 1, A$
30 FIELD 1, 256 AS B$
40 FOR R = 1 TO LOF(1)
50 GET 1, R
60 PRINT B$
70 NEXT R
```

For CRT display, you could include the "press any key to continue" technique to control the pace of the display.

```
65 LINE INPUT ""; C$
```

(a) In line 50, how is the record number to GET determined? ____________

(a) By the FOR NEXT loop control variable (whose value goes from 1 to the value of the length of file, which is the same as the last record number in the file).

CHAPTER 7 SELF-TEST

1. Write a program to create a random access data file that contains the inventory of products carried by an imaginary business. Each random access record contains the following data for one item of inventory in the order shown below. Numbers in parentheses indicate maximum string lengths. Since record space is not crucial, assume single precision for values assigned to numeric variables, even though some could be integer values.

P$ = product number (4)
D$ = description of inventory item (20)
S$ = supplier (20)
L = reorder point (how low the stock of item can be before reordering)
Y = reorder quantity
Q = quantity available (currently in stock)
C = cost (from supplier)
U = unit selling price (what the item is sold for)

Here is the introductory module:

```
100 REM     PROB 7-1 SOLUTION
110 :
120 REM     VARIABLES USED
130 REM       P$,PB$ = PROD. NO. (4)
140 REM       D$,DB$ = DESCRIPTION(20)
150 REM       S$,SB$ = SUPPLIER (20)
160 REM       L,LB$ = RECORDER POINT
170 REM       Y,YB$ = RECORDER QUANTITY
180 REM       Q,QB$ = QUANTITY
190 REM       C,CB$ = COST
200 REM       U,UB$ = UNIT SELLING PRICE
210 :         R$ = USER RESPONSE
220 REM     FILES USED
230 REM       PRODUCTS R-A FILE
240 :
```

Using the program, create a random access file. Make up your own data for 20 records (inventory items) and enter them into the file. This file will be used in Chapter 8 examples and activities.

Use as much scratch paper as needed to draft your solution programs for all problems in the self-test.

2. Write two programs, one to create and another to read/display a *sequential* file named POINT, which has two data items per dataset. The first data item is the product number *only* from each dataset in PRODUCT, and the second data item is a value that corresponds to the record number in the PRODUCT file where that product number is stored. There should be exactly as many datasets in the sequential file POINT as there are records in the random access file PRODUCT. Your file creating program must input an entire dataset from the *random access* file named PRODUCT, while only the first data item and the record number are output to the *sequential* file named POINT. This file will be used in a Chapter 8 application.

3. Write a program to make a copy of the random access file that you transferred from a sequential file in the last example program in Chapter 7. The copy should be another random access file.

Here is the introductory module:

```
100         R-A TO R-A FILE COPY
110 :
120 REM       VARIABLES USED
130 REM         NB$,NC$ = CUST. #(5)
140 REM         PB$,PC$ = PHONE # (10)
150 REM         CB$,CF$ = CREDIT STATUS
150 REM         BB$,BF$ = B-LANCE OWED
170 :
180 REM       FILES USED
190 REM         CUST = R-A FILE
200 REM         CUST1 = R-A FILE
```

4. Write a program or program module to display the contents of the original data file and the copy in the previous problem (3), for verification of the completeness and accuracy of the copy. The program should display the data in record 1 of the original file, and then the data from record 1 in the file copy, then the data from record 2 in the original file, followed by the data from record 2 in the copy, and so on to the end of the files.

5. For application in Chapter 8, write one program to create and then read/display a *sequential* data file with this dataset:

C = Check number or deposit slip number
Y$ = date (8) (format: xx/xx/xx)
W$ = party to whom check is written, or source of deposit (20)
A$ = account number from chart of accounts (4)
D = dollar amount

For your financial records, you create a file at the beginning of each month containing last month's money transactions, as shown in your checkbook register of checks written and deposits made. Since you will have a separate data file for each month of the year, use the LETTER# file name creating technique (see page 133 in the Chapter 4 Self-Test problem 6). The file named MONTH1 is all January checks and deposits, MONTH2 is all February checks and deposits, etc. Use your own checkbook register (or your imagination) to create one or more MONTH# sequential files. Select A$ (the appropriate account number) for each dataset from the chart of accounts on page 272.

6. Write one program to create three different *random access* files which contain your budget estimates for the coming year. Your budget has forty-six categories of income and expenses as listed in the chart of accounts on page 272. Your budget files are named BUDGET1, BUDGET2, and BUDGET3, and you use the LETTER# technique for creating the file names. BUDGET1 will have six records (account chart numbers 1001 to 1006); BUDGET2 will have twenty-eight records (account chart numbers 2001 to 2028); and BUDGET3 will have twelve records (3001 to 3012). The dataset is as follows:

NF$ = Account Chart Number (4)
DF$ = Account name from Chart of Accounts (20)
BF$ = Budgeted amount for this category (annual budget estimate) (4)
EF$ = Amount spent or earned (year-to-date) (4)

Use your program to create, then read/display, three separate BUDGET# files as you would at the beginning of a new year, using as data the account chart numbers and names (page 272), your own values for budgeted amount, and zero for the amount expended or earned to date. The BUDGET# files will be used in Chapter 8.

Answer Key

Also see Final Self-test Problem 5

1.
```
100 REM      PROB 7-1
110 :
120 REM     VARIABLES USED
130 REM      P$,PB$ = PROD. NO. (4)
140 REM      D$,DB$ = DESCRIPTION(20)
150 REM      S$,SB$ = SUPPLIER(20)
160 REM      L,LB$ = REORDER POINT
170 REM      Y,YB$ = REORDER QUANTITY
180 REM      Q,QB$ = QUANTITY
190 REM      C,CB$ = COST
200 REM      U,UB$ = UNIT SELLING PRICE
210 REM      R$ = USER RESPONSE TO CONTINUE ENTRIES
220 :
230 REM      FILES USED
240 REM      PRODUCT - RA FILE
250 REM      INITIALIZE
260 CLEAR 1000
270 OPEN "R", 1, "PRODUCT"
280 FIELD 1, 4 AS PB$, 20 AS DB$, 20 AS SB$, 4 AS LB$, 4 AS YB$, 4 AS
    QB$, 4 AS CB$, 4 AS UB$
290 :
300 REM    DATA ENTRY MODULE-DATA ENTRY TESTS OMITTED
310 LINE INPUT "ENTER PRODUCT NUMBER (4 DIGITS):"; P$
320 REM*** DATA ENTRY TESTS GO HERE
330 LINE INPUT "ENTER PRODUCT DESCRIPTION (20 CHAR. MAX.)"; D$
340 REM *** DATA ENTRY TESTS GO HERE
350 LINE INPUT "ENTER NAME OF SUPPLIER (20 CHAR. MAX.)"; S$
360 REM *** DATA ENTRY TESTS GO HERE
370 INPUT "REORDER POINT"; L
380 REM *** DATA ENTRY TESTS GO HERE
390 INPUT "REORDER QUANTITY"; Y
400 REM *** DATA ENTRY TESTS GO HERE
410 INPUT "QUANTITY NOW IN STOCK"; Q
420 REM *** DATA ENTRY TESTS GO HERE
430 INPUT "WHOLESALE COST"; C
440 REM *** DATA ENTRY TESTS GO HERE
450 INPUT "UNIT SELLING PRICE"; U
460 REM *** DATA ENTRY TESTS GO HERE
470 REM *** DATA ENTRY CHECKS DELETED TO SHOW PROGRAM STRUTURE
480 :
490 REM    MOVE VALUES TO BUFFER
500 LSET PB$ = P$
510 LSET DB$ = D$
520 LSET SB$ = S$
530 LSET LB$ = MKS$(L)
540 LSET YB$ = MKS$(Y)
550 LSET QB$ = MKS$(Q)
560 LSET CB$ = MKS$(C)
570 LSET UB$ = MKS$(U)
580 :
590 PUT 1
600 :
610 LINE INPUT "MORE DATA (TYPE YES OR NO)?"; R$
620 IF LEFT$(R$,1) = "Y" THEN CLS : GOTO 310
630 :
640 REM    CLOSE FILE
650 CLOSE
660 PRINT "FILE CLOSED."
670 END
```

2.
```
100 REM     PROB 7-2 SOLUTION
110 REM    CREATE A POINTER FILE NAMED 'POINT' FOR RANDOM
           ACCESS FILE 'PRODUCT'
120 :
130 REM    VARIABLES USED
140 REM      P$ = PROD. NO. (4)
150 REM      D$ = DESCRIPTION (20)
160 REM      S$ = NAME OF SUPPLIER (20)
170 REM      L = REORDER POINT (4)
180 REM      Y = REORDER QUANTITY (4)
190 REM      Q = QUANTITY IN STOCK (4)
200 REM      C = WHOLESALE COST (4)
210 REM      U = UNIT SELLING PRICE (4)
220 REM      R$ = USER RESPONSE VARIABLE
230 REM      R = RECORD NUMBER
240 :
250 REM    FILES USED
260 REM      RANDOM ACCESS FILE NAME: PRODUCT
270 REM      DATASET FORMAT: P$,D$,S$,L,Y,Q,C,U
280 REM      SEQUENTIAL FILE NAME: POINT
290 REM    DATASET FORMAT: P$,R
300:
310 REM    INITIALIZE
320 OPEN "R", 1, "PRODUCT"
330 FIELD 1, 4 AS PF$, 20 AS DF$, 20 AS SF$, 4 AS LF$,
    4 AS YF$, 4 AS QF$, 4 AS CF$, 4 AS UF$
340 OPEN "O", 2, "POINT"
350 :
360 REM    READ 'PRODUCT' AND WRITE 'POINT'
370 FOR R = 1 TO LOF(1)
380 GET 1, R
390 PRINT#2, PB$, ","; R
400 NEXT R
410 :
420 REM CLOSE FILES
430 CLOSE
440 PRINT: PRINT "FILES CLOSED"
450 :
460 REM    READ/DISPLAY 'POINT'
470 OPEN "I", 1, "POINT"
480 IF EOF(1) THEN 540
490 INPUT#1, P$, R
500 PRINT P$; R,
510 GOTO 480
520 :
530 REM  CLOSE FILE
540 CLOSE


550 PRINT: PRINT "ALL"; R; "DATASETS DISPLAYED AND FILE CLOSED"
```

3.
```
100 REM PROB 7-3 SOLUTION
110 :
120 REM      R-A TO R-A FILE COPY
130 :
140 REM     VARIABLES USED
150 REM       NB$, NC$ = CUST. #(5)
160 REM       PB$, PC$ = PHONE # (10)
170 REM       CB$, CF$ = CREDIT STATUS
180 REM       BB$, BF$ = BALANCE OWED
190 :
200 REM     FILES USED
210 REM       CUST1 = R-A FILE
220 REM       CUST2 = R-A FILE
230 :
240 REM     INITIALIZE
250 OPEN "R", 1, "CUST1"
260 OPEN "R", 2, "CUST2"
270 FIELD 1, 5 AS NB$, 10 AS PB$, 4 AS CB$, 4 AS BB$
280 FIELD 2, 5 AS NC$, 10 AS PC$, 4 AS CF$, 4 AS BF$
290 :
300 :
310 REM   MAKE COPY
320 FOR X = 1 TO LOF(1)
330 GET 1
340 LSET NC$ = NB$
350 LSET PC$ = PB$
360 LSET CF$ = CB$
370 LSET BF$ = BB$
380 PUT 2
390 NEXT X
400 :
410 CLOSE 1,2
420 PRINT "FILES CLOSED. COPY COMPLETE."
430 END
```

4.
```
100 REM     PROB 7-4 SOLUTION
110 :
120 REM     RA FILE PRINT
130 :
140 REM     VARIABLES USED
150 REM       NB$, NC$ = CUST. #(5)
160 REM       PB$, PC$ = PHONE # (10)
170 REM       CB$, CF$ = CREDIT STATUS
180 REM       BB$, BF$ = BALANCE OWED
190 :
200 REM     FILES USED
210 REM       CUST = R-A FILE
220 REM       CUST1 = R-A FILE
230 :
240 REM     INITIALIZE
250 OPEN "R", 1, "CUST"
260 OPEN "R", 2, "CUST1"
270 FIELD 1, 5 AS NB$, 10 AS PB$, 4 AS CB$, 4 AS BB$
280 FIELD 2, 5 AS NC$, 10 AS PC$, 4 AS CF$, 4 AS BF$
290 :
300 :
310 REM     DISPLAY CONTENTS
320 FOR X = 1 TO LOF(1)
```

continued on next page

```
330 PRINT "FILE 1", "FILE 2"
340 GET 1: GET 2
350 PRINT NB$, NC$
360 PRINT PB$, PC$
370 PRINT CVS(CB$), CVS(CF$)
380 PRINT CVS(BB$), CVS(BF$)
390 LINE INPUT "PRESS ENTER FOR NEXT ITEM"; R$
400 NEXT X
410 :
420 CLOSE
430 PRINT: PRINT "ALL ITEMS DISPLAYED AND FILES CLOSED."
440 END
```

5.
```
100 REM       PROB 7-5 SOLUTION
110 REM    CREATE THEN READ/DISPLAY 'MONTH#' FILES OF
           CHECKBOOK TRANSACTIONS; REFER TO CHART OF ACCOUNT
           PAGE 272
120 :
130 REM    VARIABLES USED
140 REM       C = CHECK OR DEPOSIT SLIP NUMBER
150 REM       Y$ = DATE (8) (FORMAT: XX/XX/XX)
160 REM       W$ = PARTY TO WHOM CHECK IS WRITTEN OR SOURCE
                 OF DEPOSIT (20)
170 REM       A$ = ACCOUNT NUMBER FROM CHART OF ACCOUNTS (4)
180 REM       D = DOLLAR AMOUNT
190 :
200 REM  FILE USED
210 REM    SEQUENTIAL FILE NAME: MONTH#, WHERE '#' IS USER
           SELECTED (1 TO 12)
220 REM    DATASET FORMAT: C, Y$, W$, A$, D
230 :
240 REM    INITIALIZE
250 LINE INPUT "WHICH MONTH (1 TO 12)"; F$
260 IF VAL(F$) < 1 OR VAL(F$) > 12 THEN PRINT : PRINT
    "ENTER A NUMBER BETWEEN 1 AND 12, WHERE 1 = JAN, 2 = FEB,
     ETC.": PRINT : GOTO 250
270 LET F$ = "MONTH"   F$
280 OPEN "O", 1, F$
290 :
300 REM    DATA ENTRY MODULE
310 INPUT "CHECK OR DEPOSIT SLIP NUMBER"; C
320 REM    DATA ENTRY TESTS GO HERE
330 LINE INPUT "DATE OF CHECK OR DEPOSIT (XX/XX/XX)?"; Y$
340 REM    DATA ENTRY TESTS GO HERE
350 LINE INPUT "PARTY TO WHOM CHECK IS WRITTEN OR SOURCE OF
    DEPOSIT?"; W$
360 REM    DATA ENTRY TESTS GO HERE
370 LINE INPUT "CHART OF ACCOUNTS NUMBER FOR THIS
    TRANSACTION?"; A$
380 IF LEN(A$) <> 4 THEN PRINT : PRINT "CHART OF ACCOUNTS
    NUMBERS ARE 4 DIGITS. PLEASE REENTER" : PRINT  : GOTO 370
390 IF VAL(A$) < 1001 OR VAL(A$) > 3012 THEN PRINT : PRINT
    "ACCOUNT # "; A$; "DOES NOT EXIST. PLEASE REENTER":
    PRINT : GOTO 370
400 REM    OTHER DATA ENTRY TESTS GO HERE
410 INPUT "DOLLAR AMOUNT"; D
```

continued on next page

```
420 REM     DATA ENTRY TESTS GO HERE
430 :
440 REM     WRITE TO FILE
450 PRINT#1, C; ","; Y$; ","; W$; ","; A$; ","; D
460 LINE INPUT "ANOTHER TRANSACTION ENTRY (Y OR N)?"; R$
470 IF LEFT$(R$,1) <> "N" AND LEFT$(R$,1) <> "Y" THEN PRINT;
    PRINT "ENTER 'Y' FOR YES OR 'N' FOR NO" : PRINT : GOTO 460
480 IF LEFT$(R$,1) = "Y"THEN 310
490 REM     CLOSE FILE
500 CLOSE
510 PRINT : PRINT "FILE CLOSED" : PRINT
520 LINE INPUT "DISPLAY  CONTENTS OF FILE (Y OR N)?"; R$
530 REM     Y OR N CHECK GOES HERE
540 IF R$ = "N" THEN END
550 OPEN "I", 1, F$
560 IF EOF(1) THEN 680
570 INPUT#1, O, Y$, W$, A$. D
580 PRINT "CHECK OR DEPOSIT #: "; C
590 PRINT "DATE WRITTEN OR RECEIVED: "; Y$
600 PRINT "WRITTEN TO OR RECEIVED FROM: "; W$
610 PRINT "ACCOUNT CHART NUMBER: "; A$
620 PRINT "AMOUNT: $"; D
630 PRINT
640 LINE INPUT "PRESS 'ENTER' FOR NEXT DATASET"; R$
650 PRINT : GOTO 560
660 :
670 REM     CLOSE FILE
680 CLOSE
690 PRINT : PRINT "FILE DISPLAYED AND CLOSED"
```

7.

```
100 REM     PROB 7-6 SOLUTION
110 REM     CREATE THEN READ/DISPLAY R-A FILE 'BUDGET#'
120 :
130 REM     VARIABLES USED
140 REM       N$ = NF$ = ACCOUNT CHART NUMBER (4)
150 REM       D$ = DF$ = ACCOUNT NAME FROM CHART OF ACCOUNTS (20)
160 REM       B$ = BF$ = BUDGETED AMOUNT OR EXPECTED INCOME FOR
              THIS CATEGORY (YEARLY BUDGET ESTIMATE) (4)
170 REM       E$ = EF$ = AMOUNT SPENT OR EARNED (YEAR-TO-DATE) (4)
180 REM       F$ = FILE NAME
190 REM       R$ = USER RESPONSE VARIABLE
200 REM       R = RECORD NUMBER
210 REM     FILE USED
220 REM      RANDOM ACCESS FILE NAME; BUDGET# (WHERE # = 1, 2, OR
             3 AND IS USER SELECTED)
230 :
240 REM     INITIALIZE
250 LINE INPUT "WHICH BUDGET# FILE (1, 2, OR 3)?"; F$
260 IF VAL(F$) < 1 OR VAL(F$) > 3 THEN PRINT : PRINT "ENTER ONE
    DIGIT NUMBER 1, 2, OR 3 ONLY" : PRINT : GOTO 250
270 IF F$ = "1" THEN F = 6
280 IF F$ = "2" THEN F = 28
290 IF F$ = "3" THEN F = 12
300 LET F$ = "BUDGET"  F$
310 OPEN "R", 1, F$
320 FIELD 1, 4 AS NF$, 20 AS DF$, 4 AS BF$, 4 AS EF$
330 :
```

continued on next page

```
340 REM     DATA ENTRY MODULE
350 LINE INPUT "ENTER CHART OF ACCOUNTS NUMBER:"; N$
360 IF LEN(N$) <> 4 THEN PRINT : PRINT "ENTRY ERROR. "; N$; "IS
    NOT A 4 DIGIT ACCOUNT NUMBER." : PRINT : GOTO 350
370 IF LEFT$(N,1) <> RIGHT$(F$,1) THEN PRINT : PRINT "ENTRY ERROR.
    "; N$;  "IS NOT AN ACCOUNT NUMBER FOR "; F$ : PRINT : GOTO 350
380 IF VAL(RIGHT$(N$,3)) < 1 OR VAL(RIGHT$(N$,3)) > F THEN PRINT :
    PRINT "ENTRY ERROR." ; N$;  "IS NOT AN ACCOUNT NUMBER FOR" ;
    F$ : PRINT : GOTO 350
390 LINE INPUT "ENTER ACCOUNT NAME:"; D$
400 IF LEN(D$) > 20 THEN PRINT : PRINT "ENTRY TOO LONG.
    ABBREVIATE TO 20 CHARACTERS OR LESS.": PRINT : GOTO 390
410 REM     OTHER ENTRY TESTS GO HERE
420 LINE INPUT "ENTER BUDGETED AMOUNT OR EXPECTED INCOME FOR
    THIS FOR THIS CATEGORY FOR THIS YEAR:"; B$
430 REM     DATA ENTRY TESTS GO HERE
440 LINE INPUT "AMOUNT SPENT OR EARNED (YEAR TO DATE):"; E$
450 REM     DATA ENTRY TESTS GO HERE
460 :
470 REM     WRITE TO FILE
480 LSET NF$ = N$
490 LSET DF$ = D$
500 LSET BF$ = MKS$(VAL(B$))
510 LSET EF$ = MKS$(VAL(E$))
520 PUT 1, VAL(RIGHT$(N$,3))
530 PRINT
540 LINE INPUT "ANOTHER ENTRY (Y OR N)?"; R$
550 IF R$ <> "Y" AND R$ <> "N" THEN PRINT : PRINT "ENTER 'Y' FOR
    YES OR 'N' FOR NO" : PRINT : GOTO 540
560 IF R$ = "Y" THEN 350
570 :
580 REM     CLOSE FILE
590 CLOSE
600 PRINT : PRINT "FILE CLOSED" : PRINT
610 :
620 LINE INPUT "DISPLAY THIS FILE (Y OR N)?"; R$
630 REM     Y OR N TEST GOES HERE
640 IF R$ = "N" THEN END
650 :
660 REM     READ/DISPLAY MODULE
670 OPEN "R", 1, F$
680 FIELD 1, 4 AS NF$, 20 AS DF$, 4 AS BF$, 4 AS EF$
690 FOR R = 1 TO EOF(1)
700 GET 1, R
710 PRINT
720 PRINT "ACCT NUMBER: "; NF$
730 PRINT "ACCT NAME: "; DF$
740 PRINT "BUDGET AMOUNT: $"; CVS(BF$)
750 PRINT "YEAR-TO-DATE: $"; CVS(EF$)
760 PRINT
770 LINE INPUT "PRESS 'ENTER' TO DISCPLAY NEXT CATEGORY"; R$
780 NEXT R
790 :
800 REM     CLOSE FILE
810 CLOSE
820 PRINT : PRINT "ALL DATA DISPLAYED AND FILE CLOSED."
```

CHAPTER EIGHT

Random Access File Applications

Objectives: In this chapter you will learn expanded techniques for random access data file applications and how to use sequential "pointer" data files as an index for a random access data file.

Two file applications are designed to be somewhat typical of the programs you might encounter as you design your own computer software systems and write your own programs. The programs are not really long, as you might expect, but they are only one component of a larger software system composed of many programs.

The first application is an inventory control application that uses both a sequential file and a random access file in the same program. The objective is to show how to use a sequential "pointer" file and how to change data located in a random access file record. The application could as well have been a mailing list, a credit information file, or any sort of master file application.

In this case, all the data regarding the inventory of products carried are stored in a random access file(s). Each random access record contains the following data for one item of inventory in the order shown below:

```
P$ = PROD # (4)
D$ = DESCRIPTION (20)
S$ = SUPPLIER (20)
L = REORDER POINT
Y = REORDER QUANTITY
Q = QUANTITY AVAILABLE
C = COST
U = UNIT SELLING PRICE
```

If you wanted to change some data for product number 9827, you would have to search through the random access file records one at a time, until you found product number 9827. You could then make your changes – a very inefficient use of random access files. To increase efficiency, you could add a sequential "pointer" file that contains the product numbers (in a string variable) followed by the record number where the proper datum is located in the random access file. To change the cost and selling price data in the random access file, follow these steps:

1. Enter product number and new cost and price data.
2. Quickly search the sequential pointer file for the product number that gives the record location.
3. Access the correct random access record.
4. Make the changes in the random access file record.

It looks easy, but there are a few "tricks." Here is the first part of the program. Read it through carefully.

```
100 REM   R-A/SEQ INVENTORY FILE PROGRAM
103 REM   THIS PROGRAM PERMITS THE USER TO CHANGE THE COST AND
105 REM   UNIT SELLING PRICE FOR AN EXISTING INVENTORY ITEM IN FILE.
110 :
120 REM   VARIABLES USED
130 REM      R$ = DATA ENTRY STRING
140 REM      P1$ = PROD # (4)
150 REM      R = RECORD #
160 REM      P$ = PROD # (4)
170 REM      D$ = DESCRIPTION (20)
180 REM      S$ = SUPPLIER (20)
190 REM      L = REORDER POINT
200 REM      Y = REORDER QUANTITY
210 REM      Q = QUANTITY AVAILABLE
220 REM      C = COST
230 REM      U = UNIT SELLING PRICE
240 :
250 :
260 REM   FILES USED
270 REM      POINT = SEQ POINTER FILE
280 REM      INVEN = R-A FILE
290 :
300 REM   FILE INITIALIZATION
310 OPEN "I", 1, "POINT"
320 OPEN "R", 2, "INVEN"
330 FIELD 2, 4 AS PF$, 20 AS DF$, 20 AS SF$, 4 AS LF$, 4 AS YF$, 4 AS
    QF$, 4 AS CF$, 4 AS UF$
340 :
350 REM   DATA ENTRY MODULE
360 CLS
370 LINE INPUT "ENTER PROD #:"; R$
380 REM   DATA ENTRY TESTS
390 INPUT "ENTER NEW COST:"; C
400 REM   DATA ENTRY TESTS
410 INPUT "ENTER NEW SELLING PRICE"; U
420 REM   DATA ENTRY TESTS
430 :
```

All data have been entered and tested. It is time to search the sequential file for the record location of the data in the random access file. On the chance that the operator made an entry error that escaped the error tests, include an error trap in case you read all the way to the end of the sequential file and find no matching product number. This error message is shown below in lines 690 through 700. You fill in lines 450, 460, and 470.

(a)
```
430 :
440 REM   SEARCH POINTER FILE
```

```
450                                          :REM    EOF TO 690
460                                          :REM    READ THE SEQ FILE
470                                          :REM    CHECK ENTERED #
                                                     WITH FILE #
480 :                                        :REM    USE THIS LINE IF
                                                     YOU NEED IT.

670 :
680 REM    ERROR TRAPS
690 PRINT "THIS PRODUCT # NOT IN OUR FILE"
700 PRINT "CHECK YOUR NUMBERS AND REENTER"
710 GOTO 610             :REM   RETURN TO MORE DATA TEST
720 :
```

(b) In which variable is the record number of the random access file located? _______

(a)

```
430 :
440 REM     SEARCH POINTER FILE
450 IF EOF(1) THEN 690
460 INPUT #1, P1$, R
470 IF P1$ <> R$ THEN 450
480 :
```

(b) R

Before you get the record contents and copy them to the buffer, test that the record number in the sequential file is valid in the random access file (better safe than sorry!). Test record validity using the LOF function. The error message is shown below in lines 730 and 740. You fill in lines 500 and 510.

(a)

```
480 :
490 REM     GET RECORD FROM R-A FILE
500                                     :REM    LOF TEST FOR RECORD #
510                                     :REM    GET THE RECORD
520 :
680 REM     ERROR TRAPS
720 :
730 PRINT "RECORD # ERROR IN POINTER FILE"
740 PRINT "PROCEED TO NEXT ENTRY AND NOTIFY SUPV"
750 GOTO 610             :REM    RETURN TO MORE DATA TEST
```

(a)

```
480 :
490 REM     GET RECORD FROM R-A FILE
500 IF R > LOF(2) THEN 730
510 GET 2, R
520 :
```

There is not much else to do.

(a) What is the next step before you copy the buffer back out to the file? ______

(a) Convert the cost and price numbers to string variables and place them in the buffer.

Complete lines 540, 550, and 580 below. You can refer back to the field statement in line 330 for proper placement of the data.

(a)
```
520 :
530 REM      COPY CHANGES TO BUFFER
540                                          :REM     COPY C
550                                                   TO BUFFER
                                             :REM     COPY U
                                                      TO BUFFER
560 :
570 REM      COPY BUFFER BACK TO FILE
580                                          :REM     COPY BUFFER
                                                      TO FILE
590 :
```

(a)
```
520 :
530 REM      COPY CHANGES TO BUFFER
540 LSET CF$ = MKS$(C)
550 LSET UF$ = MKS$(U)
560 :
570 REM      COPY BUFFER BACK TO FILE
580 PUT 2, R
590 :
```

If line 580 said only 580 PUT 2, you made a serious error. You would have placed the data in the NEXT file record beyond R (R + 1). Each time a GET or PUT statement is executed, the current record number is increased by one (1). When you know which record you want to GET or PUT, include it in your statement as done in lines 510 and 580. Don't count on chance!

The remainder of the program looks like this:

```
590 :
600 REM    MORE DATA?/CLOSE FILE
610 LINE INPUT "MORE ENTRIES:"; R$
```

```
620 IF LEFT$(R$,1) <> "Y" THEN 650
630 CLOSE 1: OPEN "I", 1, "POINT": GOTO 360
640 :
650 CLOSE 1
660 GOTO 760
670 :
760 END
```

(a) Look closely at line 630. Why was it necessary to CLOSE and reOPEN the sequential file?

(a) If the first file search went to the middle of the sequential file, that is where the file pointer would stop. If the second file search was for a product number placed earlier in the file, the pointer would search from the present pointer location to the file end, resulting in the "INVALID PRODUCT NUMBER" error message.

To put it another way, the purpose of line 630 is to reset the file pointer to the beginning of the sequential file. This action is not necessary for random access files.

That completes the first random access file application; one part of an entire product inventory application.

(a) What other programs are needed to complete this series of application programs?

(a) 1) Add new inventory items. 2) Delete inventory items. 3) Change supplier and/ or description. 4) Change reorder point, etc., to name a few.

PERSONAL MONEY MANAGEMENT APPLICATION

The second program could form part of a large home financial management software package. The example gives some hints for setting up your own home finance programs. The objectives of this application are to show you how to process a "transaction" file and to demonstrate how account numbers can be used to point out the file and record in a random access file.

The first step is to decide exactly what expenditures you want to computerize. Record all income and all expenditures into particular accounts. Include the capability to discern taxable from non-taxable items so these records can be used as data for your income tax returns. To keep things simple, the following chart of accounts has been prepared for this application:

```
1001        TAXABLE SALARIES
1002        TAXABLE INTEREST
1003        TAXABLE DIVIDENDS
1004        TAXABLE OTHER INCOME
1005        NON-TAXABLE INCOME
1006        MISC. NON-TAXABLE MONEYS
2001        GROCERIES
2002        NON FOOD STAPLES
2003        MORTGAGE
2004        GAS/ELECTRICITY
2005        WATER & GARBAGE
2006        TELEPHONE
2007        HOME INSURANCE
2008        PROPERTY TAXES
2009        FURNITURE
2010        AUTO PAYMENTS
2011        GAS AND OIL
2012        AUTO REPAIR
2013        PARKING/TOLLS
2014        AUTO INSURANCE
2015        FATHER'S CLOTHES
2016        MOTHER'S CLOTHES
2017        SON'S CLOTHES
2018        DAUGHTER'S CLOTHES
2019        CLOTHING REPAIR/CLEANING
2020        SPORTS FEES/TICKETS
2021        SPORTS EQUIPMENT
2022        MAGAZINES/BOOKS
2023        MOVIES/PLAYS
2024        ALCOHOL
2025        DINING OUT
2026        VACATION EXPENSES
2027        POSTAGE
2028        SCHOOL/HOUSEHOLD SUPPLIES
3001        LEGAL/ACCTG. FEES
3002        LIFE INSURANCE
3003        MEDICAL INSURANCE
3004        DENTAL INSURANCE
3005        UNREIMBURSED MEDICAL EXPENSES
3006        DRUG EXPENSES
3007        EDUCATIONAL FEES AND TUITIONS
3008        BOOKS AND SUPPLIES
3009        EXCESS SALES TAXES PAID
3010        CONTRIBUTIONS
3011        SAVINGS DEPOSITS
3012        INVESTMENTS
```

The account number has important significance. The first digit of the account number is the number of the random access file in which the account details can be found. All random access files are called BUDGET#. The details of the taxable salaries account are found in file BUDGET1 (1001). The details of the telephone account are in file BUDGET2 (2008).

(a) Which file contains the details of the dining out account? ______________

- - - - - - - - - - - - - - - -

(a) BUDGET2(2006)

The last three digits of the account number indicate the record number of the random access file containing the account details. The investment account (3010) will be found in file BUDGET3, record number 10.

(a) The legal/accounting account details are found in file ______________

record number ______________ .

- - - - - - - - - - - - - - - -

(a) BUDGET2, record 30

For convenience, the account number is always entered as a string variable so that you can use the LEFT$ and RIGHT$ functions to separate the file number and record number.

To demonstrate the file number concept, we use three separate files for this small list of accounts. Of course, all these accounts could be placed in one file, but that will not be the case when your account list grows. At that point you may want to use this scheme.

The random access files (BUDGET#) contain the details of each account. Each record contains the following information in the order shown. The name of the buffer variable used and the size of the buffer variable in bytes are indicated.

```
NF$ = ACCOUNT # (4)
DF$ = ACCOUNT NAME (20)
BF$ = BUDGETED AMOUNT (4). ANNUAL BUDGET
EF$ = EXPENDED/EARNED AMOUNT (4). YEAR-TO-DATE
```

Each month a new sequential transaction file is created containing the information found in your checking account check register. For the month of January, the file is called MONTH1. March is MONTH3, etc. You may keep "old" files on your disk for other analyses you may want to do. Each month you will create a transaction file, then process or "post" it to the BUDGET# file. Each sequential transaction file entry includes the following information in the order shown:

```
C = CHECK #/DEPOSIT SLIP #
Y$ = DATE (6)
W$ = PARTY TO WHOM CHECK IS DRAWN/SOURCE OF FUNDS (20)
A$ = ACCOUNT # (4)
D = DOLLAR AMOUNT
```

Notice that the format is set up to be used with deposits and payments and that the transaction file includes more information than you will actually be using. This file, however, can be used for other things as well, so all this information is included.

Let's review the application. Each year, create random access files that contain the beginning status of all your personal accounts. This status includes a yearly budget estimate. Each month create a sequential file (MONTH#) using the information found in your checkbook register. After the MONTH# file is completed, process or post it to the BUDGET# files. Periodically, you can print a status report of the BUDGET# files.

The task is to write the program that processes the monthly transaction file. Here is the introductory module with the file initialization module:

```
100 REM    PERSONAL MONEY MANAGEMENT
110 REM    SEQ/R-A FILE APPLICATION
120 :
130 REM    VARIABLES USED
140 REM       A$ = N$ = ACCT. # (4)
150 REM       D$ = ACCT. NAME (20)
160 REM       Y$ = DATE (8)
170 REM       W$ = CHECK WRITTEN TO/SOURCE OF FUNDS (20)
180 REM       M$ = MONTH SELECTED (2)
190 REM       C = CHECK #/DEPOSIT SLIP #
200 REM       D = DOLLAR AMT. OF CHECK OR DEPOSIT
210 REM       B = BUDGETED AMT.
220 REM       E = AMT EXPENDED TO DATE
230 REM       F$ = SEQ. FILE NAME
240 REM       F2$ = F1$ = R-A FILE NAME
250 REM       R = RECORD NUMBER
260 :
270 REM    FILES USED
280 REM       MONTH# = SEQ/TRANSACTION FILE. # IS USER SELECTED.
290 REM       BUDGET# = R-A FILE. # IS FUNCTION OF A/C # AND
300 REM          CHANGES WITH EACH TRANSACTION
310 REM     INITIALIZE
320 CLEAR 500
330 LINE INPUT "WHAT IS THE MONTH # TO BE PROCESSED?"; M$
340 REM    DATA ENTRY TESTS
350 LET F$ = "MONTH" + M$
360 CLEAR 300
370 OPEN "I", 1, F$
380 REM    R-A FILE IS OPENED/FIELDED WITH EACH TRANSACTION
390 :
```

(a) In lines 330 through 360, if the user enters 3 for M$, what is the file name F$ in line 350? ____________________

(a) MONTH3.
(A word of caution: In line 330, the file number is entered into a string variable M$). If it had been entered into a numeric variable and then changed into a string variable using the STR$ function, the resulting F$ would be MONTH 3. A space is reserved for the sign of a number when you use the STR$ function. The program would never find file MONTH 3 (with a space).

```
390 :
400 REM     PROCESS TRANSACTIONS
410 :
420 REM     READ SEQ. FILE TRANSACTION
430 IF EOF(1) THEN 730
440 INPUT #1, C, Y$, W$, A$, D
450 :
460 REM     EXTRACT FILE #/INITIALIZE R-A FILE
470                           :REM    EXTRACT FILE # INTO F2$
480 REM     F2$ DATA TESTS
490 LET F1$ = "BUDGET" + F2$
500 OPEN "R", 2, F1$
510 FIELD 2, 4 AS NF$, 20 AS DF$, 4 AS BF$, 4 AS EF$
```

Line 430 tests for the end of the transaction file. When that file is complete, so is the program (CLOSE and END). Line 440 reads an entire dataset from the transaction file. In the next section, the file number is "extracted" from the account number to be used in line 490 to make the complete BUDGET file name. Complete line 470, extracting the file number from the account number (it's the first digit of A$).

(a) 470 ____________________

- - - - - - - - - - - - - - -

(a)
```
470 LET F2$ = LEFT$(A$,1)
```

The next section extracts the record number from the account number (the last three digits of A$), tests for the validity of the record number in line 550, and, if the record is determined invalid, prints an error message and closes the BUDGET# file. Fill in line 540.

(a)
```
520 :
530 REM     EXTRACT RECORD #/CONVERT TO #
540                                      :REM    EXTRACT
                                                 RECORD # (R)
550 IF R <= LOF(2) THEN 620       :REM    RECORD VALIDITY TEST
560 PRINT "RECORD # ERROR ON CHECK #"; C
570 PRINT "TRANSACTION IS NOT PROCESSED"
580 CLOSE 2                  :REM    CLOSE R-A FILE
590 GOTO 430                 :REM    RETURN FOR NEXT TRANSACTION
600 :
```

- - - - - - - - - - - - - - -

(a)
```
540 LET R = VAL(RIGHT$(A$,3))
```
(Warning: Don't forget the double closing parentheses.)

The remaining module copies the proper record to the buffer, updates the amount expended/earned, and prints the new value back to the file. Follow the remark clues and complete this module:

(a)
```
600 :
610 REM    COPY AND CHANGE R-A FILE RECORD
620                                          :REM    COPY RECORD TO
                                                     BUFFER
630                                          :REM    CONVERT EXPENDED
                                                     $ TO NUMBER
640                                          :REM    ADD CHECK AMT. TO
                                                     OLD EXPENDED AMT.
650                                          :REM    LSET INTO BUFFER
660                                          :REM    COPY BUFFER TO FILE
670 CLOSE 2
680 :
```

(a)
```
600 :
610 REM    COPY AND CHANGE R-A FILE RECORD
620 GET 2, R
630 LET E = CVS(EF$)
640 LET E = E + D
650 LSET EF$ = MKS$(E)
660 PUT 2, R
670 CLOSE 2
680 :
690 REM    RETURN FOR NEXT TRANS
700 GOTO 430
710 :
720 REM    CLOSE FILES
730 CLOSE
740 END
```

This completes the program. It will continue reading checking transactions and processing them until the end of the transaction file is reached, at which point files are closed and the program ends. This program keeps your disk drive working, but does nothing on your screen or printer.

The way the current program is written, each transaction OPENs and CLOSEs a file – not very efficient use of a disk drive. Professional programmers would scorn the program because it causes so much activity on the disk drive. Always attempt to minimize the number of disk accesses in your programs.

(a) If you were told that most of the transactions in this program take place in file BUDGET2, show how you would change the program to minimize the use of OPEN and CLOSE statements.

(a) Your solution may be different from ours. Read ours carefully, however; it contains some necessary, though tricky, statements.

```
 390 :
 400 REM     PROCESS TRANSACTIONS
√405 LET F3$ = "X":        REM   DUMMY VALUE FOR FIRST TIME
 410 :
 420 REM     READ SEQ. FILE TRANSACTION
 430 IF EOF(1) THEN 730
 440 INPUT #1, C, Y$, W$, A$, D
 450 :
 460 REM     EXTRACT FILE #/ INITIALIZE R-A FILE
 470 LET F2$ = LEFT$(A$,1)
√480 IF F2$ = F3$ THEN 540        REM    IF SAME FILE, SKIP THE OPEN
√485 LET F3$ = F2$:        REM      RESET F3$ FOR NEXT TIME
 490 LET F1$ = "BUDGET" + F2$
 500 OPEN "R", 2, F1$
 510 FIELD 2, 4 AS NF$, 20 AS DF$, 4 AS BF$, 4 AS EF$
 520 :
 530 REM     EXTRACT RECORD #/ CONVERT TO #
 540 LET R = VAL(RIGHT$(A$,3))
 550 IF R<= LOF(2) THEN 620       :REM    RECORD VALIDITY TEST
 560 PRINT "RECORD # ERROR ON CHECK #"; C
 570 PRINT "TRANSACTION IS NOT PROCESSED"
√580 :
 590 GOTO 430            :REM    RETURN FOR NEXT TRANSACTION
 600 :
 610 REM     COPY AND CHANGE R-A FILE RECORD
 620 GET 2, R
 630 LET E = CVS(EF$)
 640 LET E = E + D
 650 LSET EF$ = MKS$(E)
 660 PUT 2, R
√670 GOTO 430
 680 :
 690 REM     RETURN FOR NEXT TRANS
 700 GOTO 430
 710 :
```

Note: (√) shows changes made.

(a) Only one small component of this application has been completed. List the other programs you would need to make a complete personal finance management system?

(a) Programs:
   1. Edit MONTH# file for errors. eckbook.
   2. Print BUDGET # files.
   3. "Exception report" showing over budget accounts or projected over budget accounts.

You have seen only fixed-record length random access files. Some versions of BASIC provide for variable-length records that make more efficient use of disk space. Another technique can be used to place multiple datasets in one random access record. Such record-splitting is explained in detail in most basic reference materials and is not included here.

We have found random access files much easier to use than sequential files. But let's not forget that sequential files have their place in computing, especially when there is need for file space efficiency.

With the knowledge gained from this book, you should now be able to read the reference manual for your computer with new understanding. You should also be able to write your own data file programs and read programs written by others.

CHAPTER 8 SELF-TEST

1. The first application in this chapter was an inventory control system. Before you continue you may want to review the system description so you are familiar with the contents of each file and how they interact.

   To this system is added a third file; a sequential transaction file in which is placed the data regarding each transaction that affects the inventory. Two types of transactions will affect inventory:

   Type 1 – units are added to inventory.
   Type 2 – units are taken from inventory.

   Data is recorded in the sequential transaction file in this format.

```
T = TRANSACTION TYPE (1 OR 2)
Y$ = DATE (6)
N$ = INVOICE # (5)
P2$ = PROD # (4)
Q1 = QUANTITY ADDED OR DEDUCTED
```

   Write a program to create, then read/display, the *sequential* data file named TRANSACT with this dataset. Make certain the product numbers entered in the file correspond to product numbers that exist in PRODUCT. Include both transaction types in your file data.

2. Write a program to process the data in TRANSACT to PRODUCT (update the quantity in stock information). For each dataset input from TRANSACT, use the *sequential* file POINT to locate the record number in PRODUCT to be updated or posted with the data from TRANSACT.

3. To the previous problem add a routine that, after all the transactions have been processed, will search the entire INVEN file and print a report of products that have fallen below the reorder point and need reordering.

Answer Key

1.
```
100 REM     CREATE THEN READ/DISPLAY SEQ. FILE NAMED 'TRANSACT'
110 :
120 REM     VARIABLES USED
130 REM       T = TRANSACTION TYPE (1 IF ADD, 2 IF SUBTRACT)
140 REM       Y$ = DATE (FORMAT: XX/XX/XX) (8)
150 REM       N$ = INVOICE NUMBER (5)
160 REM       P2$ = PRODUCT # (MUST CORRESPOND TO EXISTING # IN
                    IN 'PRODUCT' FILE) (4)
170 REM       Q1 = QUANTITY TO BE ADDED OR SUBTRACTED FROM STOCK
171 REM       R$ = USER RESPONSE VARIABLE
180 :
190 REM     FILES USED
200 REM      SEQUENTIAL FILE NAME: TRANSACT
210 REM      DATASET FORMAT: T,Y$,N$,P2$,Q1
220 :
230 REM     INITIALIZE
240 OPEN "O", 1, "TRANSACT"
250 :
260 REM DATA ENTRY MODULE
270 PRINT "TRANSACTION CODES: 1=ITEMS TO BE ADDED TO STOCK"
280 PRINT "                   2=ITEMS TO BE SUBTRACTED FROM STOCK"
290 INPUT "ENTER TRANSACTION CODE (1 OR 2):"; T
300 IF T <> 1 AND <> 2 THEN PRINT : PRINT "ENTRY ERROR.
    PLEASE REENTER.": PRINT : GOTO 270
310 LINE INPUT "ENTER TRANSACTION DATE (XX/XX/XX) :"; Y$
320 REM     DATA ENTRY TESTS GO HERE
330 LINE INPUT "ENTER INVOICE NUMBER:"; N$
340 IF LEN(N$) <> 5 THEN PRINT : PRINT "ENTRY ERROR. USE 5 DIGIT
    INVOICE NUMBER." : PRINT : GOTO 330
350 REM     OTHER DATA ENTRY CHECKS GO HERE
360 LINE INPUT "ENTER PRODUCT NUMBER:"; P2$
370 IF LEN(P2$) <> 4 THEN PRINT : PRINT "ENTRY ERROR. USE 4 DIGIT
    PRODUCT NUMBER." : PRINT : GOTO 360
380 REM     OTHER DATA ENTRY TESTS GO HERE
390 INPUT "QUANTITY TO BE ADDED OR SUBTRACTED FROM STOCK:"; Q1
400 IF Q1 <> ABS(Q1) THEN PRINT : PRINT "DO NOT USE NEGATIVE
    NUMBER. PLEASE REENTER.": PRINT : GOTO 390
410 REM     OTHER DATA ENTRY TESTS GO HERE
420 :
430 REM     WRITE TO FILE
440 PRINT#1, T; ","; Y$; ","; N$; ","; P2$; ","; Q1
450 LINE INPUT "MORE TRANSACTIONS (Y OR N) ?"; R$
460 IF R$ <> "Y" AND R$ <> "N" THEN PRINT : PRINT "TYPE 'Y' FOR
    YES OR 'N' FOR NO"  : PRINT : GOTO 450
470 IF R$ = "Y" THEN 270
480 :
490 REM     CLOSE FILE
500 CLOSE
510 :
520 LINE INPUT "DISPLAY THIS FILE (Y OR N) ?"; R$
530 REM     Y OR N TEST GOES HERE
540 IF R$ = "N" THEN END
550 OPEN "I", 1, "TRANSACT"
555 IF EOF (1) THEN 670
560 INPUT#1, T,Y$,N$,P2$,Q1
570 PRINT
```

continued on next page

```
580 PRINT "TRANSACTION TYPE: "; T
590 PRINT "TRANSACTION DATE: "; Y$
600 PRINT "INVOICE # : "; N$
610 PRINT "PRODUCT # : "; P2$
620 PRINT "QUANTITY : "; Q1
630 PRINT : LINE INPUT "PRESS 'ENTER' FOR NEXT INVOICE"; R$
640 PRINT : GOTO 555
650 :
660 REM    CLOSE FILE
670 CLOSE
680 PRINT : PRINT "ALL DATA DISPLAYED AND FILE CLOSED"
```

2.
```
100 REM  PROB 8-2 SOLUTION
110 REM    POSTS TRANSACTION FILE NAMED 'TRANSACT' TO
    'PRODUCT' FILE
120 REM    VARIABLES USED
130 REM      R$ = USER RESPONSE VARIABLE
140 REM      P1$ = P2$ = PROD # (4)
150 REM      R = RECORD #
160 REM      P$ = PROD # (4)
170 REM      D$ = DESCRIPTION(20)
180 REM      S$ = SUPPLIER (20)
190 REM      L = REORDER POINT
200 REM      Y = REORDER QUANTITY
210 REM      Q = QUANTITY IN STOCK
220 REM      C = COST
230 REM      U = UNIT SELLING PRICE
240 REM      Y$ = DATE (8)
250 REM      N$ = INVOICE # (5)
260 REM      Q1 = QUANTITY ADDED OR DEDUCTED
270 REM      T = TRANSACTION TYPE
280 :
290 :
300 REM    FILES USED
310 REM      POINT = SEQ POINTER FILE
320 REM      PRODUCT = R-A FILE
330 REM      TRANSACT = SEQ. TRANSACTION FILE
340 :
350 REM    FILE INITIALIZATION
360 PRINT "WORKING"
370 CLEAR 300
380 OPEN "I", 1, "POINT"
390 OPEN "R", 2, "PRODUCT"
400 FIELD 2, 4 AS PF$, 20 AS DF$, 20 AS SF$, 4 AS LF$, 4 AS YF$, 4 AS
    QF$, 4 AS CF$, 4 AS UF$
410 OPEN "I", 3, "TRANSACT"
420 :
430 REM   READ TRANSACTION FILE
440 IF EOF(3) THEN 850
450 INPUT #3, T, Y$, N$, P2$, Q1
460 :
470 REM   READ POINTER FILE
480 IF EOF(1) THEN 790
490 INPUT #1, P1$, R
500 IF P1$ <> THEN 480
510 :
520 REM   GET R-A FILE RECORD
530 IF R > LOF(2) THEN 750
540 GET 2, R
550 LSET Q = CVS(QF$)
560 IF T = 2 THEN 600   :          REM   TEST TRANSACTION TYPE
570 LET Q = Q + Q1:        REM   ADD NEW QUANTITY
580 GOTO 620
590 :
600 LET Q = Q - Q1:        REM   DEDUCT QUANTITY TAKEN
610 IF Q < 0 THEN LET Q = Q + Q1: GOTO 690   :REM   ERROR TEST
620 LET QF$ = MKS$(Q)
```

(continued on next page)

```
630 PUT 2, R
640 :
650 REM    RESET POINTER IN POINTER FILE
660 CLOSE 1: OPEN "I", 1, "POINT": GOTO 440
670 :
680 REM    ERROR MESSAGE
690 PRINT "INVALID ENTRY. TOO FEW GOODS"
700 PRINT "TRANSACTION DATED "; Y$;"  FOR PROD: "; P2$
710 PRINT "NOT PROCESSED"
720 GOTO 660
730 :
740 REM    ERROR MESSAGE
750 PRINT "RECORD # ERROR IN POINTER FILE"
760 GOTO 800
770 :
780 REM    ERROR MESSAGES
790 PRINT "PRODUCT # NOT IN POINTER FILE"
800 PRINT "TRANSACTION DATED "; Y$;"  FOR PROD # "; P2$
810 PRINT "NOT PROCESSED"
820 GOTO 440
830 :
840 REM    CLOSE FILES
850 CLOSE
860 END
```

3.

```
860 :
870 REM    REORDER REPORT GENERATOR
880 :
890 LINE INPUT "REORDER REPORT (Y OR N) ?"; R$
900 REM     Y OR N TEST GOES HERE
910 IF LEFT$(R$,1) <> "Y" THEN 1090
920 OPEN "R". 2, "PRODUCT"
930 FIELD 2. 4 AS PF$. 20 AS DF$. 20 AS SF$, 4 AS LF$,
    4 AS YF$, 4 AS QF$, 4 AS CF$, 4 AS UF$
940 FOR X = 1 TO LOF(2)
950 GET 2
960 LET L = CUS(LF$)
970 LET Y = CUS(YF$)
980 LET Q = CUS(QF$)
990 LET C = CUS(CF$)
1000 IF Q > L THEN 1080
1010 PRINT "REORDER PROD #: "; PF$
1020 PRINT "ITEM: "; DF$
1030 PRINT "SOURCE: "; SF$
1040 PRINT "ON HAND: "; Q
1050 PRINT "REORDER QUANTITY: "; Y
1060 PRINT "LAST COST: $"; C
1070 PRINT : LINE INPUT "PRESS 'ENTER' FOR NEXT ITEM";
     R$ : PRINT
1080 NEXT X
1090 CLOSE
1100 END
```

Final Self-Test

1. Write a program to create a sequential disk file named PHONE1, containing the following data concatenated into one string in fields as indicated:

   last name (fifteen character maximum)
   first name (fifteen character maximum)
   area code (three digits)
   phone number (eight characters, including hyphen between third and fourth character)

```
110 :
120 REM     VARIABLES USED
130 REM      L$ = LAST NAME (15)
140 REM      F$ = FIRST NAME (15)
150 REM      A$ = AREA CODE (3)
160 REM      N$ = NUMBER (8 CHARACTERS INCLUDING HYPHEN)
170 REM      D$ = CONCATENATED DATASET
180 :
190 REM     FILES USED
200 REM     PHONE1 = NAME & PHONE NUMBER DIRECTORY
```

2. Write a program to display all the datasets in PHONE1, with the data items separated (undo concatenation) under headings as follows:

LAST NAME FIRST NAME AREA CODE PHONE NUMBER

```
110 :
120 REM     VARIABLES USED
130 REM       D$ = ONE COMPLETE DATASET
140 :
150 REM     FILE USED = PHONE1
160 :
```

3. Write a program that will select and display all names and numbers in a user-selected area code from PHONE1, with the option to continue or STOP when the display is complete.

```
110 :
120 REM     VARIABLES USED
130 REM     A$ = AREA CODE (USER REQUESTED)
140 REM     D$ = ONE COMPLETE DATASET
150 REM     R$ = USER RESPONSE TO CONTINUE
160 :
170 REM     FILE USED = PHONE1
180 :
```

4. Write a program to display the contents of the random access disk file named PRODUCT that you created in the Chapter 7 Self-Test problems 1 and 2.

```
110 :
120 REM     VARIABLES USED
130 REM      P$,PB$ = PROD. NO. (4)
140 REM      D$,DB$ = DESCRIPTION(20)
150 REM      S$,SB$ = SUPPLIER(20)
160 REM      L,LB$ = REORDER POINT
170 REM      Y,YB$ = REORDER QUANTITY
180 REM      Q,QB$ = QUANTITY
190 REM      C,CB$ = COST
200 REM      U,UB$ = UNIT SELLING PRICE
210 REM      R$ = PRESS 'ENTER' TO CONTINUE VARIABLE
220 :
230 REM      FILES USED
240 REM      PRODUCT - RA FILE
250 :
```

5. Write a program to change each dataset in PRODUCT by increasing the unit sales price of each item by 10 percent. The program should display the product number, the old price, and the new price.

```
110 :
120 REM     VARIABLES USED
130 REM      P$,PB$ = PROD. NO. (4)
140 REM      D$,DB$ = DESCRIPTION(20)
150 REM      S$,SB$ = SUPPLIER(20)
160 REM      L.LB$ = REORDER POINT
170 REM      Y,YB$ = REORDER QUANTITY
180 REM      Q,QB$ = QUANTITY
190 REM      C,CB$ = COST
200 REM      U,UB$ = UNIT SELLING PRICE
210 REM      R$ = USER RESPONSE TO CONTINUE ENTRIES
220 REM      U1 = CHANGED UNIT SALES PRICE
230 :
240 REM      FILES USED
250 REM      PRODUCT - RA FILE
260 :
```

Answer Key

1.

```
100 REM   FINAL SELF TEST PROB 1
110 :
120 REM    VARIABLES USED
130 REM     L$ = LAST NAME (15)
140 REM     F$ = FIRST NAME (15)
150 REM     A$ = AREA CODE (3)
160 REM     N$ = NUMBER (8 CHARACTERS INCLUDING HYPHEN)
170 REM     D$ = CONCATENATED DATASET
180 :
190 REM   FILES USED
200 REM   PHONE1 = NAME & PHONE NUMBER DIRECTORY
210 REM   INITIALIZATION
220 CLEAR 500
230 OPEN "O", 1, "PHONE1"
240 :
250 REM    DATA ENTRY MODULE
260 PRINT "TYPE 'STOP' IF NO MORE ENTRIES."
270 LINE INPUT "ENTER LAST NAME (15 CHAR. MAX.):"; L$
280 IF L$ =  STOP  THEN 540
290 IF LEN(L$) = 0 THEN PRINT "NO ENTRY MADE. PLEASE MAKE AN ENTRY.":
    GOTO 260
300 IF LEN(L$) > 15 THEN PRINT "ENTRY TOO LONG. ONLY 15 LETTERS
    ALLOWED.": GOTO 260
310 IF LEN(L$) < 15 THEN LET L$ = L$ + " ": GOTO 310
320 :
330 LINE INPUT "ENTER FIRST NAME (15 CHAR. MAX.):"; F$
340 IF LEN(F$) = 0 THEN PRINT "NO ENTRY MADE. PLEASE MAKE AN ENTRY.":
    GOTO 330
350 IF LEN(F$) > 15 THEN PRINT "ENTRY TOO LONG. ONLY 15 LETTERS
    ALLOWED.": GOTO 330
360 IF LEN(F$) < 15 THEN LET F$ = F$ + " ": GOTO 360
370 :
380 LINE INPUT "ENTER AREA CODE (3 DIGITS ONLY):"; A$
390 IF LEN(A$) <> 3 THEN PRINT "AREA CODE MUST HAVE THREE DIGITS ONLY.
    DO NOT USE PARENTHESES.": GOTO 380
400 :
410 PRINT "ENTER PHONE NUMBER USING THIS FORMAT: 999-9999"
420 LINE INPUT "WHAT IS THE PHONE NUMBER?"; N$
430 IF LEN(N$) = 0 THEN PRINT "NO ENTRY MADE. PLEASE ENTER AS
    REQUESTED.": GOTO 410
440 IF LEN(N$) <> 8 THEN PRINT "ENTRY ERROR. YOU ENTERED"; N$ : GOTO 410
450 IF ASC(MID$(N$,4,1)) <> 45 THEN PRINT "USE A HYPHEN (DASH) BETWEEN
    THE 3RD AND 4TH DIGITS.": GOTO 410
460 :
470 REM   CONCATENATE AND PRINT DATASET TO FILE
480 LET D$ = L$ + F$ + A$ + N$
490 PRINT #1, D$
500 CLS
510 GOTO 260
520 :
530 REM    CLOSE FILE
540 CLOSE
550 PRINT "FILE CLOSED."
560 END
```

2.

```
100 REM   FINAL SELF TEST PROBLEM 2 SOLUTION
110 :
120 REM    VARIABLES USED
130 REM      D$ = ONE COMPLETE DATASET
140 :
150 REM   FILE USED = PHONE 1
160 :
170 REM   INITIALIZATION
180 CLEAR 500
190 OPEN "I", 1, "PHONE1"
200 :
210 PRINT "LAST NAME", "FIRST NAME", "AREA CODE", "PHONE NUMBER"
220 PRINT
230 REM   READ AND DISPLAY DATA
240 IF EOF(1) THEN 290
250 INPUT #1, D$
260 PRINT LEFT$(D$,15), MID$(D$,16,15), MID$(D$,31,3), RIGHT$(D$,8)
270 GOTO 240
280 REM   CLOSE FILE
290 CLOSE 1
300 PRINT : PRINT "ALL DATA DISPLAYED AND FILE CLOSED."
310 END
```

3.

```
100 REM FINAL SELF TEST PROB 3 SOLUTION
110 :
120 REM      VARIABLES USED
130 REM      A$ = AREA CODE (USER REQUESTED)
140 REM      D$ = ONE COMPLETE DATASET
150 REM      R$ = USER RESPONSE TO CONTINUE
160 :
170 REM   FILE USED = PHONE1
180 :
190 REM INITIALIZATION
200 CLEAR 500
210 OPEN "I", 1, "PHONE1"
220 :
230 REM  USER REQUEST ROUTINE
240 PRINT "ENTER AN AREA CODE AND I WILL DISPLAY ALL NAMES AND"
250 PRINT "NUMBERS FROM THAT AREA CODE."
260 LINE INPUT "ENTER AREA CODE (3 DIGITS ONLY)"; A$
270 IF LEN(A$) <> 3 THEN PRINT "ENTRY ERROR. YOU ENTERED"; A$ : GOTO 260
280 :
290 REM  INPUT, SELECT AND DISPLAY DATA
300 CLS
310 PRINT "LAST NAME", "FIRST NAME", "AREA CODE", "PHONE NUMBER"
320 IF EOF(1) THEN 380
330 INPUT $1, D$
340 IF A$ <> MID$(D$,31,3) THEN 320
350 PRINT LEFT$(D$,15), MID$(D$,16,15), A$, RIGHT$(D$,8)
360 GOTO 320
370 :
380 PRINT : PRINT "ALL"; A$; "NUMBERS DISPLAYED." : PRINT
390 LINE INPUT "ANOTHER AREA CODE (TYPE YES OR NO)?"; R$
400 IF LEFT$(R$,1) = "N" THEN 460
410 :
420 REM  RESET DATA POINTER TO BEGINNING OF FILE
430 CLOSE 1 : OPEN "I", 1, "PHONE1" : GOTO 260
440 :
```

continued on next page

```
450 REM   CLOSE FILE
460 CLOSE 1
470 PRINT : PRINT "FILE CLOSED."
480 END
```

4.

```
100 REM FINAL SELF TEST PROB 4 SOLUTION
110 :
120 REM   VARIABLES USED
130 REM    P$,PB$ = PROD. NO. (4)
140 REM    D$,DB$ = DESCRIPTION (20)
150 REM    S$,SB$ = SUPPLIER (20)
160 REM    L,LB$ = REORDER POINT
170 REM    Y,YB$ = REORDER QUANTITY
180 REM    Q,QB$ = QUANTITY
190 REM    C,CB$ = COST
200 REM    U,UB$ = UNIT SELLING PRICE
210 REM    R$ = PRESS 'ENTER' TO CONTINUE VARIABLE
220 :
230 REM    FILES USED
240 REM    PRODUCT - RA FILE
250 :
260 REM   INITIALIZE
265 CLEAR 300
270 OPEN "R", 1, "PRODUCT"
280 FIELD 1, 4 AS PB$, 20 AS DB$, 20 AS SB$, 4 AS LB$, 4 AS YB$, 4 AS
    QB$, 4 AS CB$, 4 AS UB$
290 :
300 REM   READ, CONVERT, AND DISPLAY ONE DATASET AT A TIME
310 PRINT "PRESS 'ENTER' TO DISPLAY NEXT DATASET."
320 PRINT
330 FOR X = 1 TO LOF(1)
340 GET 1
350 LET L = CVS(LB$)
360 LET Y = CVS(YB$)
370 LET Q = CVS(QB$)
380 LET C = CVS(CB$)
390 LET U = CVS(UB$)
400 PRINT PB$; DB$; SB$; L; Y; Q; C; U
410 LINE INPUT ""; R$
420 NEXT X
430 :
440 REM   CLOSE FILE
450 PRINT : PRINT "ALL DATASETS DISPLAYED."
460 CLOSE 1
470 PRINT "FILE CLOSED."
480 END
```

5.

```
100 REM     FINAL SELF TEST PROB 5 SOLUTION
110 :
120 REM     VARIABLES USED
130 REM      P$,PB$ = PROD. NO. (4)
140 REM      D$,DB$ = DESCRIPTION (20)
150 REM      S$,SB$ = SUPPLIER (20)
160 REM      L,LB$ = REORDER POINT
170 REM      Y,YB$ = REORDER QUANTITY
180 REM      Q,QB$ = QUANTITY
190 REM      C,CB$ = COST
200 REM      U,UB$ = UNIT SELLING PRICE
210 REM      R$ = USER RESPONSE TO CONTINUE ENTRIES
220 REM      U1 = CHANGED UNIT SALES PRICE
230 :
240 REM      FILES USED
250 REM      PRODUCT - RA FILE
260 :
270 REM      INITIALIZE
275 CLEAR 300
280 OPEN "R", 1, "PRODUCT"
290 FIELD 1, 4 AS PB$, 20 AS DB$, 20 AS SB$, 4 AS LB$, 4 AS YB$, 4 AS
    QB$, 4 AS CB$, 4 AS UB$
300 :
310 PRINT "PRODUCT #", "OLD UNIT PRICE", "NEW UNIT PRICE"
320 PRINT
330 FOR X = 1 TO LOF(1)
340 GET 1, X
350 LET U = CVS(UB$)
360 LET U1 = U + (U*.1)
370 LSET UB$ = MKS$(U1)
380 PRINT PB$, U, U1
390 PUT 1, X
400 NEXT X
410 :
420 REM   CLOSE FILE
430 CLOSE 1
440 PRINT "PRICE CHANGES COMPLETED. FILE CLOSED."
450 END
```

APPENDIX A

BASIC Reference Guide for Statements Introduced in This Book

ASC (X$) – Gives the ASCII code number value for the first character in X$.

CHR$(X) – Converts X to the corresponding ASCII code.

CLOSE n – Terminates the file buffer assignments and forces the buffer to flush its contents.

CVI(BF$) – Restores random file buffer string BF$ to a numeric value. "I" is for integer number.

CVS(BF$) – S is for single precision number.

CVD(BF$) – D is for double precision number.

EOF(n) – End-of-file detector.

FIELD #n – Organize random access file buffer field n into string variable sections.

GET n,r – Load into the random file buffer n, the contents of record r.

INPUT #n, X, Y$ – Read data from sequential file n into variables X and Y$.

LEFT$(X$,n) – Select the leftmost n characters in X$.

LEN(X$) – Gives the actual number of characters in X$.

LINE INPUT – Allows user to enter just one string variable with ENTER being the only allowed delimiter.

LOF(n) – Gives the number of the last or highest numbered record used in a file.

LSET BF$ – Left-justifies information into buffer variable BF$.

MID$(X$,y,n) – Replace or select n characters of X$ beginning with character position y.

MKI$(X) – Converts numeric value X to a string for placement in the random file buffer. "I" is for integer number. Makes a two-byte string.

MKS$(X) – "S" for single precision number. Makes a four-byte string.

MKD$(X) – "D" for double precision number. Makes an eight-byte string.

OPEN "M", n, "name" – Assigns buffer number n to file "name", in access mode M. Mode I is sequential input, O is sequential output, R is random access input/output.

PRINT #n, X$; ","; Y – Print onto sequential file n the values for X$ and Y.

PUT n, r – Write the contents of buffer n to random access file record r.

RSET BF$ – Right-justifies data into buffer string BF$.

RIGHT$(X$, n) – Selects the rightmost n characters in X$.

STR$(X) – Converts the numeric expression X to a string.

VAL(X$) – Converts X$ to a numeric value.

WRITE #n, X$, Y – Print onto file n the values for X$ and Y. Used in BASIC-80 only.

APPENDIX B

ASCII Chart

Decimal	Character	Decimal	Character	Decimal	Character
000	NUL	031	US	062	>
001	SO11	032	SPACE	063	?
002	STX	033	!	064	@
003	ETX	034	“	065	A
004	EOT	035	#	066	B
005	ENQ	036	$	067	C
006	ACK	037	%	068	D
007	BEL	038	&	069	E
008	BS	039	'	070	F
009	HT	040	(	071	G
010	LF	041	)	072	H
011	VT	042	*	073	I
012	FF	043	+	074	J
013	CR	044	‘	075	K
014	SO	045	—	076	L
015	SI	046	.	077	M
016	DLE	047	/	078	N
017	DC1	048	0	079	O
018	DC2	049	1	080	P
019	DC3	050	2	081	Q
020	DC4	051	3	082	R
021	NAK	052	4	083	S
022	SYN	053	5	084	T
023	ETB	054	6	085	U
024	CAN	055	7	086	V
025	EM	056	8	087	W
026	SUB	057	9	088	X
027	ESCAPE	058	:	089	Y
028	FS	059	;	090	Z
029	GS	060	<	091	[
030	RS	061	=	092	\

LF = Line Feed FF = Form Feed CR = Carriage Return DEL = Delete

Decimal	Character	Decimal	Character	Decimal	Character
093	]	105	i	117	u
094	↑	106	j	118	v
095	←	107	k	119	w
096	`	108	l	120	x
097	a	109	m	121	y
098	b	110	n	122	z
099	c	111	o	123	{
100	d	112	p	124	|
101	e	113	q	125	}
102	f	114	r	126	~
103	g	115	s	127	DEL
104	h	116	t		

APPENDIX C

List of Data File Example Programs

Chapter Four

p. 100-101; Creates a sequential file named PROPERTY for a home inventory. Dataset format: D$, N, V
p. 103-104; Reads/displays PROPERTY
p. 107; Creates, then summarizes and displays Quality Control data. Dataset format: N% (integer value). File name is user selected.
p. 108-109; Data file demonstration. Self-contained file creating and displaying program. Sequential file name: DEMO1. Dataset format: D$ (one string)

Chapter Four Self-Test

p. 128; Creates a sequential file named GROCERY. Dataset format: A$, B
p. 128-129; Reads/displays GROCERY.
p. 129-130; Creates a file of customer credit information. Sequential file name is user selected. Dataset format: C$, N$, R where C$ is five digit customer number, N$ is 20 char. max. customer name, R is one digit credit rating (1 to 5).
p. 130; Reads/displays customer credit file
p. 127; Creates a sequential file named PROB1. Dataset format: A$, B$, C, D
p. 127; Reads/displays PROB1
p. 130-131; Creates a sequential file of money transactions. File name is user selected. Dataset format: D$ (one concatenated string) from A$ (char. positions 1 to 5), T$ (char. positions 6, 7), and C$ (char. positions 8-14).
p. 131; Reads/displays the transaction file
p. 132; Creates a sequential file named ADDRESS. Dataset format: one fielded string, concatenated from name (char, positions 1-20), street address (char. positions 21-40), city (char. positions 41-50), state code (char. positions 51, 52), and zip code (char. positions 53-57)
p. 132-133; Reads/displays ADDRESS
p. 133; Creates files of form letter texts. Sequential file name is formed by concatenating LETTER + a user selected number. Dataset format: R$ (one line of text, 255 char. max. each)
p. 133-134; Reads/displays LETTER#

Chapter Five

p. 136-137; Sequential file copying program. Uses Chapter 4 Self-test Problem 1 data file. File name is user selected.
p. 143-144; Adding data to the end of an existing sequential file. Uses GROCERY from Chapter 4 Self-test problem 2, and temporary file named TEMPFIL
p. 151-152; First version of Credit File Changer program, to select dataset by customer number and option to change customer name. Uses customer credit file (name is user selected) from Chapter 4 Self-test problem 3. Temporary sequential file name: TEMPFIL
p. 155; Read/displays the customer credit file using the PRESS ENTER TO CONTINUE technique
p. 156; Second version of Credit File Changer program, using the customer credit file (name is user selected) and temporary sequential file named TEMPFIL. Uses PRESS ENTER TO CONTINUE technique, with option to change customer number.
p. 161-163; Third version of Credit File Editor program allows changes to all data items in dataset, inserting new datasets, or deleting datasets from the file. Sequential file name is user selected. Temporary file named TEMPFIL.
p. 172-174; File merging program. Uses two sequential files with same format. Account numbers in each file are in ascending numeric order. File names are user selected, including output sequential file name. The original sequential files to merge are from Chapter 4 Self-test problem 4. Displays contents of merged file.
p. 183-184; Letter writing program. Uses sequential file ADDRESS created in Chapter 4 Self-test problem 5, and the LETTER# sequential files from Chapter 4 Self-test problem 6.

Chapter Five Self-Test

p. 191; Makes a copy of ADDRESS file. Sequential file copy name is user selected.
p. 191-192; Creates two files from two alphabetized lists of magazine titles. Dataset format: T$. Sequential file names are user selected.
p. 192-193; Program to merge the magazine title files into one merged file maintaining alphabetical order. Original sequential file names and name for merged file are user selected. Displays merged data.
p. 193-194; Program to create and/or add to or delete from a sequential file of household maintenance tasks. Dataset format: M$ Sequential file name is user selected. Temporary file name: TEMPFIL

Chapter Six

p. 198-199; Cassette version of PROPERTY file creating program.
p. 201-202; Reads PROPERTY file from cassette.
p. 204; Creates a cassette file (referred to as STAT1) of statistical data. Dataset format; M (single value)
p. 206-207; Makes a copy of STAT1 on a separate cassette.
p. 207-208; Program to add data to end of existing cassette file. Uses STAT1.
p. 211; Program to add data to cassette file version of GROCERY, by placing new data into an array.

Chapter Six Self-Test

p. 220; Cassette version to create a file as in Chapter 4 Self-test problem. 1. Dataset format: A$, B$, C, D
p. 220; Cassette version to read/display the file created in previous problem
p. 220-221; Creates a cassette file for a shopping list
p. 221; Cassette file reads/displays program for shopping list file
p. 221-222; Creates a cassette file version of ADDRESS, with concatenated dataset
p. 222; Reads/displays the cassette file version of ADDRESS
p. 222-223; Makes a copy on a separate cassette of cassette file version of ADDRESS

Chapter Seven

p. 235-236; Creates a random access file named INVEN (parts inventory). Dataset format: N$, D$ (N$ is part number — 6 characters, D$ is part description —20 characters)
p. 237-238; Reads/displays random access file INVEN
p. 239-240; Program to create and/or add data to a random access file named PHONE. Dataset format: N$, C$, P$ where N$ is customer number (5 characters), C$ is customer name (20 characters) and P$ is phone number 10 characters
p. 240; Program module to read/display PHONE
p. 242-244; Program to create, then read/display, a new version of INVEN called INVEN2 that includes a single precision quantity of "parts in stock" Dataset format: N$, D$, Q
p. 245; User provided program to create random access file named MASTER. Dataset format: G$ (20), S$ (8), Q (4 - single precision value), M$ (30)
p. 246-247; Program to copy random access file MASTER. Random access copy file name: STORE1
p. 249-250; Random access file editing program using INVEN. Dataset format: C$, D$, which allows changing either data item in a dataset, deleting a dataset, or no change to dataset
p. 254-255; Program to make a random access file copy of a sequential file. The sequential file named CUST is created by modifying the program to create a customer credit file in Chapter 4 Self-test problem 3. Dataset format: N$, P$, C, B. Random access file copy name: CUST1, with the same dataset format, C and D stored as single precision values
p. 255; Program to change one complete random access file record from one record to a different one in the same file
p. 256; Program to display the contents of any random access file one complete record at a time

Chapter Seven Self-Test

p. 261; Program to create a random access business inventory file named PRODUCT. Dataset format, P$, D$, S$, L, Y, Q, C, U
p. 262; Programs to create and read/display a sequential file named POINT, which has one data item copied from random access file PRODUCT's dataset, and also the record number of that dataset. Sequential file dataset format: P$, R
p. 263; Program to make a random access file copy from another random access file. Source file name: CUST1 (from p. 254-255). Copy file name: CUST2
p. 263-264; Program to read/display both CUST1 and CUST2, dataset by dataset, for

comparison/verification of accurate copy
p. 264-265; Program to create checkbook register transaction files for each past month, for use in Chapter 8. These are *sequential* files named MONTH#. Dataset format: C, Y$, W$, A$, D Includes module to read/display the file created by the program. A$ selected from chart of accounts on p. 272.
p. 265-266; Program to create random access files named BUDGET# (three files) for use in Chapter 8. Account chart numbers and name are from p. 272. Dataset format: N$, D$, B, E, single precision values for B and E. Program includes module to read/display the file just created.

Chapter Eight
p. 268-271; Program to change the cost and unit selling price in random access file PRODUCT, using sequential file POINT to "look up" the record number in product for the dataset needing change. Programs for creating the files used are in Chapter 7 Self-test.
p. 274-276; Program to modify random access file BUDGET# data using data from sequential files MONTH#. Posts checkbook transactions to BUDGET# files. Uses chart of accounts numbers to identify both the BUDGET# file name and the record number in that file where transaction is to be posted.

Chapter Eight Self-Test
p. 283-284; Problem solution requires a program to create an inventory transaction sequential file of items added to or taken from inventory, named TRANSACT. Dataset format: T, Y$, N$, P2$, Q1. Solution program processes or posts the inventory transactions to PRODUCT, using the product number in TRANSACT to locate the record number in POINT for the dataset in PRODUCT where the change is to be posted.
p. 284; Program that examines PRODUCT and generates a report of inventory items that have fallen below the reorder point

Final Self-Test
p. 292-293; Program creates a sequential file named PHONE1 with last name, first name, area code, and phone number concatenated into one string. Dataset format: D$
p. 293; Displays data from PHONE1, undoing the concatenated dataset
p. 293-294; Program to display only those datasets in PHONE1 containing a user-selected area code
p. 294; Program to read/display PRODUCT
p. 295; Program to increase all unit selling prices in PRODUCT by 10% and display old and new unit selling prices

Index

NOTES

NOTES

NOTES

NOTES